Nepal
Votes for Peace

Bhojraj Pokharel
Shrishti Rana

FOUNDATION®
BOOKS

Delhi • Bengaluru • Mumbai • Kolkata • Chennai • Hyderabad
Pune • Thiruvananthapuram

Published by
Cambridge University Press India Pvt. Ltd.
under the imprint of Foundation Books
Cambridge House, 4381/4 Ansari Road, Daryaganj, **New Delhi** 110 002

Cambridge University Press India Pvt. Ltd.
C-22, C-Block, Brigade M.M., K.R. Road, Jayanagar, **Bengaluru** 560 070
Plot No. 80, Service Industries, Shirvane, Sector-1, Nerul, **Navi Mumbai** 400 706
10 Raja Subodh Mullick Square, 2nd Floor, **Kolkata** 700 013
21/1 (New No. 49), 1st Floor, Model School Road, Thousand Lights, **Chennai** 600 006
House No. 3-5-874/6/4, (Near Apollo Hospital), Hyderguda, **Hyderabad** 500 029
Agarwal Pride, 'A' Wing, 1308 Kasba Peth, Near Surya Hospital, **Pune** 411 011
T.C. 25/ 2731 Lukes Lane, Ambujavilasam Road, **Thiruvananthapuram** 695 001

First Published 2013

ISBN 978-93-82993-03-2 (Paperback)

Published by Manas Saikia for Cambridge University Press India Pvt. Ltd. and printed at Shree Maitrey Printech Pvt. Ltd., Noida

Cover Image Credit: Zzvet / Shutterstock.com

Contents

List of Figures and Tables

Figures

Tables

Acknowledgements

First and foremost, we would like to thank IFES Director Peter Erben without whom this book would not have been possible. It was Mr Erben who supported the research through the IFES/USAID (from October to December 2008), which played a vital role in getting this project underway.

We would also like to thank International IDEA Asia Regional Director, Leena Rikkila for supporting research on the Constituent Assembly elections (from March to June 2009), an equally important element of this book.

We are highly indebted to Baburam Bhattarai, Girija Prasad Koirala, Gyanendra Shah, Pushpa Kamal Dahal and others for giving us time from their busy schedules to conduct a series of interviews.

We also want to extend our deepest gratitude to Ms Indira Acharya (Girija Prasad Koirala's youngest sister) for trusting us with her unpublished diary, which contained many important and previously unknown facts about modern Nepalese history.

We would also like to thank Amresh Kumar Singh for providing us with useful political insight. Likewise, we would like to thank Khimlal Devkota, Minendra Rijal and Shekhar Koirala, who all have been a great support to us.

The inspiration to write this book came from Ian Martin. We extend our special thanks for his invaluable contribution to the book. Similarly, we are grateful to Madhavlal Maharjan for his technical support for this book. We thank C.K. Lal for his guidance at critical junctures.

We also want to thank people who provided many valuable inputs for the book: Adheep Pokhrel, Apporva Lal, Binod Sijapati, Edi Thomas, Eli Lewien, Hari Sharma, James Sharrock, Kåre Vollan, Krishna Khanal, Lucille Buldoc, Mahendra Dhoj Singh, Rafael Pintor, Sashi Bikram Rana, Sebastian Einsiedel and Trish O' Hare. Thanks also to Sheila Padmanabhan for helping us at a crucial time. Their suggestions and comments were immensely valuable in improving our initial drafts of the book. Special thanks to Anirban Roy for letting us use information from his book "Prachanda".

We would like to thank Amuda Pokharel, Monjushree Thapa, Dhurbahari Adhikari, Haribahadur Thapa and Kiran Bhandari for their encouragement in writing this book.

Most importantly, we would also like to extend our gratitude to Debjani Mazumder, Raju Dutta, Suvadip Bhattacharjee, Sushmita Banerjee and the team members of Cambridge University Press. Thanks also to Judy Wall for her editorial support for the book.

Last, but not the least, we want to thank someone who does not want his name to be acknowledged—despite being our guide throughout the writing of this book—A. Sharma.

Chronology of the Key Events

April 1990	Multiparty democracy restored through the People's Movement
February 1996	The protracted armed struggle known as the People's War, started by the CPN-Maoist party
June 2001	Assassination of King Birendra and his entire family; throne succeeded by his brother, Gyanendra Shah
August 2001	The government and the Maoist party begin their first formal peace talks, which failed within months
November 2001	A state of emergency imposed by the government led by Sher Bahadur Deuba to tackle the Maoist insurgency
May 2002	The House of Representatives (elected in 1999) dissolved by Prime Minister Deuba before the end of its five-year term, and election announced
October 2002	King Gyanendra dismisses elected Prime Minister Deuba, and appoints a series of prime ministers of his choice over the next several months
April 2003	The second formal round of peace negotiations between the Maoist and the government begins, but fails subsequently
June 2004	King Gyanendra reinstates Deuba as Prime Minister
February 2005	King Gyanendra once again removes Prime Minister Deuba and assumes the Chairmanship of the Council of Ministers
November 2005	The Peace Understanding, known as the 12-Point Agreement, between the Seven Party Alliance (SPA) and the Maoist party is signed
April 2006	King Gyanendra's autocratic regime overthrown by the second People's Movement
May 2006	Proclamation made by reinstated Parliament, which stripped the King of all his powers, and declared Nepal a secular country

November 2006	A six-point peace agreement between the SPA and the Maoists is signed, and a commitment made to hold the Constituent Assembly election by June 2007
November 2006	The Comprehensive Peace Agreement signed, which officially ended the Maoists' protracted armed struggle
January 2007	The Interim Constitution promulgated and the Interim Legislature Parliament with the Maoists is formed
January 2007	The United Nations Mission in Nepal (UNMIN) formally established in Nepal
January–February 2007	The first Madhesi uprising
March 2007	UNMIN submits the results of the first phase of the registration of the Maoist combatants
April 2007	The Maoist party joins the government and the election scheduled for June is postponed
May–June 2007	Agitation by ethnic groups starts
August 2007	The government signs negotiated Agreements with ethnic groups
September 2007	The Maoists withdraw from the government and the Nepali Congress party announces its unification with the Nepali Congress-Democratic party
October 2007	The election scheduled for November 2007 is called off
December 2007	A 23-point peace agreement is signed between the SPA and the Maoists, leading to the declaration of a new election date of 10 April 2008
February 2008	New agitation by the Madhesi community affects the election programmes, which ended after a negotiated settlement known as the Eight Point Agreement
March 2008	Election campaign begins
10 April 2008	The Constituent Assembly election is held
May 2008	The results for the Constituent Assembly elections are announced and the first meeting of the Constituent Assembly declares Nepal a republic
July 2008	Ram Baran Yadav is elected as the first President of Federal Republic of Nepal
August 2008	The Maoist Chairman, Pushpa Kamal Dahal, becomes Prime Minister

May 2009	Dahal resigns and Madhav Kumar Nepal, of the Unified Marxist Leninist (UML) party, succeeds him
January 2011	UNMIN departs from the country, leaving the management of the Maoist combatants to be resolved by the Special Committee
February 2011	Jhalnath Khanal from UML succeeds Madhav Kumar Nepal as prime minister
August 2011	Baburam Bhattarai becomes prime minister and a seven-point peace agreement is signed, paving the way for the management of the Maoist combatants
November 2011	The Supreme Court rules that the extension of the Constituent Assembly to 27 May 2012 would be the last extension
May 2012	The Constituent Assembly is dissolved after parties fail to finalise the new constitution

List of Abbreviations

ANFREL	Asian Network for Free Elections
AusAID	The Australian Agency for International Development
CA	Constituent Assembly
CAE	Constituent Assembly Election
CPN-M or Maoist	Communist Party of Nepal (Maoist)
CPN-ML	Communist Party Nepal (Marxist Leninist)
CPN-UML or UML	Communist Party of Nepal-Unified Marxist Leninist
Danida/HUGOU	Danish International Development Agency Human Rights and Governance Unit
DFID	Department for International Development
EC	Election Commission
ECN	Election Commission of Nepal
EU	European Union
EUEOM	European Union Election Observation Mission
FPTP	First-Past-The-Post
JICA	Japan International Cooperation Agency
KOICA	Korea International Cooperation Agency
LTO	Long Term Observer
MJF	Madhesh Janadhikar Forum, Nepal
MMPR	Mixed Member Proportional Representation
NC	Nepali Congress
NC-D	Nepali Congress-Democratic
NDI	National Democratic Institute
NEMA	National Election Monitoring Alliance
NEOC	National Election Observation Committee

NGO	Non-governmental organisation
NSP-A	Nepal Sadhvawana Party-Anandidevi
NWPP	Nepal Workers' and Peasants' Party
PLA	People's Liberation Army
PR	Proportional Representation
RPP	Rashtriya Prajatantra Party
SP	Sadhbhavana Party
STO	Short Term Observer
TAF	The Asia Foundation
TCC	The Carter Center
TMLP	Tarai Madhesh Lokatantrik Party
ULF	United Left Front
UMDF	United Democratic Madheshi Front
UN	United Nations
UNDP	United Nations Development Programme
UNHCHR	United Nations High Commissioner for Human Rights
UNMIN	United Nations Mission in Nepal
UPFN	United People's Front, Nepal
YCL	Young Communist League

The political map of Nepal

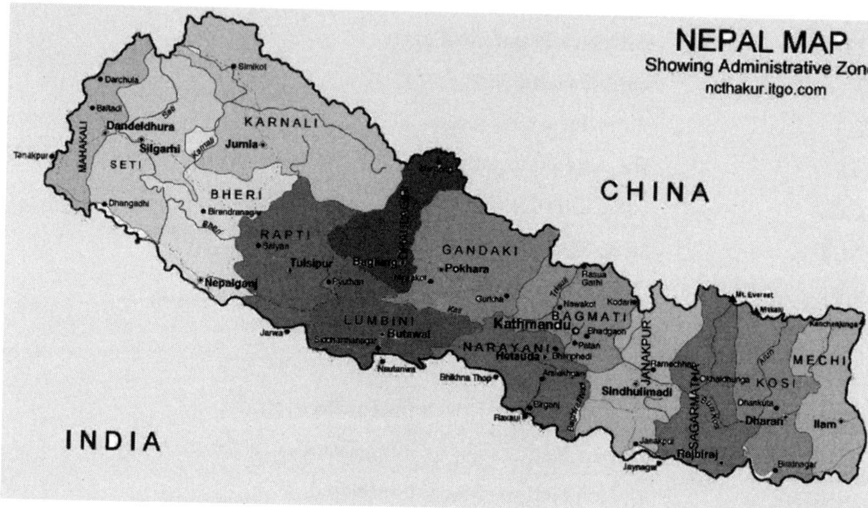

Source: Downloaded with permission from http://ncthakur.itgo.com/map.html on 2 February 2013.

Introduction

Hemmed in between the two twenty-first century superpowers—China and India—Nepal is home to nearly 26.5 million people of different ethnicity, caste and religious groups. They inhabit an area of around 147,000 sq km, which stretches from low flatlands—an extension of the Gangetic plains of present-day India in the south, to high mountains soaring to nearly 9,000 metres in the north. The Nepalese speak over 100 languages, and have different festivals, attire and food habits. But in contrast to its cultural richness, Nepal is considered poor in economic terms. The United Nations (UN) has designated Nepal as a least developed country; over 60 per cent of its population lives on less than two dollars a day and around 35 per cent is illiterate. Unsurprisingly, Nepal is said to reflect the socio-economic and political features of troubled sub-Saharan Africa.

Nepal emerged as a modern state in the mid-eighteenth century, when a number of small warring principalities were consolidated into a united kingdom. Prithivinarayan Shah, former King of the old House of Gorkha, led the consolidation process, which was achieved by a combination of war and diplomacy. He is also credited with utilising clever political strategies to keep the British colonialists, who were sweeping through South Asia, at bay. Prithivinarayan Shah's astute state building skills institutionalised the sovereignty of the Shah King in Nepal, who wielded supreme authority and power as an absolute ruler.

However, in the mid-nineteenth century, the power of the Shah King was usurped by the royal courtier Jang Bahadur Rana, and the monarchy was reduced to a ceremonial role. In 1856 Jang Bahadur received the title of Maharaja by royal edict and very significantly, gained power over the King himself. This royal edict also provided a legal basis for the establishment of a hereditary prime ministership for the Rana family, which conferred Jang Bahadur and his successors absolute authority on all affairs of state, including foreign relations. The Rana regime was prolonged by adopting a strategy of severe repression of civil and political rights, in order to retain control. Even access to modern education was restricted to the Rana family and their supporters. The regime also thrived on support from the British Raj.

In the early twentieth century, India's independence struggle inspired educated Nepalese youths to organise a movement against the Rana regime. This anti-Rana movement was also supported by the then Shah King, Tribhuvan. In 1950, an armed uprising, orchestrated by the newly-formed democratic Nepali Congress (NC) party, led to a power sharing arrangement between the King, the ruling Rana family and the emerging democratic forces. The system of hereditary prime ministership of the Rana family, and their control of all state affairs, was at an end.

Soon after, an Interim Constitution, which combined parliamentary democracy and constitutional monarchy, was promulgated and an election was announced to form a Constituent Assembly. Unfortunately, the election was abandoned after resistance from King Mahendra, who had succeeded his father King Tribhuvan in 1955. Nevertheless, parliamentary elections were later held, in 1959. Over four million people voted in this first democratic election in Nepal. The Nepali Congress party secured a two-thirds majority, and its leader Bishweshwar Prasad Koirala became the country's first democratically elected prime minister.

However, this experiment in democracy ended quickly when, in 1960, King Mahendra assumed executive control with the backing of the Nepal Army. All pro-democratic leaders, including emerging communist activists, were either imprisoned or sent into exile. In 1962, King Mahendra promulgated a new constitution, which established a panchayat system of governance. Even though this system was supposed to be an exercise in grass-roots democracy, in practice all powers were vested in the King. The panchayat system could not effectively silence people's desire for multiparty democracy, which was being triggered by the spread of education and modernisation across Nepal. The struggle continued, despite repression. The panchayat system also strongly fostered a monolithic national identity centred on the language, culture, dress and religion of the ruling elite. This alienated the majority of Nepal's multiethnic, multireligious and multilingual population. For these people an inclusive democracy, and not a panchayat system, was the only hope.

After nearly thirty years of an autocratic panchayat system, in 1990 multiparty democracy was restored. The new constitution rendered King Birendra—who succeeded King Mahendra in 1972—the constitutional monarch and established a parliamentary system of governance. But six years later a radical Maoist group launched a protracted armed struggle, known as the People's War, claiming that the existing system had failed to meet the expectations of the majority of the Nepalese people. They attacked police posts, government headquarters, local offices and other party workers, and gradually set up bases in the countryside with the intention of seizing central power. Finally, in February 2001, following their national conference, the Maoist party initiated talks with national and international political groups including the Royal Palace.

But before the formal talks had begun there was an unexpected turn of events. On 1 June 2001 King Birendra and his entire family were killed during a shoot-out in the Palace. According to the official report, Crown Prince Dipendra killed his father and other royals and then shot and mortally wounded himself. A few days later, King Birendra's brother Gyanendra succeeded to the throne. There were two immediate consequences. Firstly, the Maoists' demand for a republic was strengthened. And secondly, Nepal lost an experienced head of state, who was also the supreme commander of the Royal Nepal Army.

In August 2001, the Maoist party entered into formal peace talks with the government. But these talks failed because the government was reluctant to accept their demand for a Constituent Assembly election. A government facilitator, present at the talks, said the government objected because a Constituent Assembly election was outside the framework of the constitution—and so beyond the mandate of its negotiating team.

Following the miserable failure of its first ever negotiation with the state, the Maoist party intensified their attacks on government personnel and security forces, including army garrisons. The government reacted in November 2001 by imposing a state of emergency, which led to incalculable loss of life and property and the disappearance of many citizens, rendering the conflict one of the most intense in the world at the time.

This critical security situation prompted national and international actors to encourage the Maoists to agree to peace talks. However, while several peace initiatives were progressing, King Gyanendra assumed all executive control with the backing of the state army on 1 February 2005. Pro-democratic leaders were again imprisoned and many were forced to flee to India, rekindling memories of his father King Mahendra's takeover. This takeover prompted parliamentary parties to collaborate with the Maoists, in order to overthrow the King. In November 2005, an agreement was signed between the Maoists and the Alliance of Pro-democratic Parliamentary Parties,that called for an end to the autocratic monarchy.

Five months later, in April 2006, a People's Movement was organised. The Nepalese people were mobilised, taking to the streets to call for an end to the King's autocratic rule. After 19 days of continuous demonstration King Gyanendra finally gave up and handed over executive control to the agitating parties. By this time around 17,000 people had died in the armed conflict.

After the success of the People's Movement, a ceasefire was declared by the Maoists, and in November 2006 a Comprehensive Peace Agreement was signed, officially ending the Maoist People's War. One of the central tenets of this peace agreement was the election of the Constitution Assembly, which would provide a framework to end armed violence and create a new Nepal.

The Constituent Assembly elections were held on 10 April 2008, after two postponements. Over 10 million Nepalese women and men voted to elect their representatives, who would draft a new constitution. Disappointingly, after nearly four years of political negotiation, in May 2012 the Constituent Assembly got dissolved before it could finalise the long-awaited constitution. A new Constituent Assembly election has been declared.

This book was written immediately after the April 2008 election, drawing mainly on the experiences of the former Chief Election Commissioner. But this is not a memoir. This book was drafted by two authors—the reason behind it not being written in the first person. However, the intention has been to *bring out* the personal voice of the former Chief as much as possible. Accordingly, the book is divided into a background, main sections, and a final section in which the former Chief writes specifically about the features of the election process, analyses the reasons for the failure of the Constituent Assembly, and evaluates the current political situation.

The background section describes the political context of the Constituent Assembly election. It begins with King Gyanendra's takeover on 1 February 2005, because this event triggered sweeping changes in the country. In this section, short biographies of the key political actors who were instrumental in the Constituent Assembly election process have been also presented. This is significant, because their personalities largely shaped political developments leading up to the election.

After the background section, the main story begins. This part is set in the context of Nepal's peace process, which began in 2005. We have attempted to identify the political challenges to the Constituent Assembly election, and the reasons for the two postponements. We have also presented the *behind the scenes* negotiations, and outlined the roles of the various national and international actors including the United Nations, who contributed to the successful holding of the election.

Lastly, we must also admit that we did not foresee the dissolution of the Constituent Assembly. We had hoped this would be a narrative of the transition of Nepal from a traditional centralised unitary state into a modern federal state, or *New Nepal*. This has not yet happened. We can only hope that this book offers useful insights to those in similar post-conflict contexts.

Prologue: Flying the Flag

On 28 May 2008, a few hours before midnight, and just 20 days after the Election Commission of Nepal announced the results of the historic Constituent Assembly polls, the first meeting of the Assembly declared the abolition of the country's 239-year-old monarchy. It resulted in a magical and rare outburst of collective emotions. Traditional and staunchly monarchical, the Kingdom of Nepal became the youngest republic in the world—without a single bullet being fired. A twenty-first century republic!

All day, Kathmandu was celebration personified. Political party activists staged rallies in different corners of the city, waving flags and chanting republican slogans. Cultural events—traditional dance, songs and recitations—were performed throughout the city. Many young students painted their faces with the slogan *Republican Nepal.* Some radical activists even burnt effigies of the deposed King—their *bête noire.*

There was unending public enthusiasm. In the evening, thousands of candles were lit and firecrackers set off across the blue-black sky, adding to the festivities. Many people illuminated their houses, to celebrate the birth of a republic.

The historic declaration of the republic was made in the Birendra International Convention Centre which was named after the late king and was inaugurated by him 15 years ago. The Centre's Sagarmatha Hall was chosen to host the first official meeting of the new Constituent Assembly, signalling the end of the rule of the Shah dynasty.

Visibly excited newly elected representatives walked on the red carpet proudly, as they entered the Sagarmatha Hall. Unlike in the previous parliament, where the use of *labeda surwal* (the traditional costume of the dominant group in Nepal) and the Nepali language were mandatory for elected representatives, the Constituent Assembly saw its members wearing a range of attires—*kurta-*

pyajama, bakhu, sarong, western casuals and formals and speaking different languages. To a large extent, they reflected the cultural, religious, linguistic and ethnic diversity of Nepal. Most impressive was the participation of women—who constituted one-third of the legislative body.

The official opening, scheduled for 11 o'clock in the morning, was delayed by ten hours due to the last minute differences between the political parties about issues related to the declaration of the republic. One of the main concerns was the type of president that Nepal should have. The Maoists wanted an executive president, whereas the other parties called for a ceremonial one. Although the Maoists had agreed on a ceremonial president the day before, they were still undecided about the nature of presidential powers and duties.

Finally, around 9 o'clock in the evening the Chair, Kul Bahadur Gurung, announced the opening of the first meeting of the Constituent Assembly. The Interim Head of State and Prime Minister Girija Prasad Koirala, supported by an assistant, came to the podium. In a measured but confident tone, Koirala said:

> Only once in an era comes a day when a nation transforms itself. Today is that day…In the last few years many have become orphans, many widows…now violence must stop and Nepal has to move towards peace and stability.

His ill health did not permit him to speak for long so the Peace Minister, Ram Chandra Poudyal, finished reading Koirala's speech. Then the Home Minister, Krishna Prasad Sitaula, tabled a motion on behalf of the prime minister, proclaiming the republic.

A few elected representatives spoke on the issue of abolishing monarchy. Only Chandra Bahadur Gurung, from the pro-monarchy Rastriya Prajatantra Party-Nepal (RPP-Nepal), spoke in favour of retaining the monarchy. He said that the monarchy had played an important role in the history of Nepal and should not be abolished. After a brief discussion, the Chair called for a vote. Five hundred and sixty elected representatives voted in favour of a republic; only four Constituent Assembly members, from the RPP-Nepal, voted against it. Nepal was immediately declared a federal republic, amid thunderous applause. This historic meeting ended with an instruction to the King to vacate the Royal Palace within the next fifteen days.

At around the same time, a few kilometres from the International Convention Hall, the King was watching television in his private chamber at the Royal Palace. The following day, he ordered his aide-de-camp to remove the royal standard outside the Palace and replace it with the national flag of Nepal, to demonstrate that he had accepted the popular verdict.

That a day like this would come was unimaginable for many Nepalese. The King had been worshipped as an avatar of Bishnu, one of the Hindu Trinity. Many Nepalese cared deeply for the monarch, who was seen as the pillar of national unity, a guardian and a father figure for the common people.

Was this a happy moment in a proud nation's history? Or chapter failure? Indeed, how did this day come about?

The Setting:
The Kingdom in the Clouds

Chapter 1

Only a few years before the first meeting of the elected Constituent Assembly, the political scene in Nepal had been radically different. The most momentous event was that which occurred on 1 February 2005, triggering extensive changes across the Himalayan kingdom.

On that cold February morning, the day started with the usual rituals at the Narayanhiti Royal Palace, the centre of power in Nepal at that time. The palace staff were busy doing their chores. Over 1,800 of the best trained soldiers of the Royal Nepal Army, who were protecting the Palace and its regal residents, were preparing for their day after the reveille. Other staff were tending cows, and thorough bred horses of Arabian, English and Nepalese strains, in the animal shelters. One of the prized horses was a personal gift from Queen Elizabeth of Great Britain.

At ten, King Gyanendra entered a studio in the palace precincts. The palace staff kowtowed to His Majesty as he passed. A select group of journalists and photographers were eagerly waiting for him. Flash lights blazed and there was a rush towards His Majesty.

The King nodded a stern acknowledgement as he entered the room, appearing all set to make a live nationwide telecast. As King Gyanendra took his seat, the triangular national flag hung limply on his right side, and the square-shaped royal standard jutted obtrusively on his left. Both were crimson in colour, signifying military power—the strength of the Nepalese monarchy. Behind his chair was the coat of arms, the official seal of His Majesty's Government of Nepal.

The proclamation began with King Gyanendra's glorification of the Shah Dynasty's proud tradition of respecting the people's desires. Then, with his usual tinge of arrogance, he criticised the Nepalese political parties for ignoring the people, bickering for power, misusing the state apparatus and competing for individual or partisan interests at the cost of the nation.

The King also declared that he had consulted the common people, senior citizens, civil society members and political leaders, to ascertain the wishes of the Nepalese citizens. He remarked, "The people clearly wish for ethical democratic practice, a free-market economy, good governance, and the rule of law."

The King's face was ablaze with pride and political defiance as he went on to claim:

> The close ties between the King and the people are the shields of protection for Nepal's freedom, unity, and any onslaught on sovereignty. Our wish is that no Nepalese should suffer any pain and all of you should get economic, social, and political justice. The monarchy is not guided by cheap populism but by the welfare and progress of the people and the country.

The King's features hardened as he lambasted the Maoists as a terrorist group. He denounced them for destroying the country's infra-structure and accused them of extorting donations, and terrorising and killing innocent people. The King added:

> I am fighting against the Nepalese Maoists specifically but this is part of a common fight of nations against terrorism, just like the US war on terror post the 9/11 attacks.

Brightening up somewhat, the King eventually proclaimed his actual intention, saying:

> Due to the responsibility vested in me to save nationalism, national unity, and sovereignty, and to establish peace and security, and save the country from any kind of further deterioration, according to the spirit of The Constitution of the Kingdom of Nepal 1990, and in keeping with the spirit of Article 27, sub-Article (3), I hereby dismiss the Council of Ministers. The new Council of Ministers will be formed under my Chairmanship. This Council of Minister's priority will be directed towards managing peace, better governance, and reactivating democracy in the coming three years.

The King's voice was deceptively soft yet deep enough to be clearly audible and his language was formal. As if to give his takeover a divine sanction he invoked the usual royal last liner with visible theocratic fervour, 'May Lord Pashupatinath protect all of us. *Jaya* [Hail] Nepal!'

After the King's short speech a troubled hush settled on the country. A state of emergency was immediately declared—suspending freedom of speech and assembly and the right to information. It legalised preventive detention, on grounds of national security. Almost instantly, phone lines and mobile phone networks were severed. Internet service providers were shut down and all satellite communication links were disabled. Even the satellite link serving commercial airlines was shut down. Airports were closed and all international flights were diverted from Kathmandu.

The soldiers of the Royal Nepal Army marched into the leading media houses to stop all operations and to seize control of independent radio and FM stations. The security forces forced into the residences of senior leaders and put them under house arrest. Around a thousand political activists, journalists and human rights workers were rounded up and jailed.

The twelfth King of the unshakeable Shah dynasty, which had withstood both the Mughals and the British imperialists, *Paramadhipati Atirathi Param Senadhipati Rashtranayak Sri Pach Maharajdhiraj* Gyanendra Bir Bikram Shah Dev had crossed the Rubicon. Did he know where he was heading?

Chapter 2

King Gyanendra's confidants claim that the King's real intention behind the takeover in February 2005 was to reduce the Maoists' military strength, reduce their bargaining power and compel them to engage in talks. The King hoped this move would establish his role as peacemaker, enhancing the position of monarchy for years to come. He believed the monarchy should play a constructive role in the process of re-building the nation.

But many of the King's close associates politely and discreetly questioned the wisdom of his adoption of the Chairmanship of the Government, which no King, except his power-hungry father, had done before. King Gyanendra justified his action by indicating that 'an extreme situation demands extreme measures…A little less would have yielded no results at all.' What happened next was far from expected, like everything else in Gyanendra's bizarrely *peculiar* life.

Gyanendra Bir Bikram Shah Dev was born in Narayanhiti durbar on 7 July 1947, the fourth child of His Royal Highness Crown Prince Mahendra Bir Bikram Shah Dev and Her Royal Highness Crown Princess Indra Rajya Laxmi Devi Shah. Amidst great celebrations, the Royal Nepal Army gave a 19-gun salute in honour of the birth of a new *Adhirajkumar*, or the prince.

Unfortunately, within a few minutes of his birth, the court astrologer ominously declared that the newborn would bring bad luck to his father. So he was sent to live with his maternal Rana grandparents in Baghdurbar (the Tiger Court, a residence of Rana rulers). At that time, court astrologers and priests held enormous sway over the Hindu kings in Nepal, as well as most of the nobility or courtiers, who were mired in superstitions and pseudo-science. All major decisions had to be vetted by these dispensers of traditional knowledge.

In 1950, when the toddler Gyanendra had barely started to speak, his mother died while giving birth to her sixth child. Within two months of this tragedy, Gyanendra's grandfather, His Majesty King Tribhuvan, and other royal family members—supportive of increasingly assertive democratic forces in the country—left the Palace for an undisclosed destination, where they could lobby against the autocratic Rana regime.

Although most of his family went to India, it later emerged that Prince Gyanendra was left behind in Baghdurbar. This was done possibly because removing him may have made the Ranas suspicious. But another possible reason could be compliance with the court astrologer's suggestion. So, the young prince was left at the mercy of ruthless enemies who had manipulated the Shahs for decades. And all at once, there was a constitutional void in the Kingdom of Nepal.

On 7 November 1950, fearful of the ongoing geo-political machinations, and interference from India, the Rana coterie declared Gyanendra the ninth King of Nepal. Maharaja Mohan Sumsher—the ninth Rana Prime Minister—organised an impressive coronation ceremony and showered gold on the new King. The rare honour of a 31-gun salute, meant only for the Sovereign, was fired for the minor King by the loyal soldiers of the Royal Nepal Army, and coins were struck in his name. Rana generals in Napoleonic-style military uniforms, bejewelled helmets, medals, and swords—along with other courtiers—offered silver coins as they bowed down in *darshan* to pay him homage.

However, unexpectedly, three months later King Gyanendra was dethroned and stripped of all regal trappings and deference. Although he was too young to remember these extraordinary events, they may have instilled in him a sense of deep insecurity and lingering loss.

In February 1951, King Tribhuvan, Gyanendra's grandfather, was restored to his throne as a result of armed insurrection by anti-Rana forces and Indian pressure tactics. King Tribhuvan was the eighth successor to King Prithivinarayan Shah, whose role in the consolidation of a united kingdom had established the Shah Dynasty as a pillar of national unity.

When the Ranas usurped their power in the mid-nineteenth century, the Shahs were reduced to merely puppet kings. At the end of the Rana regime, the Shah Kings were liberated from the clutches of the Rana rulers and their pre-eminence was re-established in the Himalayan Kingdom. The only Hindu state in the world at that time, this event had a far-reaching effect.

Sensing the aspirations of his people, the reinstated King proclaimed a democratic constitution that led to the end of Rana's control in all affairs of the state. He also agreed to hold an election for a Constituent Assembly, so a new constitution for Nepal could be drafted. Through this political process Gyanendra again became third in the line of succession, reverting to his earlier position as a prince.

The fall of the Rana regime gave Gyanendra an opportunity that was previously denied to other Shah Princes—a modern education. His father, who had not been allowed to study during the Rana regime, wanted his sons to have the best education. So the three Hindu princes were sent to St Joseph's School (also known as the Harrow of the East) in Darjeeling, India.

For the Gorkhali princes, it was their first experience of the world outside the protected palace walls. While Birendra was shy and restrained, Gyanendra openly flaunted his lineage. His school friends remember him introducing himself as the former King of Nepal and always having people around him who would listen obediently to his every word. Once when the Indian Prime Minister Jawaharlal Nehru visited their school, and the Shah Princes were made to line up alongside other students to welcome him, Prince Gyanendra was said to have remarked in his recently acquired English accent: "It is for Prime Minister Nehru to receive us."

After graduating from St Joseph's College, Prince Birendra was sent to premier educational institutions like Eton College, Harvard University and finally, Tokyo University—while Prince Gyanendra, along with their younger brother Dhirendra, was asked to return home. Gyanendra got a degree—without actually attending classes (often the case in many South Asian colleges and universities)—from Tribhuvan University in Nepal, recently opened and named after his grandfather.

As a consequence of these events, Birendra experienced a wider exposure, leading to a keen understanding of the world, while Gyanendra's experiences were confined to the limited influence of the mindset prevalent in the tiny hill-station of Darjeeling, which was not much different from that of his own kingdom. The insular outlook back home in Nepal also stifled the intellectual development necessary to deal with a rapidly modernising world, and a fast-changing country.

As he had lost his mother at an early age, Gyanendra was considerably influenced by his father Mahendra. He turned into a determined and ambitious individual, just like his father. He also acquired his love for poetry from his father, who was a fine poet.

King Mahendra is seen as one of the most controversial figures in modern Nepal. With his smart political manoeuvres he managed to sideline the much-loved and internationally acclaimed Nepalese democratic leader—Bishweshwar Prasad Koirala. He substituted the multiparty democracy that Koirala envisioned with an institutional experiment, which advantaged his own position—a partyless panchayat system. Although the Nepalese people would never forgive King Mahendra for his brutal, and unrelenting attack on democracy, it cannot be denied that he was the most powerful and clever monarch of the Shah dynasty.

King Mahendra reshaped Nepal's monarchy, transforming it from a feeble entity into an almost unbeatable political force inside Nepal. Through his unbridled power, Mahendra accumulated unprecedented wealth for his royal treasury, a wealth that was vital for the continuance and supremacy of his autocracy. Thus, the Shah Kings, who had been financially weak, insecure and dependent on the Ranas till the 1950s, quickly became prosperous.

King Mahendra also raised the international profile of the Royal Family of Nepal by frequently visiting other countries as well as regularly receiving foreign guests. During his reign, the Royal Family became the epitome of grandeur, opulence and power, and above all, the most recognisable symbol of national pride. Celebrities flocked to this kingdom of Hindu Kings.

King Mahendra also modernised anachronous traditions of the *Raj durbar* (Royal Palace), which had often been exploitative, particularly when it came to marriage or sexual relationships. He was the first heir-apparent to break the Thakuri caste tradition of bigamy. Even the most restrained among the rulers were expected to marry a minimum of two wives, although technically, there was no upper limit. In affluent times, when State coffers were full, the only considerations regarding choice of marriage partners were inclination, appetite and potency. *Lyaite*, *bhitrini*, concubines and dancing girls were always plentiful. One of the Shah Kings, Rana Bahadur Shah, had over 15 legally wedded wives—most of whom committed *sati* or self-immolation, when their beloved King died. King Mahendra's aging father had also had many young wives, in addition to several younger concubines.

Mahendra was only married to Indra Rajya Laxmi for nine years, till her early death. In 1952, he re-married his wife's younger sister, Ratna Rajya Laxmi in order to honour the dying wish of his Queen. Mahendra had learnt that rifts in the palace occurred because of irreconcilable personal differences between female family members. Hence, he urged his sons to marry sisters from the same family, in order to keep feminine envy at bay.

Commanded by his father, the King, the 23-year-old Prince unquestioningly married 19 years old Komal Rajya Laxmi Rana. This meant the three princes—Birendra, Gyanendra and Dhirendra—married the three Rana sisters, Aishwarya, Komal and Preksha, in the same year (1970). Despite their internecine strife owing to their long political rivalry, the Rana–Shah marriages in the *Raj durbar* dated back to the mid-nineteenth century, when the founder of the Rana regime, Jang Bahadur, married his daughter to King Surendra, in order to consolidate his position. These politically-motivated marriages bonded two ruling families together in a strange yet complicated way.

Apart from the Ranas, the Shah Kings also married illustrious Rajputs from the desert kingships of Rajasthan in the Regent-represented British Raj. Prince Gyanendra's grandmothers, King Tribhuvan's wives, were all Rajput princesses, daughters of the Maharaja of Kashipur—a small kingdom within the United Provinces of British India. Other princes and princesses married, for example, into the Royal Houses of Jodhpur, Sikar, Mayurbhanj and Udaipur. By convention, the Royals of Nepal married Rajputs, Ranas or Thakuris. Their alliances with women of other castes were not considered legitimate, even if these marriages were actually consummated secretly.

After his marriage, Gyanendra and his new wife moved out of the Narayanhiti palace, as was the family custom, into Nirmal Niwas—a private residence a few kilometres north of the palace. His wife was neither glamorous, like her eldest sister Aishwarya, nor beautiful like the youngest one, Preksha. Unlike her sisters, who became entangled in controversy (Queen Aishwarya because of her domineering personality and Preksha because of her love affairs), Komal managed to retain her reputation and sustained an image of softness, cleanliness and focused on family.

Like his *better half*, Gyanendra refrained from doing anything which could lead to personal scandal. His extra-marital liaisons, if there were any, were discrete. While Prince Dhirendra separated from his wife to marry a British woman, Prince Gyanendra remained loyal to his marriage.

As a prince, Gyanendra did not have any executive power. His high ranking simply offered ceremonial, symbolic status—unlike his brother, King Birendra, who was the sovereign head of the country. Constitutionally, the King of Nepal had extraordinary powers, in addition to his near-divine social stature.

Now and then, when King Birendra travelled abroad, Gyanendra stood in for his brother until Crown Prince Dipendra was mature enough to assume this duty. Although this briefly acquainted him with kingly duties, such short spells in office were not sufficient to groom him to be a King.

In 1982, Gyanendra was appointed the Chairman of King Mahendra's Trust for Nature Conservation, which he took very sincerely. He became so involved in the work of the Trust that he was deeply troubled if trees were cut or the environment was harmed. This role had a profound impact on the prince, who once loved hunting and fishing, and he developed a new compassion for nature.

Besides this growing interest in nature protection, Gyanendra was said to possess good business acumen. He set up several businesses, including a tea-estate, a five-star hotel, a tobacco company and other trading companies dealing with the import of cars. Nevertheless, he paid the price for his commercial success when anti-royalist forces spread stories that he had used his royal influence to advance his business interests. There were also unconfirmed stories about him being involved in theft, smuggling and drug-trafficking, which poisoned public opinion against him.

After the historic change in 1990, that rendered Nepal's absolute monarch without power, resulting in a constitutional, but practically *toothless*, King, the popularity of Birendra's family soared, while Gyanendra's family became increasingly unpopular. In 1990, there were rumours that Gyanendra was vehemently opposed to democracy. The steady *fall from grace* of Gyanendra was also due to his only son Paras, who shamelessly ignored the social obligations that came with his royal privilege—and stories about his eccentricities, and often vile crimes, spread across the kingdom. Despite being married to a beautiful Rajput princess, Himani Rajya Laxmi, Paras' numerous extra-marital affairs worsened his reputation.

In 2000, over half a million Nepalese people sent a petition to King Birendra requesting him to strip Paras of all his royal privileges. He had been involved in a hit-and-run accident case that caused the death of a popular musician, Praveen Gurung. This had happened at a very difficult time for the Nepalese monarchy, which was already threatened like never before in its history.

King Birendra, who had already taken action against his youngest brother when he married a Christian woman, now faced having to remove Paras' royal title. But, in the end, it is said that the King was persuaded by Gyanendra in not taking any punitive action against Paras. Any such action, if taken, may have had far-reaching implications for Prince Gyanendra's life in general and his career in particular, because of the most inconceivable and dramatic event that occurred a year later.

On 1 June 2001, according to the official reports, Prince Gyanendra was in the Royal Family's Palace in Pokhara valley—a six-hour drive from the capital. On his return to Kathmandu, he was taken to a hospital and shown his two brothers, two sisters, nephew, niece and other close relatives, lying dead or seriously injured in the intensive care unit. Among them was his wife, who had a bullet in her left lung.

Crown Prince Dipendra had allegedly killed King Birendra's entire family, and then mortally wounded himself. Apparently this was because his mother would not let him marry his lover of over ten years Devyani Rana, the great-granddaughter of Maharaja Chandra Sumsher, the fifth Rana Prime Minister. After this massacre, an emergency meeting of the *Raj Parishad* (Privy Council) declared the comatose Dipendra the new King and appointed Gyanendra the Regent. Three days later, when King Dipendra died, the *Raj Parishad* proclaimed Gyanendra his successor, and he became the Twelfth King of the Shah dynasty.

This happened almost 50 years after Gyanendra had first become King of Nepal, when he was only a child. But this coronation was not an exciting occasion as the first one had been. The Royal Family and the entire nation was in deep mourning and on the day Gyanendra was crowned, there were rumours that he may have been behind the Narayanhiti massacre.

The Nepalese people refused to believe that the King's son, especially their much-liked Crown Prince Dipendra, could have killed his own family so brutally. Instead, they suspected Prince Gyanendra, the direct beneficiary of the regicide. His inexplicable absence from the family gathering on the night of the massacre, the clumsy handling of the investigation process, the casual national broadcast at the end of the enquiry, the survival of all the immediate members of Gyanendra's family, his public image as a hardliner and his son's notoriety, worked together to make people seriously doubt their new King's innocence.

However, the people of Nepal accepted his succession because they still wanted a monarchy. The institution was inalienably linked to the colour and vibrancy of the country's traditions and customs. Festivals, rituals and social and cultural events were presided over by the King, giving the Nepalese a sense of continuity which no other South Asian country enjoyed to the same extent. The King satisfied the emotional needs of a poor and ailing country. So despite protests and anti-Gyanendra slogans, his enthronement ceremony was held on 4 June 2001. The *Raj Guru* (the Royal Priest) placed the emerald-studded crown, peaked by plumes of a bird of paradise, once again onto his *blessed* head.

But what then led to the King's swift downfall, bringing an end to the monarchy? He was unable to adapt to the changing times. Even in an age of globalised democracy and decentralisation, Gyanendra wanted to be an active king with real executive powers, unlike his elder brother. He was guided by principal and military secretariats inside the palace and a few uninspiring advisors. His naturally ambitious mind made him consider the provisions of the 1990 Constitution in a different light. His new interpretation of the constitution led him, in October 2002, to dismiss the elected prime minister and assume discretionary powers himself. He sought to divide political parties by playing one against the other, and enhanced his grip on the administration and the army. In 2004, he made the parliament increase the Palace budget significantly. King Gyanendra had once again established the Narayanhiti Palace as the centre of power in Nepal. The February takeover was designed to cement this position, but finally became one of the main reasons for his downfall.

Chapter 3

A few kilometres north of where King Gyanendra made his historic Royal Proclamation of 1 February 2005, inside an ordinary two-storey urban building in Maharajgunj, an old and feeble man appeared deeply worried. His face was wrinkled by stress and advancing age. Despite his apparent physical weakness, a dozen armed men were positioned outside his house to stop him from going out.

This man was Girija Prasad Koirala, the first political leader to be placed under house arrest following the royal takeover. From a trusted army confidant he had learnt of the King's intention to stage a takeover of the government the day before the Proclamation. Ever since, he felt restless.

On that first morning of February in 2005, Koirala was discussing the possible impact of the King's intended takeover with his close associates. One of them was Nona Koirala—the octogenarian leader's closest advisor. Nona was Koirala's sister-in-law, married to one of his brothers, Keshab Prasad Koirala. Many people close to the democratic veteran claimed that after the death of his brother Keshab, widower Koirala became close to Nona. They also said that she was responsible for both the successes and failures in Koirala's political career.

Another person engaged in the discussion with Koirala that day was Sher Bahadur Deuba, one of the most controversial figures in Nepal's democratic history and Koirala's once political rival in the Nepali Congress party. A few years earlier Deuba had been a controversial prime minister. In May 2002 he sought to extend the ongoing state of emergency, imposed by the government to tackle the Maoist insurgency. His party's central committee—led by Koirala—had directed Deuba not to prolong the Emergency but he had refused to comply and instead tabled a parliamentary bill, in an attempt to extend the Emergency. Deuba was threatened with a no-confidence vote by his party, and in response he recommended the King to dissolve the parliament.

The immediate effect was that the democratically elected administration was weakened and the King's power increased. Insiders hinted that Deuba's matrimonial alliance with Arzoo Rana, the great-granddaughter of Maharaja Juddha Sumsher—who was also a relative of the King—was the main reason behind Deuba's action that led to strengthening the King's power and influence, at the cost of the elected representatives.

However, five months after the dissolution of the parliament in October 2002, the King dismissed Deuba on a charge of *incompetency*. He went on to appoint a number of prime ministers of his own choice before favouring Deuba again, and making him prime minister in June 2004. But this did not last long; on 1 February 2005 the King again dismissed Deuba, for *utter ineptitude*. It was no surprise, therefore, that Deuba turned to Koirala for guidance, despite their strong political rivalry.

Unlike Deuba and other political leaders, the seasoned politician Koirala had for some time been suspicious of the King's intentions. In an interview, he narrated one particular incident that made him wary. He said:

> In the summer of 2002, as the President of the Nepali Congress, I had gone to New Delhi to meet with the Maoist leaders. This was after my party's central committee meeting mandated me to initiate a dialogue for peace with the Maoists. We were really concerned about the indiscriminate murder of our party workers by the Maoists. The widows of the murdered were pressurising us to do something decisive about it as soon as possible. A huge number of Congress workers in the villages, whose property was captured by the Maoists, also pressurised us.
>
> In this context, I went to Delhi with Nona, Sujata and Chakra Prasad Bastola [Koirala's niece's husband, who was a Nepali Congress central committee member]. The contact person in Delhi was one of the Maoists' central committee members, Bamdev Chettri. That was the time when the Maoists were on the offensive, so meeting Maoists leaders was not that easy. All leaders were underground.
>
> Bamdev *jee* did not tell us the name of the exact venue but took us to the outskirts of Delhi. I wanted to meet the Maoist leaders in the morning before my Indian security guards came, in order to maintain the confidentiality from the Indian authorities. In a tiny house, I met the Maoist Chairman Prachanda for the first time in my life. The deputy leader of the Maoist party, Baburam Bhattarai was also there. The meeting lasted for 45 minutes, during which we discussed how to move forward.

> Following my meeting with Prachanda *jee*, the Maoists agreed to hold talks with the parliament. As far as we were concerned the five principles of the 1990 Constitution—multiparty democracy, a parliamentary system, an independent judiciary, human and civil rights and a constitutional monarchy—were not-negotiable, and the Maoists had to clarify the objectives of the Constituent Assembly.
>
> After reaching this understanding, I informed King Gyanendra, as the head of state, about the meeting with the Maoists in Delhi. King Gyanendra said it was fine with him and that the parliament should hold talks with the Maoists, but he asked me what the King's role would be. I explained to His Majesty that the parliament was none other than the King-in-Parliament. But from the King's expression, it appeared that he wanted to hold talks with the Maoists himself, in order that he, rather than the parliament, could agree on a peace process.
>
> With the King's *green light* to go ahead with the talks with the Maoists, I organised a mass rally with all the political parties represented in the parliament, on 10 May 2002. In the rally, I appealed to the Maoists to respond to the political parties within a week, to demonstrate their commitment to the peace talks. The Maoists responded within three days. Serious planning was done to move the dialogue with the Maoists and to hold formal talks thereafter. This is why the Nepali Congress central committee directed Deuba not to extend the ongoing emergency. However, this initiative for peace was halted when the King conspired with Deuba to dissolve Parliament, preventing talks with the Maoists from taking place.

Since the dissolution of the parliament in May 2002, Koirala led a democratic front of five parliamentary parties (Nepali Congress, Unified Marxist-Leninist, Nepal Sadbhavana Party-Anandidevi, Nepal Workers and Peasants Party, People's Front) which demanded the restoration of the dissolved parliament. Many people, including representatives of powerful countries like the US, the UK and India criticised Koirala and his campaign as unfeasible. The last parliament was dissolved by an elected prime minister and the Supreme Court of Nepal had later validated this action.

However, Koirala maintained that the restoration of the dissolved parliament was the only solution to the continuing political turmoil in the country. To achieve this end he travelled across the country, organising speaking tours demanding the restoration of the parliament. At times, his health deteriorated so much that he had to be rushed to Kathmandu. But such health problems were not enough to dampen the spirit of this strong-willed man or stop him fighting with missionary fervour for a multiparty democratic system.

Koirala believed that the King had two options. One was to reinstate the House of Representatives, activate the 1990 Constitution and preserve himself within a consolidated constitutional monarchy and multiparty democracy. The other—tactical and short-term—was to continue to *play* people's aspirations, but this would likely sweep the kingship away.

As a person who had always believed in constitutional monarchy, Koirala wanted the King to choose the first option. He urged national and international pressure against the King, hoping that the monarch would listen to him. But King Gyanendra chose not to, and launched his takeover on 1 February 2005.

Koirala feared this was the point of no return for King Gyanendra and unfortunately, also for the centuries-old institution of monarchy in Nepal, which he, his family, his party and the majority of the Nepalese people had supported thus far.

Chapter 4

As someone who had dealt with the Kings of Nepal since 1950, Koirala was not surprised by the royal takeover in 2005. By late twentieth century, the monarchy in Nepal was well-established, modeled on its counterparts in medieval Europe, and the struggle for democracy was marked by confrontation with the King.

In 1950, King Gyanendra's grandfather King Tribhuvan supported the ongoing democratic movement, which made the collapse of the repressive Rana regime possible without much bloodshed. Nonetheless, when the regime caved in, King Tribhuvan's intentions changed. Encouraged by his reactionary Rana relatives, he wanted to consolidate power for himself, by weakening the democratic parties. Since then this strategy has been adopted by successive monarchs. King Tribhuvan's successor, King Mahendra ruthlessly suppressed democratic forces throughout his entire reign. His policy was to divide the leftist and rightist (or centrist) democratic forces, in order to weaken the movement that challenged the palace authority. Even the benevolent and wise King Birendra was said to have a *soft spot* for the Maoist armed insurgency, which made it difficult for democratic forces to effectively confront their violence.

But in 2005 the King staged his takeover at the wrong time. The population was caught between the two armies of the State and the Maoists. For Koirala, King Gyanendra's takeover did not provide a solution but rather added to the already grave challenges facing the country because of the ongoing Maoist People's War. Koirala believed, first, the legitimate government should be restored. That's why at the age of eighty he was still fighting for democracy. His struggle had begun over half a century earlier, when the world was a different place. He now hoped democracy would triumph, so that the future generations would not have to fight. He called this struggle the *last battle in my life*.

Girija Prasad Koirala, or *Girijababu* as he was popularly known, was born in 1925 into a family that would give several political reformers and democratic fighters to Nepal including three prime ministers. Most importantly, it was his family that gave Nepal its *most beloved* leader, and the first elected Prime Minister, Bishweshwar Prasad Koirala.

Girija Prasad's father Krishna Prasad Koirala was a committed social reformer. To be a propagator of reform was a crime in the tyrannical Rana regime. After being appalled by the poverty of the Nepalese people, Krishna Prasad sent a parcel of tattered clothes to the ruling Maharaja Chandra Sumsher, to remind him of the plight of the common Nepalese. The whole Koirala family had to pay the price for his non-conformist and progressive actions. Their huge ancestral property was seized and 45 members of the Koirala family were exiled to India. They became *nomads*, wandering from place to place.

Girija Prasad Koirala's childhood was one of deprivation, because his father did not have the means to support his family in exile. Once, when Koirala was really young, he saw his mother, brothers and sisters crying together. Not understanding why, he went to a corner with his younger sister Indira and started laughing uncontrollably. Sadly, later when he grew up, he learnt that his family was crying because one of his older brothers had died of cholera and they did not have enough money for his cremation. That was the extent of poverty in which Girija Prasad grew up.

In 1929, after the death of Maharaja Chandra Sumsher, the Koirala family was allowed to return home. They experienced good times, as the family business became profitable. But much of the money earned from the business was not spent on the family but on social reforms. His father opened the first school providing free education in Biratnagar. Their ancestral house, the Koirala *niwas* (residence) in Biratnagar in eastern Nepal, was open to all. It welcomed people with open arms, a tradition that continues until today. Krishna Prasad's *mantra* was based on the service of those in need. He instilled in his children a sense of duty towards the less privileged.

This encouraged his sons to pursue lives of public service. Influenced by India's freedom fighters, Girija Prasad's brothers (notably Bishweshwar Prasad Koirala) actively participated in the freedom movement and were jailed many times. Bishweshwar believed it was important to expel the British from India, because the Raj had supported the Rana regime in Nepal. After the Second World War, when it became clear that Britain would leave India, Bishweshwar established the All India Nepali National Congress in Varanasi, and called on those in favour of democracy in Nepal for support. This organisation merged with other similar organisations in January 1947 to form the Nepali National Congress, with the goal of replacing the Rana regime with a democratic government. Bishweshwar Prasad Koirala, who was influenced by the socialist movement, led the new Congress party. His charismatic leadership attracted thousands of people as supporters, even in those harsh times of the oppressive Rana regime. Girijababu was also deeply influenced by Bishweshwar, his *san daju* (elder brother) and his commitment to the establishment of democratic rights for the people.

At this time Girija Prasad worked as a clerk in a large jute mill in Biratnagar, in which the Ranas were major stakeholders. Unable to tolerate the poor conditions of mill workers, Girija Prasad organised a strike and called for more equal treatment of all workers in the industry. The unrest spread to other factories across Biratnagar, and prompted the Nepali National Congress to encourage development of a broader movement for democracy in Nepal. Most members of the Koirala family, including democratic activists, participated in this agitation. Although most of the leaders were immediately arrested, the Rana rulers were forced to announce some new democratically oriented reforms.

While still in prison, Girija Prasad's brother Bishweshwar was diagnosed with cancer and consequently, was released. However, nearly a year later he was imprisoned again, in the most inhuman conditions. In protest, Bishweshwar went on a hunger strike. When Girija Prasad was sent from his jail to convince his brother to eat, he found his brother's body in chains and his fingers nailed to the floor. Girija Prasad was so shocked that he decided to go on a hunger strike himself. Finally, after almost 28 days of hunger strike, Bishweshwar was released. Girija Prasad derived much strength from this event, and himself went on a strike until he too was released. Nevertheless, he was soon re-arrested. This time he escaped from the army barracks where he was kept, so he could participate in the struggle for democracy that was fast gaining momentum in Nepal.

In early 1950, the Nepali National Congress, led by Bishweshwar, merged with the Nepal Democratic Congress to form the Nepali Congress (NC) party. This newly formed party adhered to the principles of democracy and socialism. Significantly, the same year, the Nepali Congress passed a resolution to launch an armed revolution to end the Rana regime. Historical accounts reveal that Bishweshwar and Girija were both against using violence, but they were forced by the leaders of the Nepal Democratic Congress to accept it as necessary;

that the harsh Rana regime could be ended by peaceful means was considered, at best, to be naïve.

When the armed insurrection was finally launched by the Nepali Congress in November 1950, the 25-year-old Girija Prasad worked as a political commissar, leading several armed attacks. But because of the pressure from India's Prime Minister Nehru, who had become nervous about communist China's annexation of Tibet, the Nepali Congress party had to quickly suspend its armed action. A peace settlement was soon reached, based on a power-sharing arrangement with the Ranas, known as the Delhi Compromise. This compromise, nevertheless, did end the 103-year Rana oligarchy.

After the democratic change in 1950, Girija's eldest brother, Matrika Prasad Koirala, became the first commoner to be appointed as prime minister of Nepal. And in 1959, when the first parliamentary elections took place, Bishweshwar Prasad Koirala became the first elected prime minister, securing a two-thirds majority. Girija Prasad did not contest the elections. Instead, he concentrated on the party organisation, as Party President of Morang district. According to Girija Prasad, he was not interested in party politics per se, after the democratic system had been established in Nepal. As his own brother was the leader, he did not have any personal political ambition. However, destiny had other plans in store for him.

In 1960, when King Mahendra usurped all the executive powers, Girija Prasad—along with other Koirala family members—was again imprisoned. He remained there for seven years, finally being released in 1967 after staging a hunger strike for 24 days. His release this time was more painful than his incarceration. Like many heroes of history, Girija Prasad had suffered greatly. He had lost the love of his life, Sushma.

Girija Prasad had met Sushma, a friend of his sister-in-law Nona, in Biratnagar. Gradually, they became close. It was Sushma who is said to have first proposed marriage. Girija Prasad wanted to get married on the day India got independence in 1947. However, a normal marriage ceremony was not possible, because his family objected to the union. Sushma already had a son from her previous, failed marriage, so Girija Prasad's mother was against him marrying her. In the end, 26-year-old Girija Prasad eloped with Sushma to Calcutta, where they were married.

Girija Prasad loved his wife deeply and their love created a new life, their daughter Sujata. Yet his commitment to democracy kept him constantly away from his family—in prison, in exile, or in hiding. A graduate from Banaras Hindu University, Sushma soon became a part of her husband's political struggle. Unfortunately, he was not destined to enjoy the love and support of his wife for long. Tragically, Sushma died while trying to save her elder sister, who was involved in an accident with a stove. Seeing her sister's clothes catch fire, Sushma had rushed to save her. Her clothes caught fire too and both sisters were badly injured.

Girija Prasad was not in town at that time. When he rushed home, he found his wife in hospital, with severe burns. She died a few days later. Although Girija Prasad had to help his daughter Sujata and adopted son Suresh to cope with the loss of their mother, he did not allow this devastating personal tragedy to destroy his commitment to democracy.

At that time, Bishweshwar Prasad Koirala and other senior Nepali Congress leaders were still in prison. Girija Prasad established contact with the King and eventually succeeded in getting them released. Bishweshwar said in his autobiography that Girija Prasad's role in this episode made senior Congress leaders realise that his youngest brother was a *good negotiator and politically astute.*

Soon after being released, most of the leaders of Nepali Congress including Bishweshwar Prasad Koirala, went into exile. Girija Prasad followed them. While on exile, Bishweshwar concluded that democracy cannot be restored in Nepal without an armed revolution. Girija Prasad and other Congress workers began making the necessary preparations. In 1973, Girija Prasad masterminded the hijacking of an airplane carrying money equivalent to 3 million Indian rupees, which could be used to fund the planned armed revolution. A few years later, the Nepali Congress decided to capture the Okhaldhunga district in Nepal through an armed attack, which resulted in the death of many Nepali Congress activists. The Nepali Congress gradually distanced itself from violence after this bad experience.

In 1976, Bishweshwar returned to Nepal with a new policy of National Reconciliation, advocating an understanding between the King and the people for the restoration of democracy. Soon afterwards, following widespread student unrest, King Birendra announced a national referendum—offering the people the chance to choose between a multiparty democracy and a reformed party-less panchayat system. On the eve of this referendum, Girija Prasad was formally appointed as the General Secretary of the Nepali Congress by the party President,

Bishweshwar. Girija Prasad continued in this key position until he became the party President. Some Congress activists claim that Girijababu's easy-going nature, energetic aura and extensive travel helped him to consolidate his personal hold on the Congress workers, which in turn, secured him the top job.

Although Girija Prasad was generally in the background while Bishweshwar was alive, he gained unique exposure as the trusted younger brother. Among the five Koirala brothers, the eldest one joined forces with the King. The other two—Tarani and Keshab—were not actively involved in politics. For many party workers, Girija Prasad offered primary access to their leader, Bishweshwar. This helped Girija Prasad to form close relationships with party workers across the country. He also learnt organisational skills, as he engaged in strategic planning. Bishweshwar's vision of democratic socialism drew large numbers of people of all ideological hues and Girija Prasad's job was to *knit* those people into the party's growing organisation.

Before dying in 1982, Bishweshwar handed leadership of the Nepali Congress party over to a troika—consisting of Ganesh Man Singh, Krishna Prasad Bhattarai (both were senior to Girija Prasad) and Girija Prasad Koirala. In the late 1980s, the Nepali Congress leadership took advantage of the geopolitical situation favouring democracy, triggered by the collapse of the Soviet Union. The Congress set up a democratic front with a coalition of moderate Left parties to organise the People's Movement for the restoration of multiparty democracy. This campaign succeeded in 1990, and the multiparty democracy was restored. The new constitution replaced the panchayat system of governance with a system which combined parliamentary democracy and constitutional monarchy.

When the Nepali Congress achieved a comfortable majority in the parliamentary elections in 1991, Girija Prasad became the prime minister. This was an unexpected development because no one had anticipated the electoral defeat of the Acting President of the Nepali Congress—Krishna Prasad Bhattarai, who was also the prime minister in the Interim Government. Many people, even those inside the Nepali Congress, suspected that Koirala was instrumental in Bhattarai's defeat. Therefore, post-1990, Koirala's energy was largely consumed by negotiating the internal differences between the Bhattarai and Koirala factions within the Nepali Congress party. In 1994, when the annual policy of his government failed to get the necessary support in parliament, due to the absence of thirty-six members of the Bhattarai faction, Koirala dissolved the parliament and announced mid-term elections.

Not unexpectedly, with all this political manoeuvring, the elections resulted in a hung parliament—a completely different political scenario. The Nepali Congress was pushed into second position, by a new coalition of moderate Left forces—known as the Unified Marxist Leninist party. Thus began a long period of instability, poor governance and blatant corruption—compounded by condemnable practices of parliamentary democracy in Nepal, such as the *buying and selling* of parliamentarians to form a government. Analysts assert that in the period after this mid-term election, the disenchantment with parliamentary democracy offered a suitable *objective condition* for the Maoist party to launch an armed struggle in 1996.

By historical coincidence in the same year Girija Prasad was elected the Nepali Congress party President, and in 1998 he became prime minister twice. It was during his prime ministership that Girija was ctiticised for allowing the *Kilo Sierra Two* operation—a brutal crackdown on the Maoists which caused the deaths of hundreds of Maoist cadres as well as innocent people. This repressive operation was cited as the main reason for the escalation of the Maoist insurgency.

Girija Prasad again became prime minister in 2000, but had to resign due to the non-cooperation of the army. That was the lowest point in Girija Prasad's political career. He was blamed for everything that went wrong in the country, mainly because the Nepali Congress party which he headed was mostly in power since 1990. Worst of all, he was personally accused of grafting. Many predicted that he would never be able to rise again politically after his resignation in 2001. But Girija Prasad Koirala confounded the pundits and the popular voice. He was not a man to be defeated easily.

The King's takeover in October 2002 prepared the ground for Girija's comeback. This would probably not have been possible otherwise. Girija Prasad was quick to capitalise on the situation, which had developed out of the royal *faux pas*. He led a large restless democratic force, which demanded the reinstatement of parliament. The takeover provided him with an extraordinary opportunity, and he quickly became the champion of populism, pitted against the King, the champion of tradition. This time he would not only be hailed as the undisputed leader of democracy but also that of peace.

Chapter 5

While the aged Koirala was toiling away for the restoration of the parliament, other things were *afoot* in this small country of huge diversity. The armed insurgency was becoming increasingly successful and the revolutionary cause was growing more popular day by day. On that cold morning of 1 February 2005 in the village of Lawang, in the *rebel infested* Rukum district, there were some interesting political developments taking place. All the checkpoints to the village were guarded by Maoist militia with home-made guns and grenades. The major checkpoints were land-mined, soldiers lay in ambush and a company of troops was encamped nearby—as a reserve force. On the hill top, ready to counter attack, were Maoist commanders with heavy guns, General Purpose Machine Guns (GPMG), mortars and powerful telescopic rifles. This impressive security operation was in place to protect a group of important people, who were meeting in a newly built mud house in the middle of the village.

In a large room on the second floor of that mud house the Maoist party was holding a politburo meeting. It had started the week before, and was being held to resolve serious internal differences in the party. This meeting was chaired by Puspha Kamal Dahal *alias* Prachanda, the Chairman of the Maoist party and the supremo of the Maoist War.

Around 35 members of the politburo, excluding those who were in prison, had gathered in Lawang to discuss a crucial resolution, entitled *On Comrade Laldhoj's Letter and Other Activities*. The main tenets of this resolution were against the deputy leader of the Maoist party—Baburam Bhattarai *alias* Laldhoj. Some enraged politburo members claimed that Comrade Laldhoj's activities not only benefited their opponents—who used the conflict within the party as propaganda—but also created confusion within the rank and file of the party, at a critical time when the Maoists had embarked on their final strategic offensive for state power.

At the end of a heated discussion, the majority of the politburo members concluded that Bhattarai's activities were clearly against the basic interests of the Maoist party. They decided to strip him of all the positions he held in the party for an indefinite period and keep him under house arrest. In the backwoods the Maoists had their own *law* and *government*.

The Royal Proclamation a few days later represented a shocking political development. Its reverberations were evident even in sleepy Lawang. The Maoist party extended the politburo meeting until 1 February 2005, continuing their discussions through the morning. They deliberated on how to move forward in the altered political context. Any decision they made would have far-reaching implications for the lives of the majority of Nepalese—so strong and influential had the Maoists become.

The powerful man who led that crucial Maoist meeting was originally called Chabilal Dahal. Born on 11 December 1954, the eldest of eight living siblings, Dahal came from a lower-middle class farmer's family, which lived in a small hamlet in western Nepal. Because of their extreme poverty his family had to move around constantly in search of work.

Chairman Dahal's childhood was the same as any other child of a rural family in Nepal. But an unfortunate incident, which occurred when he was a boy, had filled him with a deep, burning anger that may help explain the ruthlessness he displayed by fighting a tough war. This incident involved his father prostrating himself at the feet of a moneylender, begging for more time to repay his loan. The vicious moneylender was repeatedly kicking his father and was swearing at him. The child had to suppress his desperate rage because he was helpless. Recalling that experience in later life Dahal said "It was a political lesson I would never forget. It changed the course of my life."

Dahal's formal education began in a village school in Chitwan district, in the Inner Tarai Valley, or *Bhitri* Tarai, of southern Nepal. It was a pleasant area, which escaped the sultry heat and mosquitoes of the Tarai region. Battling destitution, his father had migrated there, along with many others. Somehow the family survived and in time, the children were able to go to school.

Although little Dahal did not initially show much aptitude for studies, the child soon realised the importance of education and worked hard as he entered his teens. He impressed one of his teachers so much that the latter suggested a new name for the young Chabilal—Pushpa Kamal, meaning the flower lotus. The young boy, it is said, was so excited that he immediately registered himself in his new name. So, Chabilal officially became Pushpa Kamal. It was around this time (1969–70) that he was first drawn to politics, particularly the burgeoning communist movement in agrarian Nepal.

The communist movement began with the establishment of Nepal's first Communist Party in 1949, against the political backdrop of the anti-Rana struggle. This newly formed party initially joined the armed insurrection, instigated by the Nepali Congress party against the Ranas, but later continued to fight on their own. When the Nepali Congress ended its armed uprising, after an agreement negotiated with the Rana Prime Minister, the Communist Party denounced the peace settlement as a *compromise* and called it a *betrayal of the revolution*. The party then formed a progressive front to agitate against the government. As a result of its alleged involvement in the armed revolt the Communist Party was banned in 1952 for nearly four years. The ban was lifted only after the party agreed (in writing) to accept the constitutional monarchy and to continue its activities peacefully.

Throughout this turbulent period, ideological rifts between the moderate faction of the Communist Party, which advocated peaceful transition and constitutional monarchy, and the radical faction, which pressed for the need to struggle for the Constituent Assembly elections to ensure a republic, divided the political philosophy of the Communist Party. These ideological differences led to a series of splits, which became particularly acute after King Mahendra's takeover in 1960. These splits, combined with King Mahendra's incarceration of most of the communist leaders, impacted heavily on the communist movement in Nepal.

Around the end of the 1960s prominent communist leaders, who had been released from prison, formed a *Central Nucleus*—a loose network of various communist factions, in order to bring the separate factions under one umbrella. This greatly reinvigorated the communist movement in the country. Moreover, the rapidly changing socio-economic conditions fuelled by improved education—which had raised life expectations without offering the opportunity to improve living standards—also gave an additional impetus to the spread of communism in rural Nepal. In this socio-political context, it was no surprise that the youthful Pushpa Kamal was drawn towards revolutionary communism.

Around 1971, Dahal came to Kathmandu to further his studies in science. His political association quickly increased in the capital, as he came into contact with several prominent communist leaders. Dahal's stay in Kathmandu coincided with the Jhapa uprising—an armed struggle by radical youths in eastern Nepal, near the border with West Bengal. This uprising was triggered by an anti-landlord campaign across the border in the Naxalbari area of West Bengal. The Naxalbari peasants' uprising was significant, in that it convinced radical youngsters like Dahal that there was no alternative to armed struggle when attempting to capture state power, in order to effect change. Dahal said that Naxalbari uprising was a significant influence on the communists of Nepal, who were committed to bringing about rapid change.

After completing his Intermediate degree, Dahal returned to his home district to pursue a bachelor's degree in science (agriculture). During this time, he became involved in the political activities of the CPN-Fourth Convention party, a faction of the Central Nucleus. This faction had conducted the party's fourth convention and registered itself as the Communist Party of Nepal-Fourth Convention. The emergence of this Fourth Convention party is considered to be a significant landmark in the radical communist movement of modern Nepal, as it attracted a large number of educated young men, like Dahal, into its fold.

Despite his active involvement in communist politics, Dahal was not yet a full-time party worker. Unable to find a good job, because the best employment opportunities were reserved for the well-connected elite, mainly in Kathmandu, he worked briefly on a rural development project funded by United States Agency for International Development (USAID). After resigning from this post, he took a job as a science teacher in a village school in the Gorkha district. Around the end of 1970s he gave up his teaching job to enter full time politics. By that time, he had married Sita Poudyal and fathered four children.

In the early 1980s, the CPN-Fourth Convention party split into two major factions: one known as CPN-Masal*—led by Mohan Bikram Singh—and the other known as CPN-Mashal, led by Mohan Baidya. Dahal joined Baidya's faction and was soon elected as a politburo member. Baidya was subsequently credited with being instrumental in advancing Dahal's political career.

In the mid-1980s, the CPN-Mashal initiated an armed action, attacking police posts in the capital and destroying a statue of King Tribhuvan. The government immediately arrested known party activists and their action was halted. These attacks were criticised by rank-and-file party members because they exposed their underground leaders and activists. Following this embarrassing failure,

* Both Masal and Mashal can be understood as meaning *a flaming torch* in Nepali.

Baidya resigned from his post as general secretary—paving the way for the supremacy of Pushpa Kamal Dahal, who was by then a dynamic communist leader with great political acumen, exceptional organisational skills, irrepressible revolutionary ardour and rare personal charm. It was at this point that Pushpa Kamal adopted the nom de guerre *Prachanda*, in order to protect his personal security.

Dissatisfied with the change in 1990, which heralded parliamentary democracy, Dahal brought together radical factions of the communist parties to form to a new umbrella party, the CPN-Unity Centre. This move established Dahal as a powerful leader of the radical communist movement in Nepal. It also prepared the ground for the armed struggle which would take place a few years later. Most importantly, this process unified Baburam Bhattarai, an intellectual rebel, and Dahal. Bhattarai's clever strategies combined well with Dahal's fine organisational skills. This combination strengthened the radical communist bloc in the country.

In order to fight the first elections, after the restoration of multiparty democracy in 1991, the Unity Centre established a political front. However, the party's performance in the elections was dismal, and it gained only nine seats in the 205-member parliament. Soon afterwards, the party passed a resolution to initiate *a people's war* in order to bring about a new democratic revolution in Nepal under Dahal's leadership.

In 1994, Dahal's Unity Centre suffered another split over the difficult question of whether or not the objective condition was suitable for armed struggle. Afterwards the party went completely underground and began preparations for the next phase of its struggle. The political context at that time was marked by widespread disappointment, because the democratic government could not meet the expectations of the Nepalese people. In 1995, the Unity Centre held its Third Plenum, during which the party reformulated its ideology, turning away from Marxism-Leninism-Mao Tse-Tung's thoughts towards Marxism-Leninism-Maoism (an advanced form of Maoist thought) and decided to rename itself as the Communist Party of Nepal-Maoist or CPN-Maoist. Dahal now led a new Maoist party, which launched a protracted armed struggle to establish a new *people's democracy*.

This struggle, based on the principles of *Marxism-Leninism-Maoism*, was formally launched on 13 February 1996, with a series of armed attacks in different parts of Nepal. Utilising their experience of the Chinese revolution, the

Maoists divided their People's War into three phases: strategic defence, strategic stalemate and strategic offence—implementing six plans between February 1996 and February 2001.

After the completion of the initial phase of the People's War, in February 2001 the Maoists staged their second national conference, where it was decided to create the post of Chairman for Dahal. This conference also decided to adopt the *Prachanda Path*, a set of ideas that would guide Nepal's revolution. *Prachanda Path* was interpreted as an ideological synthesis of the experiences of five years of armed struggle, with an application of Marxism-Leninism-Maoism—tailored to accommodate the specific context in Nepal. By 2004, the protracted armed struggle led by Dahal had become one of the most intense conflicts in the world—drawing the attention of many powerful countries.

What were the qualities of this extraordinary revolutionary in this South Asian land? Who was this man who altered the direction of an entire nation? Dahal's greatest strength has been his powers of persuasion. People said he could make even his worst enemies feel he was their friend. His flexibility made him a good negotiator, inside and outside his party. He had more charm than others in his party, and there was something pleasing about him, something warm, which made many Nepalese relate to him.

But understanding Chabilal or Puspha Kamal or Prachanda was not easy. He was a multifaceted man with a complex personality. A man allegedly responsible for countless deaths and atrocities, who on occasions could burst into tears in public. At times he appeared as hard as a rock. He was worldly and scholarly, well read and someone who enjoyed the pleasures of life. He had a weakness for good food, drank expensive liquor and had a desire for fashionable clothes and latest accessories. He joked, laughed and talked about women, but he was a *closed book*, difficult to predict. He could be as pleasant as he appeared or far more dangerous than anyone could imagine. That was the charisma of his personality; a combination of softness and hardness, regimen and unpredictability. He was larger-than-life for ordinary people; the Maoist supremo.

Chapter 6

On 1 February 2005, the only challenger to Prachanda's supreme position and power was locked up, under armed Maoist guards, inside a small mud house in an isolated corner of Lawang village. In a poorly-lit and unheated room, the deputy leader of the Maoists, Baburam Bhattarai lay on a small bed, reading. Detained with him was his wife Hisila Yami, who was also a Maoist leader. She appeared much stronger than her intellectual husband, and was frustrated at not being allowed to go outside. Incarcerated because of her husband's actions, she considered herself a *sati* of the twenty-first century.

Baburam Bhattarai was arrested for writing an article that had been published in the premier national broadsheet *Kantipur (Daily)* before the party had a chance to debate its content. Bhattarai's article, "Princely Tendency and Democracy", was a follow-up to another shrewdly analysed article, "Difference between Democracy and Monarchy", by Devendra Raj Pandey, a civil society activist. Bhattarai had written:

> At a time when King Gyanendra is about to proceed on a pilgrimage to Delhi to seek blessings for his direct military rule after doing away with the remaining… democratic facades and when the principal international power centres are inclined to put their bets on the King, all the genuine democratic forces ought to seriously consider the princely tendencies within themselves. (Bhattarai 2005, 12)

Although he did not explicitly state it, Bhattarai hinted that the Maoist supremo Dahal was developing a cult. More importantly, Bhattarai spoke out against the party's latest tactical line. Many Maoist leaders, Dahal included, and the party's rank and file vociferously advocated the politically *astonishing* idea that the Maoists and the Monarchy should unite to form a nationalist alliance against the parliamentary bourgeois parties. This tactic, they believed, would eventually help the Maoists achieve their ultimate goal—to capture state power. Bhattarai was against what he considered this short-sighted approach, and warned them:

> … it would be farcical, like the story of Soma Sharma's father, to dream of achieving any type of democracy or socialism in the specific historical and geo-political context of Nepal without first going through the sub-stage of a democratic republic. (Bhattarai 2005, 15)

The party had chosen to ignore Bhattarai's line completely. Worse, it decided to take disciplinary action against him. It is likely that the growing differences between Chairman Dahal and Bhattarai were the real reason behind this tough response. The dominant faction, led by Dahal, considered expansionism—in which he was referring to expansionist and neo-imperialist forces, like the US and India (within the context of Nepal)—to be the party's main enemy. Bhattarai's weaker faction, however, believed feudalism—represented by the King—to be the main enemy.

In an interview, a senior Maoist leader explained:

> Prachanda led the faction inside the party who felt that the Maoists should deal with the King, not the parliamentary parties, especially after 2002. The King had both power and the army, so initiating dialogue with the King made sense to them. This was opposed by the faction led by Baburam Bhattarai. Hence, Prachanda had taken action against Bhattarai so that Bhattarai would not prevent talks with King Gyanendra. Serious planning was already underway to initiate dialogue with the King. However, the King's takeover at that time ruined any chance of this happening. After the royal takeover the democratic republic, which Bhattarai had espoused, became inevitable for the Maoist party. Hence the article calling for a democratic republic, for which Bhattarai was disgraced and confined by the hard-liners, finally gave a new direction to Nepal's political future.

Baburam Bhattarai, the main proponent of a democratic republic for Nepal—which would eventually result in the abolition of the monarchy—was born poor. The Bhattarais lived in the remote village of Belbase, in the Gorkha district. The family had seen better days, and as members of the priestly Bahun caste they had, five centuries before, helped to install the same Shah dynasty that Baburam now bitterly opposed.

On 18 June 1954, within a few days of the tragic death of her eldest son (aged four years), Dharma Kumari Bhattarai gave birth to another son. An astrologer, unasked and insistent, as is often the case in *traditional* families, predicted that her newborn would bring much fame to the family. They promptly named him Ram, after a Hindu God—naming after deities being very common in a Hindu society—although his mother affectionately called him *babu*. Hence he became known as *Babu* Ram.

Although illiterate and oppressed like other women in Belbase, Baburam's mother was a wise woman with astute, instinctive leadership skills. She counselled the poor, the dalits and other marginalised groups in her village, and helped to solve their problems. It was this environment that exposed Baburam to injustice commonly prevalent.

When he was around seven years old, a distant relative visited Baburam's home. This was Krishna Prasad Neupane, a Nepali Congress party activist intent on evading arrest after King Mahendra's seizure of power, by hiding in Belbase. Every day, Krishna Prasad sat inside Baburam's mud-house scribbling on scraps of paper. Ever inquisitive, the boy found a way to read all these musings, which were highly critical of the King. This experience is said to have sown the first seeds of republicanism in Baburam's mind.

Meanwhile his parents toiled day and night in parched fields, trying to eke out a living and sustain a minimal lifestyle. Baburam's life would have followed the same pattern had it not been for his opportunity to get an education. In 1963, the United Mission to Nepal established an Amar Jyoti School in his village, and his schooling began.

At 16 he drew public attention by becoming the first boy from a rural area to secure the first position in the national-level School Leaving Certificate or SLC (equivalent to grade 10) examination. His father was convinced that the prediction made about Baburam becoming famous had come true. This success also introduced him to Prince Birendra, who would later be the reason for his first jail sentence. The Crown Prince personally gave awards to students with the highest SLC marks in his favourite subject, geography. In an interview Baburam admitted, "...the Crown Prince was a decent person, though the palace was not as grand as I had thought." This experience did nothing, however, to diminish his hostile feelings for the monarchy.

Further studies brought Baburam to Kathmandu. While pursuing a course at Amrit Science College, he became involved in various student activities. Later, he decided to study engineering—a subject in great demand at that time—because of his fascination with mathematics. He was awarded The Colombo

Plan, so he could study at the Chandigarh Engineering College in India. In the library of that college, he came across a name connected to a story that he found so inspirational that his life was completely changed. The story was about the revolutionary hero Ernesto Che Guevara. After reading this book, Baburam decided to devote his life to the socio-economic transformation of the Nepalese society.

Not long after this, Baburam became a full-blown political activist, and in 1977, the founder President of the All India Nepalese Student Association (AINSA). This organisation helped Baburam to befriend both prominent Nepalese and Indian leaders, like Bishweshwar Prasad Koirala, Chandra Shekhar, Girija Prasad Koirala, Karan Singh, Rishikesh Shah and Sharad Yadav. Among all, Baburam particularly respected Bishweshwar Prasad Koirala.

Of this affection, Baburam said:

> B.P. was the only Nepalese leader who really impressed me. B.P. was quite fond of me too. I would have, maybe, joined the Nepali Congress due to B.P.'s charismatic leadership had it not been for his policy of national reconciliation. I was so sure that the monarchy needed to be abolished for any modernisation in Nepal. Any compromise with the King was just not acceptable to me. So after B.P. called for reconciliation with the King, I steadily drifted towards communism. Until then I liked to identify myself as a radical democrat.

In the late 1970s Baburam joined the School of Planning and Architecture in Delhi. An outstanding student, he was frequently invited by his Indian friends to their homes. They were mostly well-off Delhites, whose apartments were looked after by Nepalese servants. He was distressed to see his fellow-countrymen working for survival in a foreign land, and this experience made him more of a radical. At the same time, he also waved a black flag at King Birendra, who was visiting Delhi, and was arrested (though he was later released).

In the early 1980s, Baburam sought admission to Jawaharlal Nehru University (JNU) in order to gain more political experience. At that time, JNU was the hotbed of leftist politics in South Asia. Around the same time, Bhattarai joined the Fourth Convention party headed by Mohan Bikram Singh. At JNU he studied Marxism and wrote a dissertation titled *The Nature of Underdevelopment and Regional Structure in Nepal*. During this period he also established contacts with influential Indian leaders.

While at JNU, Baburam also got married. He had met his future wife, Hisila Yami, in a restaurant at the Architecture School. It was not love at first sight; such *frivolity* was not possible for the aspiring celibate Baburam. Initially, they were friends. Hisila had grown up in India, and did not know much about Nepal's history and politics. Baburam taught her about politics including her own father's political struggle and Nepalese history. While discussing politics the couple fell in love. Somehow it took them a long time to realise it. Baburam expected Hisila to help him transform the Nepalese society, but before that, she was destined to transform his own life.

When Baburam left the Architecture School, Hisila was still studying. He missed her and decided the only way to end such torment was to be with her. She accepted, later saying 'He was so intense, so completely different than me, I couldn't help liking him.' When Baburam met with a serious accident while studying in Delhi, the couple decided to arrange a wedding, so that Hisila could nurse him back to health. Despite belonging to different backgrounds, their marriage was unopposed. Baburam's mother was happy that her *bairagi*, ascetic son had finally decided to settle down.

In the mid-1980s, Baburam returned home a different person. He claimed that he was equipped with an understanding of the three best scientific tools of Marxism-Leninism-Maoism, which could be used to root out gross inequality, oppression, poverty, underdevelopment and exploitation of the overwhelming majority of the population. Baburam was ready to take on the world.

As the Nepali Congress-led movement, which was striving to end the oppressive panchayat system, became stronger during the late 1980s, Baburam Bhattarai became the spokesperson of the coalition of radical left parties, the United National People's Front. Although this front did not want to join the Congress-Left Alliance due to strategic differences, it did participate in the First People's Movement. After the restoration of democracy, the radical left front denounced the compromise between the King and the Congress-Left Alliance as a betrayal, and declared that it would continue the agitation until elections to a Constituent Assembly were held. However, because of poor public support it eventually gave up its agitation.

In 1990, Baburam joined forces with the Dahal-led Unity Centre party and was elected to its politburo. During the first elections after restoration of multiparty democracy in 1991, Baburam headed the political front of the Unity Centre. Under his astute leadership, the United Front managed to become the third largest force in the parliament, despite winning only a small number of seats. Post-election, the Front, headed by Baburam, carried out several protests and agitations against the elected government, demanding a range of reforms. Baburam addressed public meetings, launched political campaigns and conducted social activities, in order to attract the public to his cause.

Instead of meeting any of their demands the government suppressed the movement, which made it easier for the Front to launch their armed struggle. In February 1996, Baburam submitted to the government a memorandum of forty demands. It spoke of the parliamentary parties' inability to address the concerns of the people of Nepal in the post-1990 democratic context, and raised issues concerning nationalism, democracy and livelihood. Before the government responded, the People's War was launched by the Maoists.

Baburam was considered to be one of the chief architects of the protracted and bloody Maoist People's War. He came to symbolise the public and international face of the Nepalese Maoists, who were fearless and devoted revolutionaries. By that time, Baburam had established himself as one of the most powerful leaders of the Maoist party. He could settle for nothing less than a republic in Nepal. His mission had become a grave threat to the institution of monarchy, and thus to the collective history of the twelve *divine* Hindu monarchs.

Chapter 7

Soon after the royal takeover on 1 February 2005, the deputy leader of the Maoists, Baburam Bhattarai was released from house arrest. In October 2005, the Maoist party held a central committee meeting in Chunwang, in the Rukum district. In the prevailing context of King Gyanendra's seizure of power, this meeting concluded that the Maoist party should collaborate with parliamentary parties to overthrow the *autocratic monarchy*. This meeting also decided to campaign for a Constituent Assembly election and ultimately, a democratic republic. This decision came after the Maoists analysed that they would not be able to capture the state through direct armed confrontation against the army.

Nearly nine months after the royal takeover, on 22 November 2005, and around 800 kilometres away from the centre of Nepal's politics, Jhalak Sharma took leave of absence from his work at a small private firm in Green Park, New Delhi. A communist at heart, although not an active party cadre, Jhalak Sharma had participated in the first People's Movement in 1990. When the new democratic system failed to create any opportunity for him, Jhalak—like many people in Nepal—migrated to India in search of work. His diploma in commerce from Delhi University got him a job that was better than the low-paid menial jobs most Nepalese had to settle for. He worked to pay his bills and take care of his family, leading an ordinary non-descript life until November 2005.

Jhalak Sharma lived in a lower-middle class apartment in Deuli Gaon, South of New Delhi, with other Nepalese migrants. His apartment was on the first floor of a 10-storey building. Because of its location it was chosen as the venue where the draft of the 12-Point Peace Understanding between the Seven Party Alliance (an alliance of parliamentary parties—namely, Nepali Congress, Unified Marxist Leninist, Nepali Congress-Democratic, Nepal Sadbhavana Party-Anandiadevi, People's Front, Unified Left Front* and Nepal Workers and Peasants Party) and

* An alliance of CPN-Marxist Leninist and People's Front United.

the Maoist Party would be finalised. The apartment initially identified for this purpose was on the fourth floor but the frail and ailing Koirala could not climb to this level. So the venue was changed at the last minute to Jhalak's apartment.

On the morning of the 22nd November, Jhalak borrowed some plastic chairs from his neighbours (without raising any suspicion) and arranged them in his small drawing room. He also bought some crackers from a nearby Mother Dairy store. At around noon, all the leaders Jhalak had only read about or seen on television, but never met, came to his apartment one by one. Within a few minutes Baburam Bhattarai, Girija Prasad Koirala, Jhal Nath Khanal, Pushpa Kamal Dahal, Madhav Kumar Nepal and other prominent leaders squeezed into Jhalak's small drawing-room.

Soon it was decided that Jhalak's bedroom, the only other room in his apartment, would be better for the meeting because it offered more privacy. All the leaders instantly moved into Jhalak's rectangular cream-walled bedroom. The door was closed and locked. After some hours the leaders came out one by one and Jhalak knew from their flushed faces that the deal was done.

The draft of the first Peace Understanding was finalised that day, bringing the parliamentary parties and the Maoist rebels together, with the intention of solving the prevailing political problems through dialogue. In this sense, the Understanding marked the beginning of the new peace process in Nepal—stressing the need to establish full democracy by ending the autocratic monarchy, resolving the 10-year armed conflict and holding a Constituent Assembly election. The Maoists committed themselves to democratic values and norms, like multiparty competition, civil liberties, human rights and the rule of law. The Seven Party Alliance or the Democratic Alliance agreed to the Maoists' demand for the Constituent Assembly election. Hence, the Understanding established the Constituent Assembly election as the common ground between the parliamentary parties and the Maoist rebels, and the means to attain peace and full democracy.

The need for the prominence of the Constituent Assembly election in the peace agreement was historically rooted. In the 1950s, after the end of the autocratic Rana regime, the major political forces in the country agreed there should be an election to form a Constituent Assembly. The proposed elected body was expected to draft a new constitution, as had happened in India. But King Mahendra opposed the holding of a Constituent Assembly election. It is said the King objected because he did not want two sovereign bodies coexisting in the country—the King and an elected Constituent Assembly. Naively, the Nepali Congress party (the largest democratic force then) compromised its position and agreed to the King. As a result a parliamentary election was held in February 1959 instead of the Constituent Assembly election, which had been promised.

This political development however, did not silence popular aspirations for a Constituent Assembly election, and the creation of a fully elected body to draft another constitution for Nepal. Again and again different political groups called for Constituent Assembly elections, with radical communist factions the most vociferous.

During the democratic movement in 1990 the Constituent Assembly became the major cause of division between the Democratic Front (an alliance of the Nepali Congress party and other moderate leftist forces) and the coalition of radical communist factions. The radical coalition did not want the new constitution to be an agreement solely negotiated between the King and the Democratic Front—as had happened before. The communist factions wanted the post-1990 constitution to be drafted by a fully-empowered Constituent Assembly. They believed in the full sovereignty of the people and their right to make the rules that will govern them.

It was against this background that the Maoist party demanded, in the mid-1990s, a new constitution drafted by an elected Constituent Assembly. Later, they claimed they had to resort to violence because the contemporary government did not accede to their *just and reasonable* demand. Thus, the issue of the Constituent Assembly election was core to the Maoists' decision to instigate what would become a violent armed uprising.

The ongoing, unresolved question about the Constitute Assembly was also central during the peace talks in 2001 and 2003. But at that time the other parliamentary political parties refused to accept it. It was only after the King's takeover in February 2005 backed by the state army, that other parliamentary parties accepted the unconditional demand by the Maoists for holding a Constituent Assembly election. This crucial political decision led to the historic 12-Point Peace Understanding. Hence, it can be said that this Peace Understanding, which would mark the beginning of a new chapter in Nepal's contemporary political history, rested on the premise of the Constituent Assembly election.

In an interview, elaborating the background of the 12-Point Understanding, the Democratic Alliance leader Koirala said:

> In many ways, the 12-point deal emerged as a reaction to King Gyanendra's takeover. After the takeover we came to the conclusion that if we wanted to restore democracy, we needed to tackle the root cause that had jeopardised democracy again and again in Nepal—the Royal Nepal Army.
>
> It was this compulsion that pushed us to explore the option of having an understanding with the Maoists, for our common interests of neutralising the army converged. So soon after the King's takeover I came up with three principles—consensus, collaboration and unity—based on Bishweshwar's policy of national reconciliation, espoused two and a half decades ago. Though Bishweshwar's reconciliation was between the King and the people, as there was no third party like the Maoists at that time, I was for reconciliation between all three sides. It was not an easy decision as the Maoists had still not given up their armed action.
>
> Immediately after being released from my three-month house arrest, after the takeover, I visited New Delhi where I met Prachanda *jee* and decided on the basic premise of the peace agreement. Then, there followed a series of telephone conversations and meetings in Nepal and India.

In another interview, the Maoist deputy Baburam Bhattarai added:

> Once dialogues between us and the Democratic Alliance progressed we walked for over 20 days from Rolpa/Rukum to Delhi, in order to finalise the 12-Point deal. We wanted to finalise the draft in Rolpa but that was not possible for security reasons.
>
> In Delhi, we arranged the meetings, because we didn't yet trust the parliamentary parties. These meetings were held mostly in farm houses in Gurgaon, Noida and Dhaula Kuan, where many Nepalese worked as security guards. These guards, who were mostly members of a Maoist front organisation for Nepalese migrants in India, arranged the venues for the meetings only after ensuring that the house owners were absent.
>
> Even though the Understanding document was finalised in New Delhi, the Democratic Alliance leaders waited to return to Nepal to sign it, but we could not do that for security reasons. The Alliance refused to sign the same document as the Maoists, as they had not given up the armed struggle.

A background narrative of the 12-Point Understanding is not complete without due consideration given to the role played by India, which was crucial in making the agreement possible. No major political decision in the Himalayan Kingdom could be sustained without India's support (due to Nepal's dependence on India). Moreover, the support of India, an emerging superpower with increasing political and economic clout, was needed in order to rally international approval.

India's entry into the peace process started around the time of the 2005 takeover. Indian policy makers were compelled to encourage an agreement between the parliamentary parties and the Maoists, because of King Gyanendra's repeated refusal to engage with democratic political parties in Nepal. Also, the King's insensitivity towards India's security concerns could have provided another trigger. With growing Maoist activities in India, particularly after the merger in 2004 of the People's War Group and the Maoist Communist Centre—to form the Communist Party of India (Maoist)—resolution of the armed conflict, spearheaded by the Maoists in Nepal, became a security interest for India.

King Gyanendra, however, failed to resolve the Maoist problem in Nepal, either by military or by peaceful means. The February takeover meant the King had ruined any chance of solving the ongoing armed conflict. Most importantly, the takeover forced Indian policy makers to revise their Two Pillars strategy—that of multiparty democracy *and* constitutional monarchy in Nepal. The takeover, they argued, proved that the Two Pillars could not coexist, as they contradicted each other.

On Indian involvement, a Nepalese leader closely engaged in the peace process said:

> In the prevailing political situation, ending the King's regime was only possible if the Seven Party Alliance and the Maoists came together. At that point, the SPA lacked the ability to mobilise people, owing to the Maoist control of the countryside. This compulsion could have pushed India to encourage and facilitate the signing of the 12-Point Understanding.

He added:

> Since the Maoists were still deemed a terrorist organisation by the Indian government, the Prime Minister's Office in India had cautiously delegated the responsibility of dealing with the Maoists to its intelligence agencies. Both the Intelligence Bureau and the Research Analysis Wing were in contact with the Maoists. Following the February takeover, these contacts grew, especially when King Gyanendra finalised an arms deal with China. Ending King Gyanendra's regime became a security interest for India.

Therefore, it can be said that the 12-Point deal emerged as a political necessity for the major actors of Nepal, in the aftermath of the royal takeover in February 2005. The deal was reached after it was realised that military confrontation was not the solution and that the parties would need to engage in dialogue to resolve their differences. The framework of this peace understanding was: *Sahamati, Sahakarya ra Ekata* [Consensus, Collaboration and Unity].

In an interview to the media after the 12-Point Understanding was signed, Koirala said:

> The international community, including the United States of America, says we should not move ahead with the Maoists as they cannot be trusted. But as democratic parties, we have the responsibility to bring the undemocratic forces into the democratic-constitutional fold. OK, let's assume for a while that I will fail; I may be unsuccessful but the country will not. But if I am successful, a small underdeveloped country that perhaps does not enjoy much importance on the world map, will set an example for the international community. And terrorists across the world will know that their problems can be resolved only through dialogue. Consider this as my political gamble. (Koirala 2007, 102)

The Story: The Rocky Road to Democracy

Chapter 8

Five months after the signing of the 12-Point Understanding, the Democratic Alliance and the Maoist party launched an agitation against the Royal government. The first point in the 12-Point Understanding called for an end to the autocratic King's rule, through the force of the People's Movement. Building on this, civil society leaders played an important role in laying the groundwork for the mass uprising, which called for democracy and goaded the political parties into action. Accordingly, in the spring of 2006, the Democratic Alliance called a general strike demanding restoration of peace and full democracy.

Thousands of ordinary Nepalese people from different parts of Nepal joined the demonstration—including farmers, labourers, workers, teachers, students, drivers, clerks, shopkeepers, housewives, doctors and lawyers. This was despite the presence of a large posse of security personnel, who had been ordered to quell the movement with tear gas, rubber bullets and even live rounds. The people were brave and defiant, and attended rallies across the country, ignoring the curfew.

The movement was also supported by the wider international community. Many western donors had cut foreign aid on the eve of the 2006 People's Movement, in order to pressurise the King to respect human rights and democratic freedom. Both moral and financial support was extended to the People's Movement by many foreign countries, especially India.

Sixteen years earlier, a similar mass movement had taken place when thousands of Nepalese people took to the streets of Kathmandu demanding the restoration of multiparty democracy. Unlike that first People's Movement, the second not only clamoured for democracy but also for the restoration of peace. The new slogan of the second People's Movement, 'Inclusive Democracy', drew people from various ethnicities and castes.

Figure 1: The People's Movement in April 2006
Source: Photo by Chandra Shekhar Karki.

Most importantly, the Maoist party, an organisation still waging an armed revolt, played a vital role in mobilising people for demonstrations. This was particularly important because they did not allow other parties access to the public at the local level. In an interview, one of the Maoist leaders, Khim Lal Devkota, said:

> The Maoist leaders could not come out openly so we asked the ordinary people in the villages to join the agitation, assuring them we would look after their work.

In the Nepalese New Year's Day message, in mid-April 2006, King Gyanendra invited the agitating political parties for a dialogue. The Democratic Alliance spurned this belated offer, claiming that the King's message had not addressed the burning issues of the country. Instead, the Alliance announced revitalised agitation. Aggressive demonstrations began throughout the country, and the Nepalese diaspora in India and other countries around the world staged rallies in cities like New Delhi, New York, London and Tokyo—calling for an early return of full democracy in their motherland.

As these demonstrations intensified 28-year-old Hira Lal Gautam was killed, when the police fired on the crowd during a demonstration in Bara district.

Hira Lal, a poor street vendor, had three young daughters and was the only member of his extended family with an income. The same day, 22-year-old Setu Sunar died when tear gas shells, which police fired to disperse the crowds in Nepalgunj, hit her face. And the next day, three young boys were killed in Kalanki *Chowk*, one of the entry points to the capital, when the police opened fire on pro-democracy protesters. Thousands of others across the country were injured or badly wounded.

As King Gyanendra showed no signs of retreat, in spite of the deaths and injuries, the Indian Prime Minister Dr. Manmohan Singh sent a special envoy, Karan Singh (the son of the deposed Maharaja of Kashmir and the leader of the Indian National Congress party) to the King, with a special message. Singh gave the King a letter from the Indian prime minister, which expressed his deep concern about the situation. The mounting international and national pressure finally forced King Gyanendra to relinquish his power.

On 21 April 2006, King Gyanendra made a televised address to the nation, urging the Democratic Alliance to form a new government. He said:

> The Executive Power of the Kingdom of Nepal, which was in our safekeeping, shall, from this day, be returned to the people and be exercised in accordance with Article 35 of the Constitution of the Kingdom of Nepal, 1990.

Nevertheless, the King's address failed to satisfy the Democratic Alliance, which rejected his offer and announced their intention to intensify the peaceful demonstrations. They claimed that the King had not fully addressed the demands of the people. The Alliance was not ready to settle for anything less than the restoration of parliament, so it continued to agitate—despite the pressure of most international partners, including India and western powers, to accept the King's offer.

Because of this continued agitation, three days later King Gyanendra was forced to address the country for the second time. This happened after a series of negotiations between the Palace and the Democratic Alliance. In his proclamation (guided by the Alliance) the King extended his condolences to the relatives of all those who had lost their lives in the People's Movement and wished the injured a speedy recovery. He said:

> I am convinced that the source of State Authority and Sovereignty of the Kingdom of Nepal is inherent in the people of Nepal, and I am cognisant of the spirit of the ongoing People's Movement as well to resolve the ongoing violent

> conflict and other problems facing the country according to the road map of the agitating Seven Party Alliance. We, through this Proclamation, reinstate the House of Representatives, which was dissolved on 22 May 2002, on the advice of the then prime minister—in accordance with the Constitution of the Kingdom of Nepal, 1990.

While the Democratic Alliance welcomed the King's offer and announced the withdrawal of its agitation, the Maoist party rejected the offer and announced the continuation of its protest, until an announcement of unconditional Constituent Assembly election was made. The Seven Party Democratic Alliance had accepted the restoration of parliament, as the route to a Constituent Assembly election, but the Maoist party wanted an all-party national conference, as a precondition to the staging of an election.

Finally, Girija Prasad Koirala managed to convince Chairman Dahal to accept the offer, saying:

> Continuity of history means moving on by the current constitution. Even if we go to a Constituent Assembly, we have to move through this constitution. It will give continuity to both history and identity.

When the Maoists finally agreed, euphoric victory rallies broke out across the country and the Maoists declared a three-month ceasefire. Three days later, the Seven Party Alliance met to appoint Girija Prasad Koirala the prime minister—making him the only elected leader to be appointed as the prime minister of Nepal for five times. For the sake of historical continuity, Koirala took his oath of office from the King, the last prime minister to do so.

The change that Nepal saw after that event altered the character of the country completely. At the first meeting of the reinstated parliament, Koirala registered a proposal to hold Constituent Assembly elections. This proposal was unanimously passed. Soon after, the bill for parliamentary proclamation approved by the newly formed Council of Ministers was tabled. Passed unanimously on 18 May 2006, this bill was hailed as Nepal's Magna Carta. It reduced the monarchy to a ceremonial position, declared the centuries-old Hindu kingdom to be a secular state, guaranteed women one-third of representation and placed the state army under the control of the parliament.

Immediately after the proclamation, His Majesty's Government became the Nepal Government, prompting changes in all official and legal documents. The Royal Nepal Army was transformed into the Nepal Army and all government institutions and diplomatic missions removed the word *Royal* from their names.

This is where Bhojraj Pokharel enters the story. A public servant, it was his role to institutionalise these changes through a Constituent Assembly election—a process expected to bring lasting peace and full democracy in Nepal.

Chapter 9

Changes in history and weather often seem analogous. The change of seasons serves on many occasions as the ideal backdrop for the march of history.

The monsoon of 2006 coincided with a sudden transformation in a retired bureaucrat's career. As the Country Director of a US-based international non-governmental organisation, Bhojraj Pokharel was striving to reduce stigma and discrimination against people afflicted by HIV and AIDS, and related groups like sex workers, intravenous drug users and homosexuals. Pokharel had no inkling of what was in store for him.

One afternoon while he was reviewing a project proposal, he received a call from Gokarna Poudel, Koirala's private secretary, requesting him to meet the prime minister. Pokharel had established a personal rapport with Koirala when he served in his government in 1992, as Home Secretary and they grew fond of each other.

The day after the phone call, Pokharel went to see Prime Minister Koirala. At around eight in the morning Pokharel passed through the silver gates of the Baluwatar fortress—the prime minister's residence. Inside the power-house there were many senior Nepali Congress members milling around, competing to prove their allegience to Koirala. Pokharel folded his hands in *Namaste* to greet these leaders and headed upstairs. He found Koirala seated in a high chair, especially made to suit his height. The two men exchanged pleasantries, over cups of tea. Then they began to talk politics. Koirala said:

> Last time our wish to appoint you as the Chief Election Commissioner failed due to the King. We again wish to offer you the same position. You ought to be mentally prepared to take charge *hai* [ok]? I have already told the present incumbent to resign.

However, while not really wanting to avoid doing his duty to the nation, Pokharel initially refused the appointment. Urged by Koirala, he eventually agreed to think it over.

Pokharel later explained:

> The reason I did not want to take up the position of the Chief Election Commissioner was mainly because of my bitter past experience. In 2003, my name was recommended for the same position. But after three months of keeping me in waiting, King Gyanendra pressurised the Constitutional Council to drop my name and recommended his trusted persons, and then appointed his own preferred person in that position. The whole episode was quite humiliating and frustrating for me. Naturally, I felt I had had enough of a shock the first time itself. There appeared no need for me to go through the tortuous experience again. Also, I had started enjoying my work as a freelancer which made it comfortable to cover my living expenses and my kids' education. This was not the case when I worked in the public service and that's the reason why I didn't want to go back to public service again.

Two months after the meeting with Koirala, in October 2006, Pokharel was again summoned to the prime minister. By this time, the Maoist and the Democratic Alliance were close to signing the six-point agreement that would determine many aspects of the peace process and the Constituent Assembly elections.

Koirala told Pokharel:

> As you know the political parties have decided to hold Constituent Assembly elections (by June 2007) and to appoint new Election Commissioners soon (by mid-October 2006). The mainstream political parties have recognised the injustice meted out to you earlier by the King, so they want to appoint you as the Chief Commissioner. Please conduct these elections.

Pokharel replied:

> Prime minister, sir, I have already rejected the position earlier so please don't force me. Why do you want to force me into something that I don't want? There are many aspirants for the office; why don't you choose from them?
>
> More importantly, there is no constitution right now. The provisions could change after the Interim Constitution is enacted. The Maoists are also not in the government. It would not be wise to make appointments to any constitutional body until the constitution is enacted.

Not prepared to accept no for an answer, Koirala said:

> This country has invested so much in you. And now when the country needs you, you are running away from your responsibilities. Aren't you betraying your motherland?

A few days later, the Constitutional Council, meeting in Baluwatar, recommended Bhojraj Pokharel for the post of Chief Election Commissioner. Soon after, Pokharel was subjected to two hours of interrogation by the parliamentary hearing committee—making him the first head nominee of any constitutional body in Nepal to be subjected to this kind of process. On 30 October 2006, the government appointed Pokharel the Chief Election Commissioner, with the onerous and unenviable task of conducting the crucial Constituent Assembly elections.

One of Pokharel's first tasks was to determine the intentions of the Maoists, as they were a key stakeholder in the elections. The Maoists were still not officially in contact with the government so the Chief did not know how to reach them. He contacted B. K. Shrestha, Dahal's close aide and asked him to arrange a meeting with the Maoist chairman. Within the hour Shrestha made the necessary arrangements.

A few days later the Chief met Dahal in Kathmandu following elaborate security instructions to reach the meeting place, a four-storey hotel in Bouddha. On the third floor the Chief was taken to a small room, furnished with only a few chairs. A few minutes later two Maoist leaders entered, Pushpa Kamal Dahal and Baburam Bhattarai. They offered him tea, and then the Chief began the discussion by saying, "Destiny has chosen me to implement your agenda. So I came here to talk about that."

Dahal replied:

> Yes, the Constituent Assembly election is our agenda. We have inquired about you from our mechanism and we have confidence in you. You will get full support from our side.

The meeting originally arranged for half-an-hour extended to one-and-a-half. They mainly talked about issues of the Interim Constitution, which was in the process of finalisation. The Maoists were concerned that the palace and the army could jeopardise the election process, but they expressed their commitment to the elections. The Chief was reassured, and was determined to progress the elections without delay.

An early election seemed indispensible, as Koirala's health was rapidly deteriorating. He told the Chief:

> I don't know how long I will survive. The Constituent Assembly elections are now my dream. If these elections don't happen in June, I will have to come as a ghost to see the elections.
>
> Bhojraj *jee* I don't know what will happen to the peace process if the elections don't happen in time. So whatever is needed from the side of the government, we will provide to you. You have to manage the elections by mid-June 2007 anyhow. This is the wish of all the political leaders.

The Maoists also wanted the election to be held early. Dahal said:

> The election must happen in June at any cost. There are many elements that don't want the peace process. If the election doesn't happen in June, then the peace process will be derailed.

The Chief later admitted:

> Within the timeframe, the constituent election in June seemed impossible. Yet I believed in what the top leadership said. They were all firm that the election must happen in June 2007. I felt that if these powerful people wanted the election then the election would happen. In such a situation, as the Chief of the Nepalese election management body, I realised that my predominant role was to make sure that a lack of technical preparations did not obstruct the leaders' political will to hold the June election.

Chapter 10

On 30 October 2006, Pokharel began working as the Chief Election Commissioner (CEC) of Nepal. At 11 o'clock he entered the Bahadur Bhavan—the home of the Election Commission, which had been built in the nineteenth century by a Rana Prime Minister. He was met by the Secretary of the Election Commission, Dolakh Bahadur Gurung, who escorted him to his office.

Gurung advised him that the first task was to get the government to finalise legal framework, including the constitution and electoral laws. But there was also the question of rebuilding the trust of the political parties and other partners, which the last election—commissioned by King Gyanendra—had destroyed. This would be difficult, given the prevailing post-conflict political environment.

Soon after the Chief took office, other commissioners were appointed—Usha Nepal, Neil Kantha Uprety, Dolakh Bahadur Gurung and Ayodhi Prasad Yadav. These appointments were *unofficially* shared between the main four political parties representatives of the Democratic bloc and the Maoist party.

As soon as the commissioners had been appointed, the Chief held a meeting. He briefed them, saying:

> Amid many challenges, we have a historical opportunity to conduct the Constituent Assembly elections pending since the 1950s. Now it's up to us to make that possible.
>
> The government and the political parties are committed to conducting the elections before the end of June 2007 so we have to speed up preparations.

The immediate major challenges were seen as

- transitional political context—political instability, weak state institutions, poor security situation-security forces were demoralised due to the many years of fighting and the continued use of violence by the Maoists.

- immature peace process—many key issues that could affect the election remained to be resolved
- no constitution—election low could not be made without a constitution being in place.
- key issues of the elections unformulated—for example, there was no agreement on the type of electoral system to be used (what); there was uncertainty about the number of seats and election constituencies there should be (where); there was no decision or announcement regarding the election date (when); and no decisions had been taken on the eligibility criteria for voters (who).
- unequal players—the Maoists had an army (thought to be cantoned in the UN-monitored camps); some political parties had electoral experience while other did not.
- no local government—the local government's term had expired in 2002 and since then no election had been held. As a result most local government office positions were vacant and the government was squeezed into the district headquarters.
- international concern—since the Constituent Assembly election had attracted global attention, the process had to comply with international standards.

To-do-list for the Election Commission of Nepal (ECN)

- Understanding the Constituent Assembly (CA) election process and training core staff (the CA was a new challenge for the ECN).
- Drafting laws necessary for the election—the main election act, six new laws, by-laws, directives and guidelines (approximately 45 such documents) were needed.
- Formulating the policy and carrying out the technical (for example, voter education and registration and political party registration) and logistical preparations—including procurement, transport and delivery of election materials.
- Identifying, training and mobilising around 234,000 poll workers, as well as other election staff.

All tasks had to be resolved within eight months, in a political environment burdened by the legacy of the armed conflict. After 10 years of armed conflict a sense of fear and insecurity prevailed amongst government officials, voters and political workers. Unfortunately, the government and political parties had made little effort to address these problems.

An administrative vacuum also challenged the success of the election, across large parts of the country. Because of the armed conflict, after the terms of office expired for local representatives in 2002, there were no elected local governing bodies in districts and villages. Because most government officials were based in the capital, offices at the local level were also vacant. The state was only present in urban centres and district headquarters.

Moreover, the police force was highly demoralised and had limited competency. Police posts that had been destroyed during the Maoist insurgency were only slowly being re-established. And the posts that had reopened were often dysfunctional, their work disrupted by local Maoist cadres. The political parties' decision to avoid dealing with integration of the Maoist combatants into the state's security apparatus, and their rehabilitation into the community until after the election added a potentially destabilising element.

In this politically fragile situation, securing the confidence of stakeholders in the election was vital. To build its institutional credibility, the Commission went beyond its traditionally limited and purely technical function and played a more proactive role. It interacted with various actors, whose support was critical if the election was to be a success—such as political parties, civil society and the media. In addition, the Commission also talked to various marginalised groups who had been identified by the peace agreement, such as various ethnic groups, including the Madhesis (an ethnic group dominant in southern Nepal), the Janjatis (indigenous groups), the Dalits (the Hindu untouchables) and women.

Of this experience, the Chief later said:

> In the transitional period it was quite difficult to reach agreement on the myriad of election issues facing the political parties, which had diverse historical backgrounds, ideologies and organisational strengths. For example, the Maoists, who had just resurfaced, were completely ignorant about the details of planning an election and the overall process. During discussions, the Maoists wore blank expressions and nodded their heads obediently, in sharp contrast to their leaders' aggressive public image and rhetoric.
>
> As the manager of the elections, I paid special attention to the Maoists because they were new to the process, and I felt it was important to convince them and make them feel comfortable. I tried to be as flexible as possible, to ensure the participation of the former rebels and this seemed to work.
>
> The Commission also frequently interacted with civil society activists and leaders, as well as the media. We encouraged the civil society leaders to petition

politicians on different election related matters. Many of them had good access to political parties. For example, when the Interim Constitution was delayed because of disagreement between parties, we requested civil society leaders to push political leaders to finalise the Constitution on time. This tactic worked.

Our contact with civil society also gave the Commission confidence. In a political transition, state institutions are generally weakened and lack confidence. This was the case here, and support from civil society was vital for boosting confidence in the process.

Moreover, in the post-conflict context, when political forces were occupied with dealing with other complex issues—like management of armed combatants—the media became an effective tool which could be used to inform people about vital election issues.

Engagement with the media helped us make the election process transparent. Nevertheless, balancing this was not easy. Post-conflict political sensitivities demanded secrecy on some issues, yet transparency was also required to ensure the credibility of the process. We walked a tight rope.

Apart from these groups, we also talked to marginalised groups, which was equally challenging. Since the Maoist armed rebellion had escalated, due to continued marginalisation of various ethnic/caste groups, I was convinced that their issues had to be taken seriously. This was important to ensure the success of the election, but also the peace process as a whole.

The problem that plagued us was related to the internal democracy of these ethnic/caste organisations, especially the NGOs. Most representatives were not elected, so it wasn't clear if they had the authority to speak for their groups. In many circumstances, a circle of elites within the groups were dominant during dialogue.

Regardless of this problem, these discussions enabled us to understand the concerns of various marginalised groups, and to ensure better representation of them in the Assembly.

In addition to these ethnic/caste groups, the Commission also interacted with discriminated and under-represented gender groups, like women. The issue of gender was closely linked to the armed rebellion, as continued discrimination was one of the reasons which attracted women to the Maoist uprising.

Interaction with the women's groups was key to securing their representation in the Constituent Assembly. Female politicians from all parties had voiced their common concerns. Non-partisan female activists also powerfully advocated their issues. As a result of this interaction the Commission could pressure political parties to guarantee women their due representation.

One women's group told us:

"We have access to most of the political leaders in some way or another. If they try to deflect from their commitment to women's representation, while drafting legislation, tell us. If need be, we will even go to their houses and suitably deal with them."

So, we exchanged information strategically with the women's leaders whenever their representation seemed under threat, and they *suitably* dealt with senior male leaders to fix any problems that arose.

Contact with women's groups also enabled the Commission to shape gender-sensitive policies. For example, a Madhesi woman leader said that Madhesi women in the Tarai region were very conservative and were hesitant to vote, since their thumbs were smeared with ink during the process, by male polling staff. She was concerned about women being touched, even on the thumbs, by any nonrelated males, and said this could discourage women from voting. On her suggestion, the Commission changed its policy and deployed only female staff for this task.

One problem for the Commission was implementing gender-sensitive policies for minority gender communities like lesbian, gay, bi-sexual, transgender and intersex groups, or the LGBTI. The LGBTI groups informed the Commission that they had faced difficulty in previous elections because polling officials would not let them vote if they were dressed as females, when their identification cards showed them to be males. They asked the Commission to recognise them as a *third gender* in the voter's and candidacy nomination lists. However, because of constitutional constraints there were no provisions for a third gender category and their demand was not met. The gender minority issue is linked to long-term peace and should have been addressed, in order to further legitimise the process.

Chapter 11

The Chief's initial days at the Commission were fully occupied with meeting different stakeholders, in order to gain their trust in the election process. These included local partners and international contacts. Trust-building was essential for a successful election, after what was one of the *highest intensity internal armed conflicts* in the world. A lot was at stake; in the context of an increasingly globalised world, the success of Nepal's post-conflict election had direct ramifications for global peace and security.

The international community had become concerned about the conflict in Nepal after the imposition of a state of emergency in November 2001. This came only months after America's 9/11, and the inception of the resulting *war on terror*. The Nepalese government had resorted to a military solution to the Maoists' insurgency, mobilising the Royal Nepal Army. This military action resulted in serious human rights violations, including arbitrary arrests, detentions and extra-judicial killings by the state. As the violence escalated, the international community became nervous and took the initiative to resolve the armed conflict in Nepal as soon as possible.

One of the first steps was taken by a Geneva-based organisation called the Centre for Humanitarian Dialogue (HD Centre), which strove to promote communication between the Maoists and the government. Padma Ratna Tuladhar, a human rights activist and facilitator of the peace process, put the Centre in touch with the palace and the Maoists. Tuladhar claimed that in early 2003 the Centre had come close to facilitating direct meetings between two representatives of the government and two senior Maoist leaders. An arrangement was made to fly these representatives to Geneva in a chartered plane. But at the last minute the then Prime Minister Lokendra Bahadur Chand, decided to cancel the meeting—due to what he called a *diplomatic exposé*. Apparently, Maoist Chairman Dahal was so desperate for the talks to take place that he said he was willing to foot the bill for the chartered plane himself.

Additionally, other international organisations, like the Atlanta-based Carter Center (CC), launched their own initiatives to stimulate peace talks in Nepal. And some countries, like Switzerland, Norway and Finland, offered to facilitate peace talks between the rebel group and the government.

With nearly a quarter of its national budget coming from aids, international partners not only carried good will but were also extremely influential in Nepal. Therefore, it was important that the Election Commission engage international partners closely during the election.

On these interactions, the Chief later said:

> In Nepal's assembly elections, rushing first to the Commission, predictably, was the *Bharatiya Rajdoot* [the Indian Ambassador], Shiv Shankar Mukherjee. He insisted in Hindi, "*Apko elections ke liye kya chahiye, kitna chahiye hume boliye, hum sab denge.*" [Whatever you need for the elections we will provide you.]
>
> Mukherjee also specifically added that "you don't need to approach any donors. Just let me know your needs, my government has allocated enough funds for this purpose."
>
> Mukherjee is a pleasant and interesting man. We often discussed the elections over a few drinks. His commitment to the peace process and the June elections was really firm.
>
> India played a proactive role in facilitating Nepal's peace process. Understandably, India was more concerned about the Constituent Assembly elections than any other international friend. Backed by their own internal insurgency experience, Indian policy makers were of the opinion that the elections would help to institutionalise the peace process and hence needed to be held as soon as possible.
>
> From my experience as Home Secretary, I was aware that India's security interests in Nepal were substantial, due to our long open border with India on three sides, and due to the fact that Nepal serves as a buffer state between India and its neighbour China.
>
> During my tenure as Home Secretary, India was in turmoil because of severe internal security challenges from the states of the Punjab and Jammu and Kashmir. The Indian intelligence agencies were rather worried that the Pakistani intelligence service—the Inter-Services Intelligence—was conducting its operations in India from Nepal. They also suspected that the underworld, including the notorious don Dawood Ibrahim, then, and now, operated from Nepal.

In most cases, Indian authorities demanded that we hand over their suspects. They complained that *madrassas* were being rapidly established in Nepal and that this trend could lead to increased fundamentalism and potentially destabilise India in the long term. At the local level, both sides had been quietly and informally extraditing criminals for many years. Since our extradition treaty was very vague, the Indians used to pressurise us to hand over the people they wanted for one reason or another. They quietly requested us to do so rather than going through any legitimate procedure. Of course, Nepalese officials also used to coordinate with Indian officials to capture Nepalese criminals who fled to India.

These types of security tensions featured in the election process as well. When accepting India's support for the elections, we had to counter-balance India's desire, or need to support the electoral process, with the Nepalese sensitivity towards India.

The Chief also explained about the role of Nepal's another powerful neighbour, China:

The *Chiniya Rajdoot* [the Chinese Ambassador] Zheng Xianglin was another important guest of the Commission. Through his young female translator, he generously conveyed, "Your Excellency, our government in Beijing is ready to support your elections. Please let us know what we can do for you." When handed with a list of twenty-two essential election-related items, the Ambassador said that he would send them to Beijing.

Unlike Western ambassadors, the Chinese Ambassador never committed to do anything without consulting with his government. Unlike Western diplomats, his speech was controlled. He never talked about informal or personal matters. Hence, meetings with him at the Commission used to take place within exactly the scheduled time. Sometimes, even if he disagreed with certain issues, he would never say so explicitly. I used to discover this by observing his ears turn red in disagreement.

I became aware of Chinese sensitivities from my experience at the Home Ministry. For them, the Tibetan refugee issue was at the top of the list of mutually-related security concerns. China was mostly concerned that the Tibetan refugees in Nepal had the backing of Western powers and also alluded indirectly to India, that they were creating a threat to China's security. For example, Tibetans would publicly celebrate the Tibetan Uprising day, but the Chinese authorities used to pressurise us to not give them that right. On the other hand, Western powers like the USA, the UK, and other EU nations were quite sensitive about the Tibetan issue, especially human rights violations. If we had taken any action against the

Figure 2: CEC with Chinese Ambassador Zheng Xianglin
Source: ECN, Photo by Suman Ghimire.

Figure 3: US Under-Secretary of State Henrietta H. Fore with Election Commissioners
Source: ECN, Photo by Suman Ghimire.

refugees and Tibetans in Nepal, international authorities and the media in the west would have created a hue and cry.

In the new political context of Nepal, after the weakening of its most trusted ally, the Nepalese monarchy, the Chinese wanted a bigger role. This led China to support the Constituent Assembly elections. More importantly, to China, is the idea that whoever is in power should be supported and should remain in a good relationship with them.

Dealing with this low-profile, and unproblematic neighbour, during the elections process would have been quite easy if it had not been for a major ethical dilemma which Nepal faced. Was it acceptable to receive support from a country that did not practice multiparty, democratic elections? Even if the answer was no, due to the dictates of conscience, Nepal could not afford to offend this massive and powerful neighbour—a world super-power that was challenging the United States. So China's support was accepted without a murmur.

The Chief reflected further on his memories of engagement with international partners:

The *Ameriki Rajdoot* [the American Ambassador], James F. Moriarty, was another enthusiastic and candid ally of the Election Commission. He had said to me, "Our government's policy is to support democracy and democratic institutions. Please feel free to ask for any support you need." But unlike Mukherjee, he had said, "Don't hurry. Focus on making the elections credible." His focus was always on the management of the Maoist combatants.

Moriarty was quite outspoken about what he thought, sometimes even at the cost of his own popularity. He openly criticised the Maoist violence at a time when many Nepalese were ready to give the rebels benefit of the doubt. He was never convinced that the Maoists would agree to a democratic election process. However, his successor Ms. Nancy Powell, a seasoned diplomat, developed good relations with the Maoists.

I knew from my Home Secretary days that the American interest in Nepal was also related to security. Those days they were keenly interested in providing support to the Nepalese security structure. They were chiefly concerned about human rights issues, most importantly the lingering Tibetan issue. Their interest in the functions of our Home Ministry focused upon what it did about security or immigration. The Americans wanted to collect as much information about Nepalese intelligence, overtly or covertly—without actually spying—as they could. As a super power, and one of Nepal's largest aid donors, the United States has always played an influential role in the internal affairs of Nepal.

It is said that Ambassador Moriarty was against any peace agreement with the Maoists, reflecting his government's position after the 9/11 terrorist attack. But the US position slowly changed and they contributed positively to holding the Constituent Assembly elections, although they were still not able to communicate directly with the Maoists, due to US law.

Another friend, who needs to be mentioned, is the *Belayeti Rajdoot* [the British Ambassador], Andrew Hall, who was also head of the European Union at that time. Ambassador Hall was quite encouraging and impartial in his dealings, compared to some other interfering or indifferent Ambassadors. Since he had spent some time in Nepal, he understood local sensitivities and played a positive role on behalf of EU members.

As the Constituent Assembly elections would evidently mark a major break with Nepal's past, the UK, politically and commercially astute, was eager to renew its historical relationship with the new political set-up.

Another EU member, I must mention, is the Danish Ambassador, Mr. Finn Thilsted. Although straightforward, and almost blunt at times, he was the Commission's strongest friend. He helped make the Constituent Assembly elections happen on time. The Norwegians were equally supportive. The Norwegian Ambassador Tore Toreng, a pleasant and soft-spoken man, was also our closest ally. He quietly played an instrumental role in bringing conflicting political parties together.

Figure 4: The EU delegates at ECN headed by the British Ambassador to Nepal
Source: ECN, Photo by Suman Ghimire.

> I must say, these Scandinavian countries played a more crucial role than the Americans or the British. This is because during that time, the Americans and the British could not engage with the Maoists—the Americans for legal reasons, and the British due to their long historical relationship with the Nepalese Army. The Scandinavian countries were engaged with the Maoists throughout and won their trust.
>
> Along with these international development partners, Japanese Ambassador Tatsuo Mizuno and the Australian Ambassador, Mr. Graeme Lade also deserve a special mention for their support of the Commission at critical moments.

Apart from working with the diplomatic missions of these countries, the Commission's interaction with international development partners also occurred through other bilateral and multilateral donor agencies, creating a wide network of support for the elections. Danish International Development Agency Human Rights and Good Governance Unit (Danida/HUGOU), USAID, the Department for International Development (DFID), the Japan International Cooperation Agency (JICA), the Korean International Cooperation Agency (KOICA) and the Australian Agency for International Development (AusAID) paid many of the Commission's bills by channelling their money through the Nepal Peace Trust Fund in the Ministry of Finance, or through direct contribution.

Similarly, international non-profit organisations like the International Foundation of Electoral Systems (IFES), The Cater Center (TCC), The Asia Foundation (TAF), and others also contributed significantly to the election process. An interesting thing about donor meetings at the Commission was that India and China were also included though sometimes some Western nations informally questioned if these countries at all deserved donor status.

Finally, the Chief summed up his experience of working with international partners in the following way:

> The international community was highly supportive of the Constituent Assembly elections, and regular interaction enabled them to assess our position and also coordinate better in mobilising resources for the elections. The presence of Heads of missions or Ambassadors during these meetings also showed the importance they attached to our post-conflict elections.
>
> We had to account for the money we were given, which is fair enough. But sometimes, we also had to tolerate the *tantrums* of these super-rich donors, their condescending attitude, their out-of-context suggestions, their unnecessary claims of expertise and their unceasing interference.

Despite this, the two big neighbours [India and China] and other international friends played a valuable role in creating an optimistic atmosphere for the success of the elections. They provided the pressure necessary to convince the Nepalese political parties to show respect for the election, instead of always focusing on their own partisan interests.

The election in Nepal was one of those rare occasions when international countries came together for a common goal, despite their varying interests. In this sense, our elections were truly global. We had Australian ink, American ballot paper, British generators, Chinese election materials, Danish computers, Indian vehicles, Japanese ballot boxes and Korean fax machines.

Chapter 12

As negotiations with a range of partners commenced, the Election Commission of Nepal also began to engage with the United Nations.

The UN's involvement in Nepal's peace process began when Secretary-General Kofi Annan visited Nepal in March 2001, two months before the palace massacre. The following year, in August 2002, in his annual report to the UN General Assembly Annan offered his *good offices*. This offer came after political leaders, including the Maoists, indicated their preference for engagement with the UN—due to its global composition.

Padma Ratna Tuladhar, one of the facilitators in the peace talks between the Maoists and the government in 2001 and 2003, recalls some interesting details about the UN's engagement in Nepal. In an interview, Tuladhar said:

> On the occasion of the UN Day celebrations, the UN Resident Coordinator, Henning Karcher, said the UN could make its offices available to assist in solving the conflict—provided that both sides made a request to this effect. It was actually Karcher's remark on UN day that encouraged most Nepalese actors to take UN involvement seriously.
>
> The day after Karcher's remarks, Prachanda called me to learn more about how the UN wanted to be involved in Nepal. Daman Nath Dhungana and I felt we had to secure international expertise during the previous peace talks in 2001. So I went to meet Henning Karcher to discuss possible UN involvement in the peace process, and a series of informal talks commenced.
>
> In July 2003, Kofi Annan had sent his Senior Political Officer Tamrat Samuel to Nepal. During this visit, although his mandate was not clearly defined, Tamrat met various government actors, political party and civil society leaders, and talked with the Maoists to see if the UN could assist with the ongoing peace process.

> From my old house in Lainchaur, Tamrat talked to the Maoist leaders on their satellite phones. During that visit, I told Tamrat about the *Indian factor*, explaining to him that initiatives for dialogue could not move forward without the consent of New Delhi. Tamrat understood and visited New Delhi. After that, he made it a point to fly to New Delhi either before or after visiting Kathmandu, in order to update the Indians regularly on the process.
>
> But it was not easy to bring the UN formally to Nepalese soil, due to sensitivity of our neighbours—India and China—who were wary of any external presence in Nepal.
>
> The First Secretary of the Indian Embassy, which is just a few meters away from my house, visited me frequently. During our talks, he used to ask me 'Why do you need the UN? India is there to give you all kinds of support.' Of course, he used to say that informally.

India was not enthusiastic about UN involvement in Nepal for mainly two reasons: firstly, if the UN succeeded in assisting the transition to democracy in Nepal it might refocus its attention on Kashmir, which India did not want. And secondly, if the UN mission to Nepal failed, and the international contingent returned home, India felt it would be left to clear up the mess in Nepal. For India it was a no-win situation.

According to Tuladhar, China's position vis-à-vis the UN, in the initial phase, was not clear. He said:

> The Chinese diplomats used to tell me that China would be concerned only if there was direct Indian military intervention. Of course, the Chinese wanted to be informed about everything, but they did not want to interfere.

At this time, China seemed less concerned about the UN involvement than India. This could have been because of the veto it enjoyed as a permanent member of the Security Council.

Tuladhar said the groundwork for the entry of the United Nations into Nepal was laid by a series of dialogues and negotiations with Nepal's internal and external political actors. To facilitate this process, an Office of the High Commissioner for Human Rights (OHCHR) was set up at Kathmandu in May 2005, headed by Tamrat's colleague from East Timor, Ian Martin. They knew each other well and together coordinated talks with political actors in Nepal. The OHCHR monitored human rights violations on both sides of the armed conflict—the governmental and the Maoists—with over a hundred national and international staff.

This was the background to the 12-Point Understanding, which hinted at the UN's involvement in the peace process. Clause Three of the Understanding said that both the Maoist and the Royal army should be supervised by the UN or a reliable international body during the Constituent Assembly election process. This was possible only after India reluctantly agreed to some kind of UN presence, other than formal mediation.

After the People's Movement in 2006 the field was clear for the UN to enter Nepal. A reliable third party was needed to monitor the Maoist combatants and their arms, in order to ensure free and fair elections. National actors lacked the credibility, neutrality and technical expertise for this role. Hence, the presence of the UN was inevitable.

After receiving an invitation from Nepal, the UN dispatched a pre-assessment mission to the country in late July 2006—led by Staffan de Mistura. The objective of this mission was to secure an agreement between the government and the Maoists on the nature and scope of the UN's role. The mission resulted in a series of discussions and negotiations between the political parties, on the precise terms of their request for UN support.

One of the major hurdles to reaching an agreement was the difference over modalities for the storage of the weapons of the Maoists. The government had insisted not only on the cantonment of the Maoist army but also that they relinquish their weapons. Since this was not part of the peace deal, the Maoists objected. Despite vigorous negotiations, no agreement was reached and the UN team had to leave Kathmandu empty-handed. Tamrat Samuel was assured that the agreement would be sent to New Delhi, where the team was headed after Kathmandu. That did not happen.

In August 2006, the parties finally agreed to seek UN assistance in five areas (leaving the storage for weapons to be discussed later). The Nepalese government and the Maoists wrote separate letters, on the same day, requesting the UN to assist in the peace process—specifically, in relation to monitoring: human rights through the OHCHR; the Code-of-Conduct during the Ceasefire; arms and armed personnel of both the sides; and observation of the Constituent Assembly elections.

Ian Martin was appointed the Personal Representative of the UN Secretary General, assisted by a small team of political, military, electoral and ceasefire monitoring advisers. The team closely engaged with important political actors, to forge an agreement on the specifics of the UN mission's role in the peace process (particularly in relation to the monitoring of the Maoists arms and combatants).

The Office of the Personal Representative, under Martin's leadership, also worked with the political parties in the lead-up to the signing of the Comprehensive Peace Agreement (CPA) on 21 November 2006. And they facilitated the Agreement on the Monitoring of the Management of Arms and Armies (AMMAA)—which was vital for the election to proceed. A Joint Monitoring Coordination Committee, chaired by the UN, was also formed to assist the signatory parties to the AMMAA to implement the agreement.

The Chief reflected on the UN's engagement in Nepal at this time:

> The Commission was continuously engaged with the UN in these processes, because they affected the election directly. Unless Maoist arms and combatants were monitored by a reliable body, the political environment necessary to conduct elections would not exist. Similarly, the legislative basis to conduct

Figure 5: SPA leader Koirala (left) and the Maoist Chairman Dahal (right) during signing of the Comprehensive Peace Agreement
Source: Photo by Chandra Shekhar Karki.

Figure 6: During the AAMMA signing process, UNMIN head Ian Martin is standing between Home Minister Krishna Sitaula (on the left) and Maoist leader Krishna Mahara (on the right) *Source*: UN, Photo by Sagar Shrestha.

elections, for example the Interim Constitution, would not be achieved if there was no political understanding on these crucial issues. That's why I closely engaged with the UN team, particularly Ian Martin.

Ian Martin was already well-known in Nepalese political circles owing to his previous role in the OHCHR, which helped us to promptly trust him. His direct access to the government and political leaders, and his personal rapport with Prachanda *jee*, was also a distinct advantage. A few leaders said he was pro-Maoist; however, my observation was that he was sympathetic to a progressive agenda rather than being inclined towards the Maoist party. Additionally, he seemed to be convinced that a change in the old order was essential for ending the armed conflict in Nepal. Martin and I worked closely together, whenever we needed to convince the government and the Maoist leadership about any issue. Not that it worked in all cases. Nevertheless, Martin was able to develop trust with the Maoist leaders, which we as local actors could not, given the sensitive, polarised political environment.

The Election Commission felt that requesting the UN for technical assistance rather than observation of the elections, would be useful. The UN also didn't want to send an observation mission, as they had not deployed one since 2000.

One of my main worries was that the Maoists would not accept the election outcome and that this would result in violence, as had happened in many other post-conflict elections, for example, in Zimbabwe, Kenya and Moldova. Like most people in insulated Kathmandu, I also believed that the Maoists' performance in the elections would be poor. The Maoists had neither any experience of elections nor any well known candidates, like the other established parties. I assumed that if they performed poorly, the Maoists would reject the legitimacy of the election process. I, therefore, needed a foolproof strategy to counter this likely threat. And the UN seemed to be the best tool for that.

The involvement of the UN in the election process, through providing technical assistance, had its distinct advantages. Firstly the UN presence in the field would help create a better political atmosphere and increase confidence among political actors; secondly, the elections would gain global attention and acceptability because of UN's participation; thirdly, the direct involvement of the UN would help to secure the required international resources and expertise for the elections; and finally, the involvement of the UN would make the elections more credible, encouraging the Maoists, and others, to accept the results.

I spoke to my colleagues and the political leaders and convinced them to ask the UN to provide their technical assistance. After strategic lobbying, the government and the Maoists were persuaded to send a revised letter asking the UN for technical assistance, instead of just election observation. The UN Secretary General then received two clear election-related mandates from the Security Council. The first was to provide technical assistance in conducting the Constituent Assembly elections, and the second was to review all technical and political aspects of the electoral process, utilising an independent team of election experts appointed by the Secretary-General.

I wanted the political parties to resolve the Maoist arms and combatants issues *before* the Constituent Assembly election. But when I brought this matter to the party leaders, they told me that managing such a complex issue would take a long time and that the parties needed the election as early as possible, in order to establish their legitimacy. I think the real political reason for postponing management of the Maoists combatants and arms was the assumption that the Maoists would perform poorly in the elections. The major parties, like the Nepali Congress, calculated that they would be able to negotiate with the Maoists on the issue of the management of the combatants from a position of strength after the election. This view was supported by international partners, including India.

Another factor behind that decision was that the Seven Parties Alliance and the Maoists felt threatened by the Royal Palace, which was perceived to be backed by the Nepalese Army. Due to this perceived threat, they took slower approach to deal with the Maoists army so that the rebel army acted as counter balance to the state army if they tried to threaten the Constituent Assembly elections.

I feel it was wrong that the political parties arranged the election before managing the future of the Maoist combatants and weapons. In the end it was not possible to ensure a level playing field among actors during the election because one party still retained an army—even though it was monitored by the UN.

Chapter 13

While all these international negotiations were continuing, on 15 January 2007, around 185 parliamentarians in the recently reinstated House of Representatives voted unanimously in favour of promulgating the Interim Constitution.

Nearly 56 years after King Tribhuvan approved the first Interim Constitution for Nepal, which included preparations for a Constituent Assembly election, this second Interim Constitution was legislated with the same mission, albeit without the involvement of the Royal Family. In fact, it was the first Constitution of Nepal that rendered the King powerless. The Interim Constitution was similar to the first one in many ways. Both subscribed to liberal democratic ideas of a representative government, adult franchise, the rule of law, and freedom and liberty for individuals and groups, and both envisaged the new state as a positive instrument for improving human welfare and social justice. However, the 1951 Interim Constitution was greatly influenced by the Indian Constitution—reflecting principles such as separation of state power, checks and balances of power, independence of judiciary, a bicameral legislature, a majoritarian election system and an executive prime minister. In contrast, the 2007 Interim Constitution was a document of compromise—influenced by the internal political dynamics of a transitional Nepal, and lacking coherent principles or cogent ideology.

This Interim Constitution vested all executive powers in the Council of Ministers; the King was stripped of his authority to govern the country and the prime minster assumed the powers of Head of State. The Interim Constitution also stipulated the formation of a Constituent Assembly with a two-year term, which would formulate the new constitution. The government would declare the date for the Assembly election. The Constituent Assembly would comprise of 425 members, of which 409 members were to be elected through a mixed election system comprised of First-Past-The-Post (FPTP) and Proportional Representation (PR). The remaining sixteen members would be nominated by the Council of Ministers, from amongst the country's prominent persons.

On the same day that the Constitution was promulgated as part of the peace process, the Interim Legislature-Parliament was formed, according to its mandate. This mandate envisaged an interim unicameral legislature, of which 209 members would be from the dissolved Parliament (restored in April 2006), 73 from the Maoist party and 48 nominated by the major political parties. The main objective of this body was to induct Maoists into the parliament. This process was important in order to ensure their participation in creating the necessary legislation for the Constituent Assembly election. One of the key facilitators of the peace process from the Maoists side, Krishna Bahadur Mahara, headed the Maoist team. Explaining how the Maoists felt about joining the mainstream political arena, Mahara said:

> We are in the parliament as a result of this epoch-making leap, and are armed with a new ideology, philosophy and a new way of thinking...The political systems that were in place in Nepal could not rightly address the different problems of the country. Therefore, we waged the ten-year war, and last year this great People's Movement, the April Movement, took place. Then we began a new process in the country so that the Nepalese would not have to go through another war or struggle for democracy time and again.

A few kilometres away from where Mahara made these remarks, in Bahadur Bhavan, the manager of the Constituent Assembly elections, the Chief, was elated. Recalling his views of the Interim Constitution, the Chief later said:

> Getting the Interim Constitution enacted was a great relief to us. The Commission finally had a firm legal footing. Otherwise we would be operating in a legal vacuum with a nearly defunct 1990 Constitution.
>
> The new constitution legally settled many issues that were necessary for the election process, like the election system, the number of seats, the voters' age limits, the cut-off date (namely the specific date by which the person must be 18 years to be eligible for registration or voting) and the party registration requirements.
>
> Major political parties had serious disagreements about these issues, for example, about the voters' age. The Maoists wanted to lower the voting age because they had a tighter grip than all other parties on the younger age group. But the Nepali Congress and the Unified Marxist Leninist party were not keen to lower the voting age.

> No wonder it took over four months to finalise this Constitution, despite the Commission's intense pressure to complete it early. The draft of the Interim Constitution was submitted to the political parties in August 2006 by the Interim Constitution Drafting Committee. However, because of the vast differences between the political parties on many important issues, negotiations went on until they signed a six-point agreement in November 2006 that led to the finalisation of the Interim Constitution.
>
> I remember Prime Minister Koirala being under tremendous pressure during those days. He confessed to me one day, 'Bhojraj *jee,* while there is tremendous political pressure on me to finalise the Constitution in time, legal experts say that the draft violates many democratic principles and needs to be suitably amended before declaring it.'
>
> Not only was the Constitution important for decisions to be made on vital election issues but also for moving the peace process forward, which was equally crucial for the election. The Maoists could join the parliament and the government only after the Constitution was enacted.
>
> Although we were happy to get the Constitution ratified, we were disappointed that the political parties ignored many necessary technical suggestions that ECN had suggested. Completely ignoring international and national practice, the government kept the right to declare the election date itself—bypassing the Commission. The newly legislated Constitution was also, conveniently, silent on many controversial election issues, like the number of ballots required for voting, the exact nature of mixed election system, how candidates would be selected, and the principles of inclusion of previously excluded groups:- issues which created many difficulties for us in such a polarised political context.

As the Interim Constitution came into effect, the Election Commission faced many unexpected impediments. One of them was the eruption of agitation by the Madhesi groups. The reason for this is historical. Although there is no accepted definition of the Madhesi community, they are generally seen as residing on the plains in the southern part of Nepal, which borders India. While the characteristics of the various individual Madhesi groups vary, they are generally a people who claim to have been ruled by Nepal for a long time. A case study of the Mithila culture could help illustrate the predicament of Madhesi communities.

The Madhesi communities in central and eastern plains of Nepal belong to Mithila culture and trace their origin to mythological times. Historically, the culture flourished under the Kingdom of Simraungarh—between eleventh and fourteenth centuries—but then fell to the Mughal rule. When present-day boundaries were created, a small part of the Mithila state found itself in Nepal and the remaining in India. Similar was the fate of the Bhojpuri-speaking people in the central region and the Awadhi-speaking population in the western part of the country.

Not surprisingly, the large majority of these people in Nepal share linguistic and cultural traits with people across the border in India. For example, they both speak Maithili, Awadhi and Bhojpuri. Cultural ties across the border are also strong, with inter-marriages and other linked economic activities. Unfortunately, these strong cultural and economic bonds with people in Northern India have been exploited by the rulers of Nepal time and again, as an instrument to create suspicion against the entire Madhesi community and to question their loyalty towards the Nepali state. The people of Madhesi identity were not recruited into any sensitive state institutions or security agencies, like the Nepal Army, and some of them were even deprived of the right to citizenship. This systematic discrimination made the Madhesi community feel like *second class citizens.*

After the People's Movement in 2006, in which the Madhesi community played a vital role, it was expected that perceived structural discrimination against these people would end and that their grievances would be addressed. However, when the Interim Constitution failed to address their concerns, the whole of Madhesi community erupted into spontaneous protest. The uprising started when some pro-Madhesi groups, like the Madhesi Janadhikar Forum (MJF), a Madhesi rights group and the Nepal Sadbhavana Party (SP), objected to the Interim Constitution's silence on federalism (a key demand of the Madhesi groups). They registered their displeasure by burning copies of the Interim Constitution.

Soon after, the Madhesi Janadhikar Forum—popularly known as the Forum—presented a 10-point document of demands to the government, which called not only for a federal system but also for a fully proportional election system. Intrinsic to Madhesi demands was an assertion of their identity and dignity. They felt that the Nepalese state owed them much, after centuries of neglect.

But somewhat surprisingly, the government, led by the Seven Party Alliance, did not address the demands of the Madhesi groups, and instead suppressed the movement through brutal police action. This resulted in the death of 16-year-old Ramesh Kumar Mahato, a grade ten student. This incident infuriated the Madhesis, who called for agitation until their demands were met.

This movement was soon joined by a cross-section of the Madhesi populace, including labourers, farmers, rickshaw pullers, shopkeepers, students and teachers. The agitation erupted into violent clashes everywhere—with activists attacking shops, government offices, police posts and political party offices, burning vehicles and blocking national highways. Tarai, the lifeline of Nepal, came to a virtual halt.

The protest and violence went on for several weeks, leaving around 24 dead and 800 wounded. According to the UN report, at least 18 deaths during the Madhesi uprising were the result of police action. After only a few weeks, the government softened, and an agreement was reached with the Madhesi group. One of the provisions of that agreement was that the number of constituencies in the majoritarian system would be increased to 240 seats in order to accommodate the population increase in some of the Tarai districts, as indicated by the 2001 census.

Immediately afterwards, the Electoral Constituency Delineation Commission (ECDC) was established, to draw up the constituency boundaries to adjust the added constituencies. While in the Himalayan region the boundaries remained more or less unchanged, the ECDC made adjustments which added 28 constituencies in the Tarai region and seven constituencies in the hilly regions.

Figure 7: Madhesi uprising
Source: UN, Photo by Subodh Singh.

This revised demarcation was designed to achieve one representative per 96,000 people, and one seat for each district—irrespective of its population size.

The Election Commission of Nepal was not prepared to handle unexpected political developments. Reflecting on the impact of the Madhesi uprising on the elections process, the Chief said:

> The Madhesi uprising took us by surprise. As it was, the Commission's schedule, to complete all preparations for the election in June 2007, was already tight. The unexpected Madhesi uprising introduced fresh challenges. The Election Commission was highly disturbed by this political development, and pressured the prime minister to redress the Madhesi's demands so that elections could be held smoothly.
>
> The uprising immediately disrupted some election preparation in the affected areas of Tarai. Plus, the Madhesi uprising also resulted in an increase in the total Constituent Assembly seats. Although political parties were not initially in the mood to increase the number of seats in the First-Past-The-Post (FPTP) or the majoritarian voting system, they were forced to review their decision after the Madhesi uprising.
>
> In post-conflict election, such unexpected challenges are likely to emerge. The Election Commission had to be prepared for these kinds of developments and remain flexible.

Chapter 14

Unaware of hostile undercurrents, the Commission started preparing for the elections, scheduled for June 2007.

The Bahadur Bhavan faced innumerable hurdles, owing to the post-conflict situation. More importantly, handling the former rebels—who threatened to walk out of the election process whenever they did not get what they wanted—was extremely difficult. For example, during the allocation of party symbols to be used during the elections, the Maoists threatened to walk out if they were not given the hammer and sickle symbol. The Commission could not oblige because the other communist parties objected, saying the hammer and sickle was the symbol of *all* communist parties. But after a series of negotiations, the Commission found a solution: granting the hammer and sickle to the Maoists—while placating the other parties by placing the common symbol inside a small circle. Despite this creative outcome the EC was criticised for pleasing the Maoists.

In addition to these post-conflict challenges, the Commission faced obstacles, owing to Nepal's geographical diversity and poor infrastructure. In more than half the country, there were no roads and the Commission had to rely on air travel. That too was not easy. In one incident, the helicopter containing training materials could not fly to the mountainous Solukhumbu district for a week, due to bad weather—meaning preparations for the training had to be redone. The biggest difficulty was created by the frequent shortage of petrol, diesel and kerosene. As a result, the Commission had to reschedule crucial trainings and other election preparations in many districts.

The international community also helped to solve these problems. For instance, the USAID and the Indian government assisted with the printing of the ballot papers. The Commission had faced a mammoth task—it needed to print around 241 types of 42 million ballot papers within a limited time frame. But none of the local security printing presses had the capacity to print such a large amount. Printing them in adjoining countries, like India or China, was not feasible due to political sensitivities, and having them printed further afield was not practical because of the cost.

In the end, the USAID and the Indian government provided technical support to increase the capacity of the security printing presses in Nepal—making it possible to print the ballot-papers locally, in time for the election.

The Chief later said:

> Almost regularly I called a donors' meeting and pleaded with them that I need this or that ... Who would provide it? Donors had also sped up their procurement procedures to meet our emergency needs. Without prompt international support, it would have been too difficult for us to complete the election preparation.

Initially, the Commission's priority was to prepare the voters' list. The Commission already had a voters' list that was last updated in April 2006. But there were questions about its accuracy. It was claimed that local secretaries had collected details without actually visiting the voters themselves, because of the security problems during the conflict. Most significantly, the list was not acceptable to the Maoists because they were not included, since they had been waging an armed insurrection when it was drawn up. The Commission decided to compile a new voter's list using the April 2006 one as a base. Even though the Maoists initially rejected this proposal, they finally agreed after a series of negotiations.

> One of the first steps was to enact the law needed to register voters. The Commission wanted to ensure that as many people be eligible to vote in the Constituent Assembly election, as possible. The mixed election system enabled some groups, who had been excluded in the past, to vote in this election.
>
> The Voter Registration law contained a provision which divided voters into permanent and temporary categories. Permanent voters were those who could vote under both the Majoritarian (FPTP) and Proportional Representation systems, whereas temporary voters were allowed to vote only in the proportional system. A separate voters' list was prepared for these temporary voters, which included government employees, electoral staff, Nepalese Army personnel, the Nepalese Police force and Armed Police, the People's Liberation Army (PLA) cadres and prisoners.

Nevertheless, deciding who would be allowed to vote was highly controversial and there were many disagreements between the major political parties. For example, the Maoists were in favour of giving full voting rights to internal migrants who mainly resided in urban, suburban and semi-urban areas as temporary residents. They included impoverished tenants, small-time shopkeepers, office workers, semi-skilled workers, vendors, poor labourers and the homeless (*sukumbasis*), who had mainly migrated from the villages. Potentially they comprised a huge group of voters who favoured the revolutionaries, because they believed they would benefit if the Maoists came to power.

On the other hand, the Congress and the Unified Marxist Leninist parties, though they agreed to give voting rights to temporary residents, were concerned about identification issues and duplicated voting. They said the election provided an opportunity for these people, who mostly worked in the cities, to go home to their villages to vote—which had not been possible during the armed conflict.

The other controversy concerned internally displaced people. In any post-conflict election, the voting right of internal refugees causes considerable concern. The international community and civil society were adamant that the internally displaced population—which ranged from a relatively low official figure of 8,000 to 1 million as claimed by some of the organisations, should have the right to vote.

On this matter, the Chief later said:

> The Election Commissioners *en bloc* also strongly felt that the internally displaced should be given voting rights, at least in the proportional election system. But, the government ignored our proposal.
>
> The international community created a hue and cry about it and sent us a long letter requesting us to give the internally displaced their voting rights. When this issue was raised with the government, Home Minister Sitaula said that the political parties thought that the election should be an occasion for these displaced people to return home—rather than linger elsewhere.
>
> There was also some resistance from the Maoists themselves about the voting rights of the internally displaced people. Because giving them voting rights would mean the Maoists would have to accept that they had displaced several such people.
>
> Still, the fact that many internally displaced people were not allowed to return home meant that they were denied the right to vote. At least they should have been given the right to vote in the proportional system, if nothing else. It was feasible for the Commission to have managed that even within the given time frame.

> Interestingly, the Voter Registration's Act extended voting rights to prisoners. When the Commission proposed the idea, none of the political parties objected, and for the first time in Nepal, prisoners were given the right to vote. This was one of the Commission's small but far-reaching reforms.

The voting rights of non-resident Nepalese were equally controversial. Most of the political parties thought that Nepalese living temporarily outside the country should be given voting rights—especially for the Constituent Assembly elections. In fact, many senior leaders had promised this to Non-Resident Nepalese (NRN) when they travelled abroad, and even received lucrative donations in return for this promise.

In retrospect, the Chief said:

> Though it had been assumed that it would be feasible to give voting rights to Nepalese living abroad in the proportional system, it did not take long to realise that it was impossible to do so within the given time. There were many technical problems, like preparing voters' lists, transporting ballots, conducting the voting amongst others. The main hurdle was tracking down voters working in the unorganised sector in India, who most likely did not have any official documents that proved their eligibility to vote.
>
> Actually, the ambiguity of the political leaders created the problem. Publicly, they said they were in favour of voting rights for NRNs. However, privately they were against it.
>
> Even during the referendum conducted by the repressive panchayat regime, there was symbolic representation of the Nepalese residing abroad in the voting. I feel that it was a big mistake to deprive them of their voting rights in the Constituent Assembly election, which would decide the future of the country.

It was not only deciding who could vote that was challenging. Identifying where those voters were located was equally daunting. 'A battle of Mahabharata,* the Chief declared.

Reflecting on some of these experiences, the Chief said:

> I had read somewhere that only the naïve rig elections on election day, while professionals target the process. So I was really sensitive about voter registration, as it was the key process that identified the people who were allowed to vote. Any tempering with it was tantamount to defrauding the entire electoral process.

* An ancient Sanskrit epic.

The transitional political context threw up many challenges. Due to the legacy of the conflict, the election staff were reluctant to go into the countryside. The Commission had to take out an insurance policy for the election staff, to make them feel more secure. I was also in frequent contact with Maoist Chairman Dahal, to get assurances that election staff would not be troubled.

Interestingly, collecting the names of the rank and file Maoists, more so than of their senior leaders, was problematic because they did not have citizenship cards or official identification papers. In many cases, our staff had to be flexible, almost to the point of violating the law, in order to ensure they met the voter's needs.

Despite their overall cooperative response, the former rebels behaved badly in a few major cities like Kathmandu, Lalitpur and Bhaktapur. Some of their objectionable activities included confiscating voters' lists and threatening the supervisory election staff, demanding that labourers, students and others living away from home should be given voting rights—despite the fact that this was against the law.

This confrontation arose due to our unclear policy on the voting rights of temporary residents. The enumerators followed different standards while registering the temporary residents in different places. Though it did not lead to a big setback, in post-conflict countries any unclear policy can lead to potential conflict. This must be avoided at all costs.

Another difficulty was created by the increasingly politically active ethnic voice. I will describe one small incident. After the completion of the voters registration process, one morning a senior Nepali Congress leader, Bal Bahadur Rai, met me with a delegation demanding that the Rai's subgroups be mentioned in the final voters' list. We were rattled, not only because the Rai had around a hundred subgroups but also because there were over another 100 ethnic groups like the Rai in Nepal—who could soon be clamouring for similar documentation.

The complexities we faced during the process of identifying voters were repeated in other election processes. It was like walking on a knife edge. If we made one wrong move the whole election process could fall apart.

The Chief summed up lessons drawn from these election processes, as follows:

- A post-conflict election is an election of compromise. A give and take scenario. The prime objective should be to support the ongoing peace process.
- The Election Commission should be flexible, able to adjust to post-conflict political complications, and ready to compromise when required—without contravening key election best practice. Election managers need to be clear

about their mission and able to focus on the larger picture, rather than being caught up in petty technical issues.

- If the Commission builds its credibility the voters, and even the international community, will respect them and excuse minor mistakes. A transparent and consultative approach, at each step of the electoral process, is the key to achieving that credibility. The consultative process should also create a sense of stakeholder ownership, which will ultimately lead to acceptability of the election results.
- Policies that may be feasible during *normal* elections may not be suitable during post-conflict elections, when time is limited and the political pressure is immense.
- Any kind of *perceived* discrimination could bring unexpected consequences in a fragile, political situation, which may affect the legitimacy of the election.

Chapter 15

A significant development that helped to create a positive atmosphere for the June elections was the formal entry of a world body—the United Nations Mission in Nepal (UNMIN)—into the Nepalese politico-electoral arena. The UNMIN was established on 23 January 2007, by Security Council Resolution 1740, with its main focus being to help conduct the Constituent Assembly election in a free and fair manner.

The UNMIN established a tangible presence by setting up an Electoral Assistance Office in Bahadur Bhavan. Fida Nasrullah, a middle-aged Lebanese woman, was appointed Chief Technical Adviser. The arrival of more international election experts in Kathmandu helped spread a *galvanic* election atmosphere throughout the country. This atmosphere was further enhanced when the UN started monitoring the weaponry of the Maoist rebels and their army personnel. This was crucial to ensure the election met international norms.

In March 2007, the UNMIN reported over 31,000 Maoist army personnel, who were placed in 28 cantonment sites under the supervision of unarmed UNMIN monitors. A total of 3,475 Maoist weapons were stored in seven main cantonment sites, under round-the-clock guard. The following month, the UNMIN registered and stored 2,855 Nepal Army weapons, again under 24 hour guard, as agreed by the peace pact.

The Chief decided to team up the newly-arrived UN international advisors to the Commission with his domestic staff in an attempt to bolster the capacity of the local operatives. It was hoped this collaboration would help achieve the common goal, of a successful election. Accordingly, nine international advisors were paired up with their national counterparts—to provide assistance to various election components—and the two UN international advisors were deployed to assist the Commission's Regional Resource Centres and the district electoral offices. This meant, in total, nearly a hundred international electoral advisors

Figure 8: Verification of Maoist combatants by UNMIN
Source: UN, Photo by Robel Mockonen.

were stationed in the districts, in readiness for the election. The Chief recalled how election officials interacted with the UN's election unit:

> It was the first time that Nepal's Election Commission took direct technical assistance from an external agency. The entire ECN crew was quite excited about having a new partner in the election process. As the Constituent Assembly election process was completely new, the Commission hoped to gain a lot from the experience and expertise of their international counterparts. However, this initial *romance* soon dissipated, when it was realised that expectations were not based on reality but on our assumptions.
>
> We had not made a study of the UN missions elsewhere, or learnt about the limitations of the UN's mandate in practice. It was simply thought that the UN, with its rich, international experience and electoral knowledge, would solve all our problems and eradicate all complications, by waving a magic wand. We also expected that UN would magically transform the capacity of the local staff within a limited time. Understandably, that would not be the case.
>
> The first problem encountered was with the language to be used in all official written or spoken communication. This was because the English language abilities of Nepalese government officials were limited, as it was mandatory for all work to be done in Nepali.

> Our staff became self-conscious about their not-so-proficient language abilities and were not comfortable enough to develop a good working relationship with the UN officials.
>
> The UN decided to hire interpreters to facilitate their work. However, Nepal did not have enough trained and experienced interpreters who could translate election jargon and election-related legal texts accurately.
>
> Although there were language difficulties, which we had not anticipated, this was not insurmountable. Linguistic *knots* were somehow minimised by mutual effort and understanding.

Nevertheless, according to the Chief, there was another, more fundamental, problem. This had nothing to do with the election process itself but, rather, was related to the inherent disparity between the wealth of the nations involved. Both the UN and the Commission were unable to resolve this difficulty. It was based on a sense of injustice, felt because of the evident inequalities in remuneration between the UN staff and the local ECN staff. This inequality led to bitter envy.

On this issue, the Chief said:

> As the exposure of our staff to UN staff increased, they were instilled with a sense of envy and deprivation, which, unfortunately, affected their overall level of motivation. Although the salaries of UN staff were not that high in relation to what is paid in rich countries, they were very high in the Nepalese context. The salary of a national member of staff, temporarily working for the UN, was up to five times more than that of the most senior government employees in Nepal.
>
> During our internal meetings, embittered comments came up. "What have these highly paid UN staff done?" and "They keep asking questions for which our working time is diverted" and "They just collect information from us and produce their reports."
>
> This is an invaluable lesson we have learnt, which we wish to share with our counterparts in other post-conflict countries.
>
> Before deciding to involve other international organisations, like the UN or external agencies, in an election process post conflict countries should consider if engaging this external expertise is worth the demotivation it may cause among local staff. This is most important in post-conflict situations, because there are multiple challenges to be faced, which demand the dedication of highly motivated officials with *staying power*.

And there was another issue that created serious friction between the two partners, for which the Commission was to blame. This resulted from a misunderstanding of the UN's role in the electoral process.

Most of the international experts who came to Nepal had prior experience in countries like Iraq and Afghanistan, where they ran the entire election. When they found a fully functioning Commission in Nepal, they did not know what their role should be.

It was our responsibility to define the roles and to inform partners of what we were expecting, but we did not do this effectively. When the UNMIN asked how we needed their support, in a typically Nepalese manner we casually made a list of things which included all the key areas of the election without doing a proper assessment of our specific capacities.

Meanwhile, with regard to the regional and district level international advisors, the Commission's hope, that their presence would help deter the fighting, was realised. It was also hoped they would help build the capacity of the local Nepalese election staff. But this outcome was more mixed—differing from individual to individual. While our staff in most districts reported that their UN counterparts were competent and supportive, in a few districts the advisors were more of a burden than an asset.

Partly, this problem arose due to the different working cultures of the national and international staff. While international staff stuck to their terms of reference (TOR), national staff often operated outside of their remit.

In retrospection, the Chief offered an insightful assessment of the overall role of the UN in the election process. He said:

Undoubtedly, the UN's monitoring of the rebel arms and armies were crucial for the elections. However, when the UN publicised the number of Maoist weapons, there was a stir around the country because the number of weapons was far less than the number of armed Maoist personnel. This became all the more alarming by reports of Maoist cadres leaving their makeshift cantonments.

So, even though the UN's monitoring of the Maoist weaponry and their army personnel helped create a positive atmosphere for the election, there were doubts about the efficacy of the monitoring, which was disturbing. This meant non-Maoist political parties and even voters, felt threatened—believing the election environment was neither free nor safe.

However, despite failing to meet our expectations sometimes, the UN's presence was indispensable for the success of the election, for many reasons. One such factor was the UN's role as the coordinator of the Joint Monitoring

Coordination Committee. The UNMIN helped to resolve many disputes between the Nepalese and Maoist armies, creating a suitable political environment for the election.

In terms of specific support for the election, the UN was tasked with both political and technical objectives. Its main political goals were: 1) to help make the Constituent Assembly election process and results credible, legitimate and acceptable; 2) to coordinate international support and resources for the elections. I can say that UNMIN succeeded 100 per cent in its political role.

Ian Martin personally inquired, almost daily, how the UN could be more supportive, and was flexible in making many adjustments according to our developing needs for the election. During times of political deadlock, Ian and I shared ideas formally and informally and agreed counter strategies to mitigate challenges. We had a good understanding and I was comfortable when asking him for frequent formal and informal assistance.

And he contributed significantly by helping to secure more funds for the election from donors. Whenever I was in doubt about which international visitor to invite to participate, or what role to give to an international partner, I was able to ask Ian for his advice. I also requested that he lobby the international community to pressurise our political parties to enact the laws necessary to stage the election on time and to create an enabling environment.

Although Ian was sometimes criticised for being too visible, his proactiveness was extremely helpful during the election process. For us at the Commission, the UN's informal role as well as visibility was clearly far more effective.

The Election Commission of Nepal, unlike most organisations in other post-conflict countries, had the capability to organise many elements of the election. Thus, the UN was most helpful in those areas where we had no prior experience, such as donor coordination, designing software for nominations and media monitoring.

There were some very committed people in the UN election unit, who were extremely helpful to us. They were very committed people in the UN election unit, who were extremely helpful to us. They often went beyond their formal role, in order to support us. For example, if we made a decision about an electoral issue, and needed to justify it with international examples, we could ask them for advice. They even worked at night to support us.

To sum up, at times it was convenient for us to criticise the UNMIN, and blame the UN for all the things that went wrong in the process. But, this criticism was unfair because the UN had not been mandated to assist in some areas where we failed. The UN's involvement, from the beginning of the peace process, was crucial in creating a politically conducive environment for credible elections.

Chapter 16

Interestingly, the UN's presence was actually the most important factor for pushing forward the elections in June 2007. The Chief realised this truth during a meeting with Indian diplomats, when the value of the UN was questioned. "What's the use of these expensive UN staff? They just take huge salaries in the name of *conflict*. Is there any *conflict* in Kathmandu where they work? We are capable of giving you any support you want. It's best to send white elephants back as soon as possible," a diplomat said to the Chief.

A few days earlier, the Indian Ambassador, Shiv Shankar Mukherjee had said Nepal could shorten the election process in order to conduct the June elections. This comment came because India was feeling increasingly uncomfortable about the UN presence in Nepal, and wanted to push hard for a June election, so the UN would leave the country without any delay. The Chief later explained:

> India is a powerful domestic factor in countries of South Asia, particularly in so-called India-locked Nepal. So, if India's interest was in holding an election in June then there was a great possibility that the election would happen at that time. Most importantly, major domestic forces also wanted the election to be held in June. I wanted to complete all technical preparations so the Commission would not be blamed for any delay.

A major barrier to these preparations was the absence of vital laws, necessary for the elections to be held. The Chief invited the Home Minister, Krishna Prasad Sitaula, to his office to discuss the bills which would have to be registered in the parliament—including the main Constituent Assembly election legislation. The Home Minister, the Commission's formal link to the government, was the fulcrum of state power.

By nature, Sitaula was calm, meditative and impassive. He lived a simple life; a vegetarian and spiritualist, he meditated many times a day. He was considered a skilful negotiator; he had been closely involved in Nepal's latest peace process—as chief negotiator for the Democratic Alliance. In the meeting with the Chief, Sitaula said, "Bhojraj *jee*, if elections don't happen in June we all will be ruined. These elections are really important for the survival of the peace process." The Chief told him that the elections could not legally move ahead without the main Constituent Assembly election legislation being in place, and requested that he act as soon as possible. Sitaula assured the Chief that the bill would be passed within a week.

Surprisingly, given this assurance, the election bill that the Commission sent to the Home Ministry was not even tabled in the parliament. Betrayed and disappointed, the Chief turned to the prime minister. At that time Koirala was not in good shape. His health was poor and he had lost his closest associate, Nona, who had died of a lingering health problem earlier that year. She had been his continuous supporter and closest advisor for decades, and the emptiness Koirala felt after her death was visible.

Amid this personal tragedy, Koirala was faced with a political complication for which he was not prepared—violent ethnic protests. Possibly due to his poor health and the fear of more political complications, Koirala was desperate to hold on to the June elections. When told that the election seemed unlikely, Koirala said, 'Don't say that. We have to manage the election some how this June, otherwise many unnecessary problems will arise.' The Chief repeated that the June election was looking increasingly unlikely and he informed the prime minister about the delay of the Election bill. Koirala asked who was delaying it and then promised to speak to the Home Minister.

But, again, nothing happened.

While political leaders, and even the Indian Ambassador, were asserting that the election must happen in June at all costs, others—middle level political leaders, civil society members and most of the international community (including UNMIN)—openly questioned the feasibility of holding elections in June. When the main election law had not been enacted by the beginning of March 2007—just three months before the planned elections—it became obvious, at last, that it would not be possible to hold the election in June.

The Chief made one last effort, inviting leaders from the thirteen parties in parliament to a meeting to discuss the election. It was hoped this would create sufficient pressure on the leaders either to agree to complete the preparations for the election in June or to postpone it without delay.

The meeting was held during the third week of March. One by one, all the powerful leaders of Nepal arrived at Bahadur Bhavan. When Democratic Alliance leader Girija Prasad Koirala—politically the most powerful—arrived, there was uproar in the building because the escalator was not working. It was difficult for him to climb the stairs but holding the hands of his assistants Koirala ascended, entered the meeting room, and sat down between Maoist Chairman Dahal and the Unified Marxist Leninist General Secretary Madhav Kumar Nepal. Facing them sat the Election Commissioners.

All the multimedia channels focused on Koirala as he spoke. He said:

> If the election is not held, I will of course be blamed, as the prime minister. But even more so, the general public will also blame the eight parties and the Commission... We have to conduct the election even if we have to shorten the election process—and the government is ready to provide anything that the Commission needs.

Dahal, as well, was concerned about the possibility of the elections getting postponed. He said:

> If the election doesn't happen in June, there will be complete chaos. The government, political parties and the Commission need to work on a *war footing* to make these elections possible.

Figure 9: Meeting with political leaders at ECN
Source: ECN, Photo by Suman Ghimire.

Figure 10: Meeting with cabinet ministers at ECN
Source: ECN, Photo by Suman Ghimire.

Figure 11: Meeting with the Speaker and the members of the State Affairs Committee of Legislature-Parliament at ECN
Source: ECN, Photo by Suman Ghimire.

Other leaders expressed similar views. The Chief said:

> Today you have to be honest with the people of Nepal about whether you are ready for the June election or not. Only one of the six laws necessary for the election has been passed. If all of you want an election on time, then you have to get all the laws passed within seven days. Otherwise the June election is not feasible.

Within a week of this meeting, the parliament passed a few election-related bills. The leaders also organised further meetings to finalise the main Constituent Assembly election bill, but on this point they made little progress. The Maoist joined the Interim Government in early April, but no progress was made on the necessary legislation. The main differences among the political parties related to their views on the implementation of the proportional system, the quotas for excluded groups and other technical matters related to the elections.

It now seemed clear the election could not take place in June. But still, no one was ready to admit it. By the beginning of April, as international observers—including former US President Carter—readied themselves to come to Nepal, the Chief decided the Commission should speak out. As a constitutional body they owed it to the people to tell the truth.

However, before taking any action, the Chief wanted to talk to Koirala one last time. He thought it would be better if the government, in consultation with the political parties, announced the postponement of the election rather than the Commission doing it by itself. By that time, the Maoists had also joined the government, so any decision the government made would likely be more acceptable to them.

The Chief told Koirala, "*Pradhanmantri jyu*, now it is not possible to hold the election. Even if you want it, the Commission will not be able to manage it in June. It would be better if the political leaders announced it publicly. If you don't, then we will. The situation has gotten out of control." Koirala replied, "Don't say that! The election has to happen at all costs." The Chief argued, "It's not possible… will you announce the postponement or shall I go ahead and do it?" Koirala relented, and said, "If you have already decided, then you should go ahead."

Koirala's easy capitulation made the Chief think he had expected the postponement. The other parties had wanted Koirala, or his government, to announce the postponement. But Koirala had been reluctant, now that the Commission had offered him a way out.

The Chief held a meeting with the other Commissioners to discuss the postponement, which had been agreed by Koirala. Some Commissioners believed it was Koirala, rather than the Chief, who had pushed for the postponement. There was also concern that the Election Commission would be blamed for the delay. One of the Commissioners pointed out, "The political parties may blame us for postponing the election, if we make the declaration. Some parties have aggressive and violent cadres; who will come to protect us if they attack?"

Another Commissioner was fearful that thousands of militant Maoist cadres would surround the Commission premises, throwing stones and waving sticks and *khukuris*, Nepalese knifes. He said, "Why should we take unnecessary risks? It's the government's duty, not ours, to announce the postponement."

Despite their reluctance, finally the Chief persuaded the Commissioners to agree to the announcement, and in the third week of April the Election Commission declared that due to the lack of a legal framework, the proposed June election could not be held. The Commission needed at least 110 days to make preparations for a future election, after the legal framework was finalised.

Reflecting on the postponement of the election, scheduled for June, the Chief said:

> Our credibility increased after we declared the postponement of the election. We were concerned that the Commission might be accused of cancelling the election due to pressure from regressive forces or the Royal Palace. Yet, finally we decided to take the risk.
>
> While analysing why the election could not be held at the scheduled time, I noticed an important shift in Koirala's earlier commitment to the elections. Something had certainly changed. I don't know if it was pressure from his own party workers on the ground, who said the Maoists would win if they went for elections then, or if Koirala's responsibilities as the party president prevailed over his responsibilities as the prime minister and guardian of peace. Or, it could have been pressure from somewhere else that compelled him to compromise on his *last dying wish*.
>
> One reason why the leaders, including Koirala, wanted to postpone the election could have been that they wanted a unification of the Nepali Congress before the election was held. Probably, Koirala feared if this did not happen then the Maoists would emerge as the largest party. This was thought likely because other parties had not been able to reach the *grass-roots* for years, owing to the Maoists' armed struggle.

There really seemed to be a convergence of interests between some of the powerful foreign forces and domestic actors, which wanted to see the rebels' strength weakened before the election was held. In an aid-dependent country like Nepal, different international powers exert great influence. That's why after the delay of the June election, I understood that there would have to be some changes before the Constituent Assembly elections could be held.

Later events would prove that the Chief was right in this assessment.

Chapter 17

There were varying reactions to the postponement of the June elections. The people of Nepal were sceptical, and wondered if the Constituent Assembly election would ever be held—mainly because of their past experience of the perpetual postponement of elections. There were reports that a joyous celebration had taken place in the Narayanhiti Palace. The last time the Constituent Assembly election was postponed, it was never rearranged.

The international community reacted variously. India was disappointed that Nepal's transition had stalled indefinitely, while others in the West, including UNMIN, were relieved that the election preparations would not be rushed.

The Maoists appeared the most agitated by the delay. Maoist cadres and combatants from the UN-monitored cantonments protested against the postponement—alleging that a conspiracy was brewing, which would completely derail the Constituent Assembly polls. Chairman Dahal said, "The delay in the election announced by the Commission heralded a great misfortune for the nation."

One effect of the delay was an increase in the activities of the royalists. King Gyanendra met with pro-monarchy political leaders, intellectuals, journalists and civil society members, and clandestine royal audiences were given to the emerging ethnic community leaders from the Madhesi and Janjati groups. Former and present army generals were also seen in the Palace precincts.

The Democratic Alliance leader Koirala was not happy about these increasing royal activities. Interestingly, despite what his family had suffered at the hands of the King, he was still in favour of saving the institution of monarchy. There were a number of reasons for this; the most important being his concern that if the monarchy was abruptly abolished this could lead to violent conflict, as had happened in other countries. After putting so much effort into the peace process, Koirala did not want to witness more bloodshed in Nepal. He envisaged a republican set-up, where the King would play a purely ceremonial role, providing a living link to the traditions and rituals of historic Nepal.

In public forums Koirala had repeatedly stated:

> Any decision about the monarchy—whether it should be retained or abolished—should be taken very carefully. A republic cannot be achieved through just a single decision—whether it's mine or of any other political party leader. A republic can be announced, one day, only after gradually removing the king's power.

After Koirala's concept of a *ceremonial king* was rejected by the people, his last hope was pinned on the *baby king*, Gyanendra's grandson Hridayendra. Koirala told King Gyanendra, "His Majesty is unpopular and the Crown Prince is even more unpopular. His Majesty should make way for the new prince Hridayendra." But the King did not accept this idea, and, much to Koirala's growing frustration, continued making public statements, visiting temples and attending festivals like he used to do before. Koirala was discouraged that the King could not see how his suggestion might have saved the institution of the monarchy. Koirala was often heard saying, "*Yo raja ta bilkulai paagal chan!* [This king is completely mad!]."

Another development after the election postponement was the increase in the proximity between the Maoist party and the Unified Marxist Leninist party—one of the members of the Seven Party Alliance. Leaders of both parties believed that the Constituent Assembly election had to be postponed because of international pressure, based on the fear of a leftist majority and that conspiracies were underway to derail the process. This shared belief led the parties to form a leftist alliance, with regard to the *republic issue*. This marked a clear split in the Seven Party Alliance's ideology, if not a break-up of the unity of the parties in the democratic bloc. With the formation of this new alliance, the energised Maoists spearheaded the launch of a pro-republican drive throughout the country. They seemed convinced that declaring a republic, ratified by parliament, was crucial to holding the Constituent Assembly election. One of their main activities was to pressurise district-level Nepali Congress party workers to encourage their own leadership to accept the idea of Nepal becoming a republic.

In May 2007, the Maoist party registered a *public interest* proposal in the Legislature-Parliament, with the immediate declaration of a republic as its first demand. They also picketed parliament and announced a plan to secure a one-million-signature petition, which called for the declaration of Nepal as a republic.

The octogenarian Koirala dealt with all these unexpected political complications in his usual astute, but *peculiar* way. When the Maoists or the Unified Marxist Leninist leaders came to pressurise him, they found him lying on his bed with an oxygen mask on his face. Looking at Koirala's frail physical condition, the leaders had no choice but to go away, having failed in their mission to secure his support. Koirala's omnipresent oxygen mask saved the peace process from falling apart many times.

Cynically, the Maoists deputy, Baburam Bhattarai, had remarked:

> Girija Prasad Koirala gives more time to foreign diplomats than to national leaders. His health improves when the US Ambassador James F. Moriarty wants to meet him but when he is needed to take decisions for the country he has to take oxygen instead.

As the issue of whether Nepal should become a republic came to occupy the centre-stage in national politics, it affected King Gyanendra the most. The government came under massive pressure to implement the decisions of the Parliamentary Proclamation that would remove the King's few remaining powers and privileges.

By the beginning of May 2007, the government had transferred all palace staff to the control of the Ministry of General Administration. Inside the Narayanhiti Palace, this administrative rearrangement created insecurity, confusion and disorder, which disrupted the systematic, luxurious and carefree life of all its inhabitants. The movement of the members of the Royal Family had become virtually impossible, as security was not available to protect them—especially since the Nepal Police were no longer cooperative.

In an interview, King Gyanendra's aide-de-camp reminisced:

> We used to have several rings for the King's security, the outermost part of which was traditionally handled by the Nepal Police. However, during those days, the Government would not communicate anything formally, and it wouldn't provide police outer protection for the movement of the royals. The army, on its own, somehow managed to provide security for the King. It was a most stressful situation.

This was the first time that the palace of the formerly *sacrosanct* Hindu kingdom had come under so much public criticism. Palace officials did not know how to deal with the open hostility that erupted everywhere, and stories about violations within the Palace became regular news items.

Despite all these difficulties, King Gyanendra tried to continue business as usual. Regarding the King's attitude, an aide-de-camp said:

> We were surprised to see how King Gyanendra acted so unperturbedly, even though he had lost so much, and was perhaps about to lose even more. Probably it was his love for the country which gave him strength. The King used to advise us, "Do things for the country, not for me." If he had given us the order, maybe we would have fought for the King.

The same official said that the King's face would turn pale if he read damaging news or lies about the palace, but he would not speak to anyone about it. Perhaps this is what royal character is about—stoicism, the stiff upper lip.

Apart from worrying about his own personal future, and that of his revered historical dynasty, King Gyanendra was concerned about the sort of misfortune that might befall his immediate family, especially his Queen and his young grandchildren. He was also worried about his mother, who was deeply distressed by recent events. She had lived during the height of her husband's power and the prominence of the Nepalese monarchy. It was particularly difficult for her to accept the changes. The former Queen had withdrawn herself, and she spoke to her family less and less.

As King Gyanendra's powers, privileges and rights were removed one by one, he himself became quieter and quieter. Many were worried by his changed manner, which was very uncharacteristic of him. They wondered whether his silence was the proverbial calm before some terrible storm.

Soon it became clear that the threat to the Constituent Assembly election would come not from the suspended King but the political parties. They blamed one another for the postponement but did nothing to move the process forward. Disagreement about whether Nepal should be declared a republic further pushed consideration of the Constituent Assembly elections into the background. A stalemate prevailed in the Himalayan capital, with no immediate resolution in sight.

The situation became even worse when Prime Minister Koirala publicly criticised the youth wing of the Maoist party, the Young Communist League

(YCL), describing it as the *young criminal league*. The YCL, established during the Maoist People's War, was revived in December 2006. Many of its members were said to be People's Liberation Army personnel who did not want to be confined to the UN-supervised cantonments. They were accused of behaving like para-militaries, using coercive tactics, physically attacking, abducting and even killing, other political party workers in order to establish Maoist dominance. The prime minister's criticism of the YCL angered Maoist leaders, who warned that the fragile eight-party coalition could collapse. And Dahal, himself, said his comments were a sign of Koirala's *criminal mentality*.

The Chief later recalled the challenges which resulted from these developments. He said:

> The political trust among the parties dipped after the postponement of the elections. As a result, no development on the actual conduct of the election was made. Assuming it was my responsibility I asked the civil society members, the international community, ambassadors, and foreign dignitaries to pressurise political parties to be serious about holding the proposed election.
>
> At that time, when political parties were guided by their own partisan interests, support from international friends was invaluable. They played a positive role in reminding the parties of their broader commitment to the peace process and also in bringing them back onto the election track. The good offices of the UN Secretary General were also used to pressurise the political parties to conduct timely elections.

With pressure from all sides the Democratic Alliance and the Maoists finally decided to put aside their differences and work together. This only became possible after the democratic bloc, in particular the Nepali Congress, consented to empower the parliament (by a two-thirds majority) to announce the abolition of the monarchy, if the king was found to be conspiring against the Constituent Assembly election. With this new understanding, the political parties agreed to hold the Constituent Assembly election by the end of November 2007.

November was selected keeping weather conditions and other constraints—agrarian, cultural and socio-economic in mind. Elections can only be held in certain specific months in Nepal. They cannot be held between July–August due to the monsoon season, and not in September or October, as major festivals fall in these months. Additionally, elections cannot be held between December–February, because of the usual heavy snowfall in the Himalayan mountains, and thick, impenetrable fog on the hills and plains. During this time movement comes to a standstill. Hence, the Nepalese political parties had only one option—November—as the next window for the election.

The political parties began working on a date for the election. In the past the Election Commission used to set a date after consulting a leading astrologer for an auspicious day. This superstitious tradition was adopted by the political parties en bloc, and supported, somewhat surprisingly, by the communists—who were supposed to be rationalists. On the recommendation of an eminent astrologer, consulted by a senior Nepali Congress leader, Koirala declared 26 November 2007 as the new date for the Constituent Assembly election.

But within a few weeks, the political parties revoked this decision and the Cabinet proposed yet another new date for the election, 22 November. This was because, supposedly, a more powerful astrologer from India had overruled the Nepalese astrologer and suggested 22 November as a more auspicious date.

Chapter 18

An issue that continued to threaten the election, and which was a constant headache for the Commission—was the electoral system.

The main Constituent Assembly Member Election Act, passed in June 2007, had established a mixed electoral system with a Constituent Assembly of 497 members—240 of whom would be elected through the First-Past-The-Post (FPTP) system and 240 through the Proportional Representation system. Additionally, seventeen members would be appointed by the Council of Ministers. Voters would get two ballots, voting separately in the FPTP and the PR races, and each element of the election would be counted separately. Decision on this process was reached by the parties after a series of negotiations.

It had to be agreed that the nature of the electoral system was critical, not least because it had been the focus of the Maoists' armed struggle. Since the restoration of multiparty parliamentary democracy, in early 1990, Nepal had adopted a majoritarian system, known as the First-Past-The-Post for its three parliamentary elections in 1991, 1994 and 1999 as well as for its two local elections in 1992 and 1997. In this system—practiced, for example, in the UK and India—candidates with the highest number of votes in a constituency are elected. Unfortunately, this system failed to meet the aspirations of Nepal's diverse society, which consisted of over 100 ethnic groups, speaking multiple languages.

The parliaments elected before failed to be socially inclusive. Around 60 per cent presence was of dominant hill groups, mainly Brahmins and Chhetris, who comprised only 30 per cent or so of Nepal's overall population. In all these parliaments, the Dalit community, for example, secured less than 1 per cent representation even though they comprised around 13 per cent of the population. Most importantly, women, who comprised over 50 per cent of the population, had less than 6 per cent of the seats in those parliaments. Hence, representation of these under-represented groups remained a major challenge.

Not surprisingly, these under-represented groups formed a major support base for the Maoist armed struggle. In this context, it was important to choose an electoral system that removed one of the reasons for the violent conflict. Therefore, the nature of the electoral system became one of the most difficult challenges to the staging of Nepal's post-conflict elections.

When the Chief Election Commissioner was appointed in October 2006, he saw the opportunity to influence the political parties in their choice of an electoral system. His main interest was to make the system as representative as possible, so that election results would be accepted by all the major political groups in the country, and controversy would be minimal.

The Chief recalled:

> Even before I formally joined the Commission, Neil, Usha and I used to meet secretly to discuss which electoral system the political parties could adopt.
>
> Both Usha and I were new to the electoral field and so we relied on Neil, who had sufficient experience of the difficult Afghanistan elections, to guide us. After days of clandestine meetings, the three of us felt, with growing assurance, that a fully proportional representation electoral system would be the best one for the upcoming Constituent Assembly election in Nepal.
>
> The proportional system, in which the overall number of votes for a party was translated into a corresponding proportion of seats in the parliament, had the following benefits. Firstly, it would ensure the proportional representation of all the groups, which was necessary for a constitution-making election. Secondly, it would encourage competition between the political parties, not merely between individual candidates, and the chances of organised violence was minimised. Thirdly, it would be easier for the Commission to manage the election, specifically to make it possible to extend voting rights to, for example, the internally displaced, temporary migrants, the landless and the homeless. Lastly, the system would be less costly.

Because of the advantages outlined above, the Election Commissioners decided to lobby for a full proportional system. Among the major parties, the Maoists and the Unified Marxist Leninist party were already in favour of a full proportional system. It was only the Nepali Congress that needed to be convinced. They resisted giving up the FPTP system, claiming that the proportional system deprived individuals of liberty to stand in an election and increased the gap between the representatives and the voters. The reluctance of the Congress was understandable, given that it had achieved its majority through the FPTP system, in three out of four previous parliamentary elections. Nepali Congress President, Koirala, would not budge. He told the Election Chief, "Bhojraj *jee*, I will not negotiate about the FPTP, vis-à-vis the proportional system, so please don't try to convince me."

It is telling how the personality of one person can affect the history of a nation. The Chief suspected someone close to Koirala had convinced him not to give up the FPTP system. Some Congress leaders believed their positions to be secure, because of the FPTP race, and were therefore vehemently against a fully proportional system.

It was Koirala's reluctance that led to the adoption of a mixed electoral system in Nepal, as a compromise between FPTP and a fully proportional system. This was decided at midnight of 7 November 2006, as part of the six-point peace agreement between the Democratic Alliance and the Maoists. According to this agreement, 205 members would be elected through FPTP, while 204 members would be elected through a proportional system. In addition, 16 members would be appointed by the Council of Ministers from among *distinguished persons* of the nation. The political parties decided to have one seat less in the proportional system, as in Nepalese culture an even number is considered inauspicious. Old beliefs die hard.

A few months later, the Madhesi uprising resulted in a change to the total number of seats. Both the FPTP and proportional system seats were increased to 240, and the number of appointed seats was increased by one to 17—again out of respect for the tradition of preferring an odd number.

Once the political parties had decided to adopt a mixed system, the next question was the type of a mixed system that would be acceptable. The parties had a choice: either a Mixed Member Proportional Representation (MMPR) system, which was close to a fully proportional system in terms of representation of political parties (used, for example, in Germany, Albania and New Zealand), or a Parallel system, which was a semi-proportional system, like those in Japan, Palestine and Armenia. The issue of whether the two races should be covered by a single ballot counted twice, or by two ballots, allowing for a split vote, was also considered.

In early 2007, the parties agreed to adopt a parallel system with two ballots. But still many questions remained unanswered. One of them was ways to ensure appropriate representation of various ethnic and minority groups in the

Constituent Assembly, as required by the six-point peace agreement. The only guideline to achieving this was the provision of Interim Constitution which specified that the proportional representation of oppressed groups, such as the Madhesis, indigenous groups, women and the dalits would be ensured. But the political parties had not considered how to implement this agreement. Thus, that responsibility was of the Election Commission's.

It was at this point that the Norwegian Kåre Vollan entered the picture. This trained mathematician was one of the top election system experts in the world. At the Commission's request he travelled to Nepal to provide support. The Commission decided to use him mainly to sort out how the proportional system should be implemented, in a way that would ensure fair representation of under-represented groups.

On the night of 25 February 2007, in a dimly lit room of the Summit Hotel in Kathmandu, Vollan began the work that would eventually change the face of the Nepalese state. His reference material included Harka Gurung's *Nepal Atlas of Ethnic and Caste Groups*, the United Nations Development Programme (UNDP)'s *Nepal Statistics and the Indigenous People and Human Development Report 2004*. Vollan was aware of the sensitivity and urgency of his task, and he had enough experience of post-conflict elections to know that any wrong move could push the country into decades of violent ethnic conflict.

That night, while the whole of Nepal slept, Vollan went through his reference materials. His sleepy eyes suddenly widened as he realised the enormity of his task. One of these challenges was to put 102 socio-ethnic groups of Nepal into five categories—Madhesi, Dalits, Oppressed castes/Indigenous groups, Backward regions and the Others specified in the peace agreement. Another serious problem he faced was the vagueness of the Interim Constitution's provision on the proportional system. It was not clear if quotas were meant for the whole of these groups or excluded groups within these larger groups. For example, it was unclear if the quotas to be applied to the Oppressed castes/ Indigenous group also meant for the elites within that group, like the Newars. Or if the quotas only meant to be applied to previously excluded groups within the Oppressed castes/Indigenous group, like the Kusunda, the Danuwar and the Kumal.

Similarly, the Others category was also confusing. It was not clear whether this should only include other excluded groups like the Muslims, or if it should include all others, except for the Madhesis, Dalits, Oppressed castes/Indigenous groups and Backward regions, specified by the political agreement. Yet another problem was related to the complicated definition of Madhesis. While some identified every one living in the southern Tarai region as Madhesis, others used linguistic and ethnic characteristics for the parameter of their definition.

Finally, Vollan submitted a nine-page document to the Commission. He made the following suggestions:

- Women should be given a 50 per cent quota (as they comprised 11,377,556 of Nepal's total population of 22,736,934, based on the 2001 Census).
- Dalits should be given between a 11.8 per cent and 14 per cent quota (based on the 2001 Census and claims made by Dalit groups).
- Deprived groups/indigenous people should be given a 31 per cent quota excluding 5.5 per cent of elites in the indigenous group like the Newars and the Thakalis.
- Backward regions should be given between a 4 per cent and 8.93 per cent quota (based on the Human Development Index and the Human Poverty Index). Nine districts—Accham, Bajura, Bajhang, Dolpa, Jagarkot, Jumla, Kalikot, Mugu, Humla—with an HDI below 0.375 were also the districts with the highest Human Poverty Index.
- Madhesis should be given a 17.2 per cent quota (Madhesis comprised around 31.3 per cent of the total population, if defined as a group. Excluding the upper castes, they formed 17.24 per cent of the total population).
- Others to be kept open (the others group should consist of groups needing specific protection, other than those groups explicitly mentioned, for example the Muslims, who represented 4 per cent of the entire Nepalese population).

The document that Vollan handed to the Chief formed the first important step towards the *Inclusive Nepal* that had so long been desired. The Election Commission used his draft to begin a series of discussions with political actors, both inside and outside the parliament. This exercise would soon change the fate of millions of marginalised Nepalese, who would see their own people in the parliament for the first time.

The negotiations on the electoral system, led by the Chief, enabled a task-force in the Parliamentary State Affairs committee to make a decision on the quotas and subsequently, to pass the necessary legislation, drafted by the Election Commission.

Minendra Rijal, one of the most talented mathematicians in the Nepalese parliament, was given the task of making this technical exercise on the quotas politically acceptable to the 330 parliamentarians. The following changes were made to the draft to ensure that:

- The Others category was overhauled, so it included *all other* groups, not only previously excluded groups, like the Muslims. Rijal maintained this had been the intention of the political parties since the six-point agreement.
- The candidates' list in the proportional system was not ranked anymore. Political parties could select whichever candidates they liked from a list after election to fill the seats won.
- The Madhesi quota was defined in broader terms, so it could include groups such as the Tharus, the Muslims and the Jains, who did not readily identify themselves as Madhesi.

The quota for the proportional part of the Constituent Assembly election, ratified by the parliament, is given in Table 1.

Table 1: Quotas for the Constituent Assembly

Group to be represented		*Percentage of candidates*
Women		50
Madhesi	Women	15.6
	Men	15.6
Dalit	Women	6.5
	Men	6.5
Janjatis	Women	18.9
	Men	18.9
Backward region (Achaham, Kalikot, Jajarkot, Jumla, Dolpa, Bajahang,Bajura, Mugu and Humla districts)	Women	2
	Men	2
Others (groups not clearly mentioned in this schedule)	Women	15.1
	Men	15.1

Source: The Election Commission of Nepal (2008, 57–58)

The international community was highly critical of these changes, particularly of the candidates' lists in the proportional race. It feared the quotas would be misused by unscrupulous party leaders. It is not hard to understand why there was such a strong reaction. According to international practice, there are mainly two types of candidate lists in a proportional electoral system—an open candidate list and a closed candidate list. In an open candidate list system voters have a say about which candidates should fill the seats, as in countries like Finland, Denmark, Sweden, the Netherlands and Peru. In a closed candidate list system the ranking of the candidate's list is pre-defined and does not change. This system is used in countries like Spain, Macedonia and Brazil. The Nepalese leaders had proposed a candidate list without ranking, in which voters had no say. As such it did not fall into either of the two previously recognised categories.

The Chief shared his memories of this time:

> When news leaked out about the parliamentary committee's decision about a non-ranked candidates' list system, international experts suggested that it would be a mistake to adopt such a policy. I immediately communicated the grave concerns, expressed by the international community, to political leaders. They, however, remained adamant that they wouldn't give in.
>
> So, we came up with a new bargain. We put a condition to the leaders, that if political parties wanted a closed candidate list without ranking they would have to comply with quotas for the selection of candidates. The selection of candidates as per quotas was then not mandatory, as the Interim Constitution had required quotas only to be used in the nominations and not the results.
>
> Political leaders chose to comply with quotas in the selection process, rather than ranking the candidate list. This could be because, as the leaders calculated, ranking could create sharp differences within the political parties before the polls.
>
> Many international election experts remained dissatisfied with the ranking provision, because it was not in accordance with international practice. President Carter also touched briefly upon this tangled issue during our first meeting. I told him that it is not necessary that we should follow all the rules of international practice, established by other countries in vastly different contexts. Nepal could invent its own system, suited to its needs, which other countries could follow if it turns out to be beneficial for them.
>
> In the beginning many parliamentarians didn't understand how the quotas would ensure representation of the previously under-represented groups. I went to the State Affairs Committee in the Parliament a number of times to explain how the proportional electoral system and its quota provision worked to enable them to reach an agreement. The Election Commission played a crucial role in this process. If we had not encouraged the political leaders to make the quotas mandatory in the selection process the Constituent Assembly might not have been as representative. Our quota system was unique and our electoral system became one of the most complicated in the world, because of all these processes.
>
> Despite these deliberations, the question of the electoral system remained unresolved. And it would become one of the reasons cited for the cancellation of the election in November.

Chapter 19

As the monsoon passed that eventful year, the political situation in Nepal worsened day by day, due to the fresh outbreak of violent agitation by the traditionally under-represented ethnic groups.

In addition to the Madhesi agitation, the Janjati groups (or indigenous nationalities) started their own agitation in the mountains. Janjati can be understood as indigenous groups/nationalities that originally came from the north and migrated into different parts of Nepal. They speak a variety of Tibeto-Burmese languages, and originally practiced various religions. The government categorised 59 groups as Janjati, ranging from privileged groups—such as Newars and Gurungs—to disadvantaged groups, like the Chepang or the Raute. Irrespective of their economic and social status, most Janjati groups were angry because they were forced to abandon their own traditions and to adopt the language, costume, customs and life-style of the ruling elite—Bahun-Chhetri group. When Janjati groups saw that their issues of identity and representation were not sufficiently addressed—despite the 2006 change—they took advantage of the political fluidity and started agitating.

The main demands of this group were for a full proportional electoral system and restructuring of the country, based on ethnicity, geography and language. They wanted their voices to be heard, and carried out violent strikes, agitation and blockades, which sometimes lasted weeks, to draw attention to their agenda.

Similarly, the Dalits and other under-represented groups also came out onto the streets demanding their fair representation. These activities worsened the already fragile security situation.

The Chief was concerned about this development and met with Prime Minister Koirala to discuss a solution. Koirala said, "I will remove Sitaula from the Home Ministry, as he is not able to handle the security situation well...

Ram Chandra Poudyal has not been able to focus enough on his work in the Peace Ministry. Maybe I will make them swap their portfolios." Koirala, who had recently been described by President Carter as *my hero*, told the Chief:

> What can I say, Bhojraj *jee*, these days even with 2,500 Nepali rupees (approx. US$30) you can get a gun. That's why if someone does not accept something they resort to using guns. So many armed groups have sprung up in the Tarai region that it is difficult for the government even to initiate a dialogue.
>
> I have already talked to the Indian Foreign Minister. He has said he will cooperate in resolving the violence in the Tarai…I have already given the responsibility of handling Janjati matters to Subash (the Speaker of Parliament who was also a Janjati). He will manage it.

It was clear that it would take time to build the trust of these agitated groups, to engage them in talks, and then to negotiate a compromise. But time was what Koirala really did not have. At 82, he was getting more and more restless for the election. He was convinced that if he died without bringing the Maoists into the newly fabricated democratic process the peaceful transformation of the Nepalese society would not be possible. He saw his role as being to bring all the forces in Nepal together for this transformation. As he felt he neared the end of his life, the Constituent Assembly election became his priority, and he was upset by anything that threatened to delay the process, for example, ethnic uprising.

But, it was not just the effect ethnic uprising had on the electoral process that worried Koirala—he detested ethnic and identity politics. His brother, Bishweshwar Prasad Koirala, had said that if a foreign power wanted to weaken the state all it had to do was mobilise ethnic groups within Nepal. Therefore, the Nepali Congress should never, Bishweshwar had believed, mobilise people along ethnic lines—even though such a strategy might yield a quick result—because this would weaken the state from within. Koirala now heeded his brother's advice and tried not to stoke ethnic sentiments (or even publicly acknowledge their existence) for fear of stirring geopolitical foul play.

With the fierce Madhesi and Janjati uprisings that year, Koirala's worst fears had come true. Even foreign forces seemed to be *fanning the fires*. Intelligence reports came to Koirala, informing him that embassies in Kathmandu—including that of a Scandinavian country—were funding the unrest. The ambassadors seemed angry that Koirala had failed to address the demands of the excluded ethnic groups. But Koirala had no time, nor the interest, to try to resolve these issues; his focus was solely on how the unrest was creating an impact on the forthcoming election.

Figure 12: Signing of the Five-Point agreement between Federal Republican National Front and the Government of Nepal
Source: UN, Photo by Sagar Shrestha.

The Chief was worried that Koirala's *quick-fix* approach to the ethnic problems could be counterproductive. Unless the government properly addressed the grievances of the ethnic groups their agitation could recur. He urged the prime minister to engage the ethnic groups in negotiations, in an attempt to quell the burgeoning civil disorder.

Soon after this meeting between the Chief and the prime minister, some progress was made. In August 2007, in order to address demands of the agitating groups, the government signed a 22-Point Agreement with the Madhesi Front and a 20-Point Agreement with the Nepal Federation of Indigenous Nationalities (NEFIN)—an *alliance* of ethnic groups. These agreements brought some relief, so far as the Commission was concerned, as much of the agitation stopped. However, sections within both the Madhesi and the Janjati groups continued to oppose the Agreement, because they wanted a fully proportional electoral system that would ensure representation of each group according to its population. The government opposed this.

In September, the situation in Tarai again intensified. In Kapilvastu district the death of a local Muslim sparked violent clashes, which took a communal turn. The Kapilvastu incident led to the death of around 14 people, and displaced thousands, with significant loss of property. This development again increased uncertainty about the election.

Later events would prove that it was not the ethnic groups that should have worried the Chief. The real threat to the election in November would instead come, surprisingly, from the main political parties.

As the ethnic violence calmed down, the bitterness between the political leaders increased sharply. The Maoists were the most agitated ones, due to a number of new developments, listed below:

- Since the first Madhesi uprising, Maoist cadres had been killed in large numbers during clashes with Madhesi groups in the Tarai region. In March 2007, 27 Maoist cadres were murdered in a place called Gaur, during a clash with a Madhesi group, the most gruesome massacre since the peace process started. This incident was soon followed by a series of killings of Maoist cadres during clashes with Madhesi groups all over the Tarai. Commentators claimed these deaths were the result of an orchestrated campaign of violence, aimed to weaken the Maoist base in the Tarai area, bordering India.
- The government continued to ignore the poor physical conditions of the Maoist combatants in the UN-monitored cantonments, despite the concern of Maoist leaders. Dahal had demanded that the government should take responsibility for the management of the cantonments, in accordance with the peace accord. Yet no concrete steps had yet been taken to do this.
- The government was reluctant to release funds to pay the Maoist combatants, despite earlier promise of giving NPR 3,000 (approx. US$38) per month to each combatant. No clear explanation was given for this delay.

The Maoists felt that the government had demonstrated a *lackadaisical* attitude towards settling these problems, so they released a list of 22 demands that had to be met before they would agree to participate in the November election. The most important of these demands were:

a. the immediate declaration of Nepal as a republic
b. the adoption of a fully proportional electoral system

Maoist Chairman Dahal also proposed, yet again, that the election should be postponed to the Nepali month of *Baisakh 2065* (mid-April 2008). He criticised other parties for postponing the June election, and said that his party had committed a mistake in signing the peace agreements with the Seven-Party Alliance. This comment seems to have been a response to the marginalisation the Maoist party was feeling during that period.

Koirala was disappointed with the Maoists' behaviour. He believed they had strategically designed their new demands so that Koirala could be held personally responsible for any postponement, yet again, of the election. The

Maoists knew their demands could not be agreed to. Even if there was the will it would not be possible to implement them before November. So, in any event, the election would have to be postponed, and the prime minister would be blamed for the delay. This situation led to a *cooling* of the relationship between the Democratic Alliance head Koirala and the Maoist Chairman Dahal, the two main actors in the peace process.

The Chief was worried that this emerging bitterness between the political parties, which until recently had been fairly united, would derail the election process. In particular, he was worried about what the Maoists would do. He conducted a series of meetings with ministers, political leaders and the international community about how the growing differences between the political parties could be reduced. One of those meetings was with Finance Minister Ram Saran Mahat, who was in charge of the release of funds to the Maoist combatants.

But when the Chief requested him to release these promised funds Mahat said:

> How can I release funds? The agreement was that we would provide money to the Maoist combatants and they would return the property they had seized during the conflict period. They have not returned the property of even a single person. How can I just release funds?

Having failed to convince the finance minister, the Chief then discussed this issue with the prime minister. The Chief thought the government should address the Maoists' demands as soon as possible, in order to win their support for the election. He explained this to the prime minister, saying:

> If you don't give them money, the combatants will get more agitated with your government. By giving them money, you can inculcate positive feelings towards your government and bring them closer to you. It's worth the investment. The first priority should be to encourage the former rebels to accept this democratic process. Once it's done, then you can deal with other issues.

The prime minister replied, "I agree with you. But the finance minister does not listen to me. Why don't you tell him that?"

The Chief later reflected:

> Times like that made me realise how weak the prime minister of Nepal could be. Even a strong and determined personality like Girija*babu* was no exception. This not only applied to the finance minister's power but he had also failed to remove

> the home minister, despite his strong desire to do. That was clearly because the prime minister was subject to different pressures, probably international.

Undeterred by this experience, the Chief continued to play the role of facilitator and he arranged to meet with the Maoists leaders, Dahal and Bhattarai in a hotel in central Kathmandu. He updated them on the Commission's preparations for the election. He said:

> I understand your difficulties, created by the government's failure to take any steps about the disappearance of your cadres, and also the government's reluctance to release money to your combatants.
>
> How can I support you as Chief Commissioner?…I think it would be best if the Democratic Alliance and the Maoists contest this election as a single front, because it is about the tussle between the forces that want change and the forces that do not want change. At least it should be possible to reach an understanding on common minimum points.

Dahal agreed, saying:

> You have analysed the situation well, as a politically astute citizen. I think that the Democratic Alliance and the Maoists should act together, too. But to what extent can we motivate the Seven Party Alliance? They have not understood the spirit of change. They just want to do things in the old way, like in the 1990s.
>
> There has been a deliberate attempt to spread the wrong message about us through the media, NGOs and international organisations. Here, things get done only after pressure from international forces. I do understand that we have to listen to them as they have supported the peace process but still...
>
> We won't run away from the peace process or go back to the jungle. We are ready to engage with the democratic process. Yet we are always doubted. Please take this message away; other political parties are acting only after international pressure.

The Maoist Chairman then asked the Chief what his view was of the position of the army and the Palace. The Chief said, "The Palace is totally silent and I don't think that the army will do anything in the name of the Palace, but if the eight parties are not united then anything could happen."

At the end of the meeting the Maoist leaders expressed their full support for the election in November, convincing the Chief that the Maoist bloc was genuinely committed to the election process.

Chapter 20

Amid the prevailing uncertainty about the elections, the Chief received an urgent telephone call requesting him to visit the prime minister. However, when he arrived he found Koirala in a relaxed mood. He said, "We have to conduct the election in November at any cost." The Chief told him, "The technical preparations from the Commission's side are progressing quite well. But probably, the Maoists need some positive incentives to contest the election."

Koirala replied:

> I have proposed that we should draw up an understanding to elect all the key Maoist leaders. Madhav Nepal (General Secretary of the UML) has agreed, so there should be no problem from the Maoists.
>
> The Maoists have assured me that they will deal with the YCL (Young Communist League) issue while we will deal with the Tarai issue. I have already talked with India's Foreign Minister regarding the agitation in the Tarai, and he has assured me that the Madhesi agitation won't pose any obstacle to the election.

The Chief said, "Many people believe that the June election was cancelled because of the delay in the unification of the Nepali Congress. When will the unification happen?"

The prime minister, who was also the President of the Nepali Congress, said:

> Sushil [Koirala] has some reservations about it. Essentially, there are some disagreements about the hierarchy of leaders...don't worry, it will be settled soon. I have told Sushil and Sher Bahadur, that one of them can become the prime minister and the other can become the president of the party.

It was clear that Koirala was confident that the Nepali Congress would win a landslide majority and that he felt sure his party would be able to appoint the next prime minister.

The Chief then raised the issue of the Congress party workers not yet being *in the field*. He questioned how an election atmosphere could be created without the political parties being on the ground. Koirala said he had instructed them to go out to meet the people but that they were afraid of the Maoists, who were still engaged in violent activities. But the Chief said the reluctance of the party workers was more due to the ambiguity of the Congress party's policy on the monarchy. The Chief said:

> When voters ask about the position of the Congress on the monarchy, what will your party workers tell them, Girija*babu*? You should immediately publicise your party's standpoint on the monarchy.

But Koirala disagreed. He said, "Our position on the monarchy is my strongest card for the election. I will speak when the time is right."

The Chief did not know what the Congress party's policy on the monarchy was at that time, but he was relieved that the parties had reached an understanding that was likely to create a better political atmosphere for the elections. After the meeting the Chief intensified his technical preparations. On the preparations for the November election, the Chief later recalled:

> The Commission's preparation for the November election was nearly done. We had appointed Returning Officers in all the constituencies, to take charge of polling in districts. We had also identified all the polling station staff we needed, including polling officers, assistant polling officers and booth officers. A range of cascade training programmes, such as those on voter education, had been completed as well.

While the Commission was immersed in election preparations, there were some positive political developments.

The Nepali Congress and Nepali Congress-Democratic parties announced their unification. The Nepali Congress party also announced its support for a republic, finally resolving the confusion of voters on this matter. The Congress party hoped to get the largest number of votes possible, capitalising on a likely split in the leftist votes between the Unified Marxist Leninist and the Maoist parties. The UML also launched its election campaign programme, confident that it could take advantage of its competitors' lack of preparation.

However, unexpectedly, on 18 September 2007 the Maoists pulled out of the government—disrupting the election process—and threatened to boycott the election if their 22-point demands were not met.

In order to make one last effort at securing a successful election, the Chief—and four other commissioners—went to Baluwatar again. Their agenda was to convince the prime minister to accept a fully proportional system: the sole remaining hope for the November elections to take place.

When the Chief and his team arrived they found the home minister, the chief secretary, and the prime minister's personal advisor with Koirala. The Chief knew what he was about to say would annoy the PM, but he felt he had little choice. *History* had placed him in a desperate position. The Chief said:

> Although it is not my role, I have come here with a request. All the forces in the country—the UML, Maoists, Madhesis, Janjatis, Dalits and the women—want a full proportional system. Why does the Congress alone want to oppose it? After all, the Nepali Congress has to secure votes from these groups too. Now that the Maoists are demanding a full proportional system, elections might be cancelled again if the Congress is stubborn about its position.
>
> The more the elections are delayed, the more complications will be created. You have brought the peace process to this point so you have to save it. If the full proportional system is not acceptable to you then you can change your position, and accept MMPR (Mixed Member Proportional system). The other parties might agree to this.
>
> The system that suited you in the past will not necessarily suit you always. Take Palestine as an example. Fatah wanted to use an electoral system they were operating before, and in the end using it benefitted Hamas.

The other commissioners pointed out that if the prime minister agreed to adopt the proportional system the pressure would be on the Maoists to contest the election. But Koirala said little, only thanking them for their advice before walking away.

A few days before the deadline for filing the nominations, the Maoists organised a mass rally and declared they would not participate in the election until their demands were taken care of. In a flurry of activity political negotiations resumed and numerous *marathon* meetings were held in Baluwatar. All these talks proved inconclusive.

The day before the nomination date deadline, the Election Commissioners were glued to the TV news, hoping that the political parties would reach an agreement at the last minute. But by late evening there had been no breakthrough. Then, just as the Chief was going to bed, he received a call from the prime minister's residence. Koirala told him:

> We are trying to build the right atmosphere for the election but today our talks were not conclusive. We might need a few more days to narrow down our differences and come to an agreement. So please extend the nomination date by seven days.

The Chief refused, saying:

> Prime Minister *jyu*, this is not possible and I won't do it. We knew that this was coming many weeks ago. Why were things dragged out until the last minute? Why didn't you do anything to solve the political problems before now?
>
> What guarantee can you give me that if I postpone the date of nominations, the election will happen? The government and political parties have lost their credibility; do you want us to lose ours? No. I can't extend the nomination date, not even for a day. You can look for another team. I am ready to give way to them.

Then the Unified Marxist Leninist leader, Madhav Kumar Nepal came on the line. He said to the Chief, "Bhojraj *jee*, all of us are here in Baluwatar to reach an understanding. Prachanda *jee* has asked for a seven-day extension. Please accept our request."

Again, the Chief refused, saying:

> We can't postpone the nomination date for technical reasons. Further, we can't lose a single day for ballot printing. If we are unable to print the necessary ballot papers for the election then the people will *hang us*. We (the Commission) can't hide from the public, like the political parties can. So I can't risk extending the declared nomination date. I would rather quit than extend the nomination date.

In the background the Chief could hear laughing. Then the Maoist Chairman came on the line. He said:

> We can't pressurise an independent institution like the Election Commission, but we can make a request. We know that the Commission has done a really good job. But the election is part of the peace process. So please support us by extending the nomination date.
>
> If you continue your nomination programme tomorrow, you have the authority to do it, but please remember that the Maoists won't participate in it.

The Chief replied:

> I am not the Commission so I cannot make this decision alone. All I can say for now is that if you truly want an extension, then the government needs to send a formal request to us by eight o'clock tomorrow morning.

The Chief felt he had been squeezed into a tight spot. If the Commission refused to extend the nomination date, the major political parties would not participate and the Commission would be blamed for the failure of the process. If the Commission agreed to their last minute request, it could lose its credibility—as the election was most likely to be postponed any way. It was probable that other political forces would blame the ECN for acting like a toy in the hands of a few political parties.

The next day, the Chief held an emergency meeting with the other commissioners. They concluded that they did not have a choice, other than to extend the nomination date as per the government's request. However, they reduced the extension to five days, instead of the requested seven. Recalling his difficulty at that time, the Chief said:

> Those five days of the extension period were torturous for us. I really felt overwhelmed. How could I face the people if the elections were cancelled after the extension? I decided I would resign, if that happened.
>
> I received all sorts of calls from international partners who were concerned about their election programmes. They were accountable to their tax payers so they needed to know if the election would happen before they started any programme. I could neither say yes nor no.
>
> In the middle of all this drama, the UML leader Madhav Nepal, called to say that the election must be held, even if the Maoists were not *on board*. Nepal questioned me, "How long can we wait?" I straightaway dismissed that idea and explained to him that the election would be meaningless without the Maoists.

In five more days, the Chief's worst fears were realised—the talks were inconclusive. The relationship between the leaders turned so sour that they had taken to verbally abusing each other. Finally, the government announced the postponement of the November election and asked the Commission to cancel all its preparations. The Commission confirmed its preparations would be cancelled, and not just postponed, given the all-pervading uncertainty at the time.

The same afternoon, the Commissioners went to the Shangri-La hotel for lunch, trying to shake off their frustration. The Chief had his resignation letter in his pocket. He planned to submit it to the prime minister after lunch. Surprisingly then the Chief received a series of phone calls from key civil society leaders and political leaders, including the prime minister, the UNMIN head and the Indian and the US Ambassadors asking him not to resign. They said it was evident that the postponement was necessary due to political reasons, for which the Commission could not be blamed. Reassured, the Chief tore up his letter.

The Chief later recalled:

> That day we felt like a bride groom whose bride had run away from the wedding. It felt like being at square one again on a snake and ladders board, after reaching the top—with much effort and good luck.

Chapter 21

It was 5 October 2007 when the election, planned for November, was finally called off. At that time, the Long Term Observers (LTOs) from the European Union Election Observation Mission (EUEOM) were boarding or waiting to board flights from various airports in London, Paris, Frankfurt, Rome, Brussels and other places in Europe; none of them expected that the election would be cancelled.

The first task for the Chief, after deciding not to resign from his post, was to attend a meeting with the Chief Observer of the European Union's Mission, Jan Mulder, who was also a Member of the European Parliament. This meeting, arranged before the postponement, was to discuss details of the election observation mobilisation.

The second pressing task for the Chief was to deal with the UN's international advisors across Nepal's 75 districts. He feared that if they went home now they might not be available when needed later. The political party leaders could decide to hold an election at any time. But if the Commission retained them, for the foreseeable future there would be no work for them to do—and this would be an unacceptable expense.

The third thing the Chief had to do was to deal with the Returning Officers, who had been sent for the November poll. An election budget had already been allocated to each of them. With the election postponed, there was the danger of overspending, misuse of funds, or even embezzlement by officials. Some dishonest Returning Officers had already taken advantage of the situation and had spent their budgets within a few days. The Commission was accountable to the Parliamentary Accounts Committee, so financial management had to be taken seriously.

After the cancellation of the election, the political debate was rekindled—particularly focusing on the future of the monarchy and proposals to change the electoral system. The Maoists were determined to have their demands fulfilled *before* they agreed to participate in the election. But Koirala was in no mood to listen to them; instead blaming the Maoists for violating peace agreements. Hence, another political deadlock was created—a common feature of Nepalese politics during the transitional period.

International *friends* were not only disappointed at this postponement of the election but also concerned about how this turn of events would impact the peace process. In his report to the Security Council, Secretary-General Ban Ki-moon said, 'Nepal's peace process now stands at a crossroads...' and he asked political parties to '...arrive at a broad road-map to carry forward the peace process' (UNMIN 2008, 67).

The prime minister invited the Chief to a meeting, to discuss ways of moving forward. Koirala was, uncharacteristically, upset about the postponement of the election. He seemed to have lost all hope of living long enough to see it take place. And he was worried that if the election never happened, he would be blamed forever.

The Chief suggested, "Why don't you accept the proportional system? The Maoists might not go for an election even after you do that, but then they will be exposed." But Koirala seemed preoccupied by his own personal standing. He said:

> There is a big conspiracy going on to weaken me. Before, the two factions of the Nepali Congress were united, the UML and the Maoists planned to form an alliance, by luring the Democratic Congress into their fold, in order to alienate the Nepali Congress and oust me...Prachanda had almost agreed to go for the November election. But someone from my own party (hinting at a senior Nepali Congress-Democratic leader) convinced Prachanda to postpone the election... Bhojraj *jee*, maybe the people from my own party want to see me fail.

Concerned, the Chief warned Koirala:

> The election has to happen by 2064 Nepali year (April 2008) otherwise all the documents and laws will have to be changed...but there is no point in declaring the election until the right political atmosphere has been created.

News reports circulating at that time backed Koirala's suspicion that some internal forces wanted to weaken him. In addition to the manoeuvrings of the Maoist leaders, members of his own Democratic Alliance, together with other party leaders called for Koirala to be replaced by another representative of the Seven-Party Alliance. This seemed linked to Koirala's deteriorating relations with India. There were unconfirmed reports that New Delhi wanted to see Koirala weakened. It was said this was because after King Gyanendra's fall it was only Girija Prasad Koirala who possessed the ability to defy the diktat of the *Delhi Durbar*.

This new political development had pushed the political parties further apart, and their frustration with each other grew. The parliamentary parties were concerned that the Maoist party continued to use violence, intimidation, extortion, abduction and other coercive tactics. On the other hand, the Maoist party was frustrated because the other parties were reluctant to introduce fundamental political and socio-economic change, and wanted to do everything the way it had been done in the 1990s. Many parts of the agreement remained to be implemented by both sides. The bitterness arising out of this situation badly affected the election. By the end of November, over a month after the postponement, political leaders were still not making any attempt to reorganise the election.

Around that time, several prominent leaders from India, including a delegation led by Digvijay Singh, the former Chief Minister of Madhya Pradesh, and a senior Indian Congress party leader, visited Nepal, offering their support to the election and the peace process. Shyam Saran came to Kathmandu, as the special envoy of the Indian Prime Minister, Dr. Manmohan Singh. Saran, a former Ambassador to Nepal, was closely involved in Nepal's peace process. During his visit, Saran met the Chief and told him he was worried about the future of the peace process. He said, "Bhojraj sir, the election has to happen at any cost by the end of 2007, as the international situation might change." I had sensed that other visiting delegates also had the same message.

Saran appeared to be hinting at the upcoming Indian elections, after which the Indian government's stand on Nepal's peace process could change. He asked the Chief if it would be possible to hold the election in December. The Chief told him that if there was political will the Commission could organise the election by then. Saran assured the Chief that Maoist Chairman Dahal was not against the election per se, and that if a fully proportional electoral system is adopted it should be possible to hold the election in December. He said, "The Maoists have two major demands—and for the sake of their image they must be met. He added that there was no *harm* in passing the proposal about the republic." The conversation the Chief had with Saran made him feel intuitively that *something was cooking*, and he became more hopeful that a political agreement could be reached.

Chapter 22

The derailment of the electoral process was of concern not only to local and regional actors but global actors as well. In November that year, President Carter came to Nepal for a four-day visit. He had been asked by the international community to explore the possibility for reconciliation among the disputing factions.

During the visit the Chief was requested, by Darren Nance, the Director of the Carter Center, for a one-to-one meeting with the President. But this invitation created a dilemma for the Chief, who was worried that the other commissioners would be suspicious of his motives if he met alone with the President. Particularly, the Chief was concerned about the commissioner backed by the Maoist party, which did not trust the US government and which could, therefore, interpret the meeting as a sign of a *conspiracy.*

Finally, it was decided to divide the one-hour meeting time with President Carter into an individual meeting with the Chief, followed by a meeting with all the commissioners. Days before the visit, the American secret service swarmed all over Bahadur Bhavan, checking everything about the proposed meeting room, the participants and the refreshments.

On 22 November 2007 President Carter arrived at 9 a.m., and the constant clicks of camera shutters opening and closing echoed along the corridors of Bahadur Bhavan. Inside a large office President Carter and the Chief sat on a sofa. The former US Ambassador to UN Peter Burleigh was also present. There was five minute photo session and a few minutes of pleasantries before the formal conversation began.

The Chief opened the meeting by warmly welcoming President Carter and thanking him for the Carter Center's continued presence in Nepal and the role it played in conflict resolution. Then President Carter asked whether the Chief was disappointed by the postponement of the election. The Chief replied, "It was a good lesson for us to realise that technical preparations alone are not enough for the election to take place."

President Carter asked, "If the election system changes, how long would it take the Commission to prepare for the election?" The Chief replied, "If they adopt the proportional system, then our preparations should be easy although the Commission needs to make some changes in the present laws."

President Carter said, "There is so much agitation going on, and there is still unrest in the Tarai region. In such a situation how will you ensure a peaceful election?"

The Chief replied, "If all the political parties join hands, there shouldn't be much of a problem."

President Carter said, "There are rumours going that the election could be held without the Maoists."

The Chief replied, "An election without the Maoists is unimaginable." He used this rare opportunity, of being alone with President Carter, to request him to pressurise the political party leaders to set a new date for the election. Then they went to meet the other four Commissioners.

President Carter briefed the Commissioners about everything he had discussed with the Chief and asked for their views. The Chief recalled:

> President Carter's visit to the Commission proved invaluable. It gave the Commission a renewed sense of self-confidence. This eighty-three-year-old President, who had once led the world's most powerful country, and who had travelled thousands of miles to help Nepal, inspired us all…It made us, at the Commission, overcome our disheartenment, caused by the November election postponement.

During his visit, President Carter also met several influential political party leaders, civil society members, marginalised group leaders, journalists and army staff. After having a private meeting with key negotiators from the three main parties—the Nepali Congress, the Unified Marxist Leninist party and the Maoists—he came up with his own proposal for a possible resolution of the outstanding issues.

Concerning the monarchy, for instance, he suggested that the Legislature-Parliament could declare a republic, which could be endorsed by a simple majority at the first meeting of the Constituent Assembly. On the election system issue, he proposed that the stalemate could be ended by allocating 70 per cent of the total seats for the proportional race and 30 per cent for the FPTP race. President Carter's visit proved to be invaluable in resolving the political deadlock.

Amid these political developments, the UNMIN completed the second phase of registration of the Maoist combatants, verifying their criteria set out by the parties. Out of the over 31,000 Maoist combatants who registered in the first phase, 19,602 were verified as meeting the criteria—15,756 men and 3,846 women. Some of the registered combatants did not appear for interview and others did not meet the criteria; around 4,000 were found to be minors and late recruits.

Around the same time political leaders reached an understanding that finally ended the political stalemate and led to the signing of a new 23-Point Peace Agreement (in December 2008). By this Agreement, the Seven Party Alliance and the Maoists committed themselves to:

- declaring Nepal as a federal democratic republic, to be implemented at the first meeting of the Constituent Assembly;
- increasing the total number of Constituent Assembly seats from 497 to 601—335 through the proportional system, 240 through the FPTP and 26 seats to be appointed by the Council of Ministers;

Figure 13: Discharge of verified minors and late recruits from the cantonments
Source: UN, Photo by Chandrasekhar Karki.

- creating new Commissions, in accordance with the provisions of the peace agreement—including the Commission for the Investigation of the Disappeared, and the Truth and Reconciliation Commission;
- requesting the National Human Rights Commission (NHRC) to monitor the distribution of relief, by mid-February 2008, to the families of people killed or had disappeared in the conflict;
- releasing funds owed to Maoist combatants by 12 February 2008, and thereafter, making regular monthly payments to them.

It appeared that the Agreement, which addressed most of their demands, would encourage the Maoists to participate in the election. This was a significant achievement, facilitated mainly by Carter, which resolved the major issues responsible for the postponement of the November election. The Maoists re-joined the government at the end of December and the Democratic Alliance decided to hold joint public rallies with them, in order to create a positive atmosphere for the election. A new election date was immediately declared, 10 April 2008.

Chapter 23

As soon as the new date was declared, the Commission moved quickly to arrange the nomination deadline. Unfortunately, before the election managers could *catch their breath* different ethnic groups, mainly from within the Madhesi community, re-started their agitation, which severely affected districts in the Tarai region. The Madhesi groups blamed the eight parties—the SPA and the Maoists—for failing to implement the 22-Point Agreement, which promised them greater representation. The resistance was fostered by the emergence of new Madhesi-based regional parties and cross-party alliances.

Senior Nepali Congress leader Mahanta Thakur quit his party to form his own party known as the Tarai Madhesh Lokatantrik Party (TMLP) or Lokatantrik party. He accused the mainstream parties of being insensitive to Madhesi concerns and of being indifferent to the under-representation of Madhesis in all state agencies and political parties. Thakur said he had no option other than to quit the Nepali Congress and to start a new party, which was committed to the interests of the Madhesis. Other Madhesi leaders, and parliamentarians from the mainstream parties, followed suit and joined the growing number of new Madhesi-based regional parties.

The Lokatantrik party immediately created a working alliance with a joint forum of two Madhesi-based parties—the Sadbhavana party and the Madhesi Forum party. (The Madhesi Janadhikar Forum or the Madhesi People's Rights Forum – a civil society organisation registered itself as a political party. It became known as the Madhesi Forum Party.) The alliance between these three parties became known as the United Democratic Madhesi Front (UDMF), or the Madhesi Front. In early 2008, the Front submitted a six-point demand to the government, which included a pledge for an autonomous Madhesi state with the right to self-determination, and a declaration which recognised as martyrs the people who had been killed during the Madhesi uprising the previous year.

Angered that the government was not taking steps to address their demands, the Madhesi Front called for an indefinite strike in the Tarai region, in the second week of February 2008. The strike was supported by around twenty armed groups, including the Jantantrik Tarai Mukti Morcha, the Madhesi Mukti Tigers and the Tarai Cobra. The groups threatened to thwart the Constituent Assembly election, and carry out other violent acts, if their demands were not met before the polls. Groups like these were spreading terror in the Tarai region, through abductions, robbery, pillage and confiscation of land belonging to their rivals.

As these Madhesi groups demonstrated their agitation, offices, schools, businesses, banks and markets in the lowlands were shut down. The arterial highways of Nepal that run through the Tarai, were blocked. This not only brought the whole country to a halt but also caused an acute shortage of fuel and food, resulting in soaring prices. Because of this there was a breakdown of law and order, which threatened to postpone or even cancel the Constituent Assembly election. As the agitation intensified, district election offices were attacked and election material and vehicles were burnt. In Bara and Nepalgunj, election offices were bombed, injuring election staff and Commission personnel were pressurised by landlords to vacate offices they had rented in the Tarai region. Voter education programmes had to be stopped when election volunteers were chased away by hooligans wielding clubs and knives, who claimed allegiance to various Madhesi armed groups.

Worse still, the agitation took on a communal slant, when Madhesis attacked non-Madhesis, and vice versa. As a result, all election-related activities in the plains were halted.

On these political complications, caused by the Madhesi uprising, the Chief later said:

> Immediately after the agitation started, election staff deployed in various Tarai districts, like Siraha, Saptarai and Rautahat, came up with excuses to support their pleas for transfers to safer hilly districts. A few staff members went as far as getting fake medical certificates, with unusual recommendations by doctors not to deploy them in the Tarai for health reasons.
>
> Apparently, the armed groups operating in the Tarai region had threatened election staff and asked them for hefty donations from their limited election budgets. The police couldn't provide security. They either hid or just disappeared.
>
> To counter this problem, the Election Commission decided to deploy election staff of Madhesi origin in the affected areas. Nonetheless, these staff also

> refused to work. Their non-cooperation may have been because of the pressure they faced from the agitators.
>
> Finally, we were forced to revise our policy and instructed Returning and Polling Officers in the Tarai to enrol whoever was interested in working as election staff, regardless of the Commission's eligibility criteria for such positions.

In the midst of this crisis, the Chief requested the Indian Ambassador, Shiv Shankar Mukherjee, to talk with his government about subduing the violence in the Tarai region. The Indian government's role was crucial, as it could control trans-border movement and other logistical support of the armed groups.

When the Chief and Mukherjee met, Mukherjee again emphasised that the elections had to take place in April, at any cost.

The Chief answered:

> How can we conduct the election when the entire Tarai is burning? The armed groups openly threaten our election staff. It is not possible to hold the election in the Tarai.

Mukherjee said:

> I don't think that the Madhesi groups will ever want to take the blame for disrupting the election... *Aare Sahib, aap kyu chinta lete hai. Hum aap ko assure karte hai ke Madhesi ke vajay se elections nahi rukengy par Maobadi ka hume pata nahi.* [Hey officer, why are you worried? I can assure you that the election won't be disrupted due to Madhesis, although I can't say anything about the Maoists.]

Mukherjee added:

> *Kya kare sahib, aapke neeta log bhi gajab ke hai. Bade bade neta log hamare pas aate hai, aur gidgidake kehte hai ki hume ek baar kuch dino ke liye bhi ho prime minister bana dijiye? Yaha saab logo ke liye prime minister ka position chahiye.* [What can I do if your leaders act so strangely? Senior leaders come and beg me to make them prime ministers, even if for a few days. All your leaders seem to want primeministership.]

After the meeting with Mukherjee, the Chief went to see Koirala, to brief him, and to try to pressurise him to resolve the Madhesi issue. Koirala's health had again deteriorated and he was suffering from a high fever and a chest infection.

The Chief said:

> If the Tarai problem is not solved soon then it won't be possible to hold the election there. How can we guarantee protection for our election staff, the candidates and the voters?

Koirala said:

> I have just talked with the Indian Prime Minister, Man Mohan Singh, and the Foreign Minister Pranab Mukherjee. Things should be solved soon…I also talked to the Chief Ministers of UP and Bihar asking for their support in dealing with these trans-border armed groups. They think they can help…But this Tarai issue may make it difficult for us to conduct the election. Who knows which foreign power is funding all this?

The Chief and Koirala eventually agreed a contingency plan for the Tarai region, which meant the election could be held there in a second phase, after completion of the election in other parts of the country.

Despite the continuing Tarai problem, the major political parties complied with the nomination deadline and filed their candidatures on time. However, in the Eastern Tarai districts violence continued to disrupt the process, with two people killed and many injured. Some of the candidates from the Nepali Congress and other parties had to use helicopters to file their papers as angry mobs in Tarai blocked access to election offices. In Dhanusa, the Returning Officer had to enter his office through a rear window to collect the nomination papers. And in another Tarai district, the election officer concealed himself in his office for three days, in order to make the nominations possible.

As not one Madhesi party had submitted its nomination, the deadline was extended for a few more days. But this did not help. Still none of the Madhesi parties filed their nominations—threatening the election again.

But when all hope seemed to have been lost, after weeks of violent civil unrest, the government and the agitating Madhesi Front finally reached an eight-point agreement—after the government acceded to the Madhesi's core demand for a fully autonomous Madhesi state. This key agreement included a promise of medical treatment for those injured in the agitation, compensation for the families of those killed, and a commitment to set up an overall monitoring committee to safeguard implementation of the Agreement.

The election legislation was amended to relax the quota rule for political parties who fielded less than 30 per cent of the maximum of 335 proportional candidates. This meant that the parties submitting less than 100 candidates, in the proportional race, did not have to follow quota rules—although female representation up to 50 per cent still applied. The Madhesi parties had made this demand because they wanted to nominate only Madhesis in their proportional system's candidate list.

After this agreement was ratified, the government asked the Commission to once again extend the nomination deadline, in order to accommodate the Madhesi parties who had boycotted the nominations. At the end of the process 3,130 candidates from 54 political parties, and 816 independent candidates filed their nominations for the FPTP poll, and 5,701 candidates from 54 political parties were nominated for the proportional poll.

On the nominations for the Constituent Assembly election, the Chief later said:

> The nomination process was quite stressful due to the challenges of transitional politics. We had to extend the nomination deadline twice. I did not know if such a repeated extension of nomination dates was acceptable according to international standards, so I consulted international experts before getting back to the government.
>
> Professor Rafael Pintor, the UN's election monitoring head, told me that being rigid about a technical process was not advisable, or even possible, in a post-conflict situation. He said it was okay to extend nomination deadlines if there was political understanding.
>
> We faced other difficulties too. There was a complication for senior Maoist leader Ram Bahadur Thapa, known as Badal. He did not check to see if his name was in the voters' list, and only found out it wasn't at the last minute—when his candidacy was about to be rejected. The election law required a candidate to be in the voter's list.
>
> The Maoist party created hue and cry about this, claiming that it was a deliberate attempt to put a senior and popular Maoist leader out of the elections. They threatened to walk out of the election unless his name was listed.
>
> The ECN was in a really difficult position – if Bodal's name is not in the list the Maoists could use it as an excuse to walk out of the election, but the prevailing law did not allow to add any new names at this stage in the voter's list. We didn't have a lot of time to decide what to do.

Finally, an hour before the nomination deadline, the government ended our dilemma by introducing an ordinance that exempted candidates from political parties from having to be in the voters' list. Of course, I was disappointed to see how political parties could manipulate the laws they themselves had made, but I did not make a fuss about it as that could have fouled things up. In a normal election, this would not have been acceptable.

In the political atmosphere of post-conflict elections, such *allowances* are inevitable. As an election manager, I considered political understanding to be my guiding principle, even though it sometimes came into direct conflict with the values I had adhered to throughout my career, and my life.

Chapter 24

The campaign for the long awaited Constituent Assembly election began in March 2008. In South Asia, election campaigns are usually marked by a high level of violence. Because of the relative weakness of the Nepalese government, vis-à-vis security matters, the potential for intense and widespread violence was high during the Constituent Assembly election. In an attempt to counter this, the Chief conceived an internal strategy, which consisted of appointing a Maoist-backed commissioner as the head of the election Code-of-Conduct (CoC) monitoring team. Most violations were expected to come from the former rebels, and it was hoped that the Commissioner would be able to pressurise them into adhering to the Code-of-Conduct. Moreover, if the Commission acted on the CoC Head's recommendations, the Maoists would not be able to say that the Commission was biased against them.

However, this strategy failed miserably.

Initially, all seemed well, and the political atmosphere became highly charged as nearly 10,000 candidates from fifty-four political parties geared up to contest what was viewed as a historically decisive electoral competition.

The political parties organised large rallies, cultural programmes, street corner meetings and door-to-door canvassing. They even used motorcades, comprised of open vehicles with loudspeakers, banner paintings and posters. Musically gifted party workers roamed around the cities and the countryside singing songs with catchy tunes and simple words about plausible dreams—that had instant popular appeal. Red, white and green party flags hung inside houses or fluttered from the rooftops of party supporters.

The party that drew the most attention during the campaign was the *debutant* in the election field—the Maoists. Like other established political parties the Maoist party formed Central, Regional, District, Municipal and Village committees to run their campaign. And funds were raised centrally and locally, in a way similar to other parties. The Maoist party presented itself as an agent of far-reaching change, their slogans declaring *patak patak arulai, yo patak hamilai* [time and again you voted for others, this time vote for us].

According to one of the Commission's internal reports, the Maoist party was the first to conduct an election campaign planning meeting. After this confidential meeting at party office, which ran into the early hours of the morning, campaign instructions were given to the *foot soldiers* in the Maoist area committees, its sister organisations, class organisations and other party cadres. The party approached the election as it would a military campaign. The Maoists were ready to use both violent and peaceful means, whichever served their interests in winning the elections.

In an attempt to woo voters, the Maoists visited the families of people who had been killed during the armed uprising. They wanted to assure them that, should they win the election, their priority would be to fulfil the dreams of their relatives, the *martyrs*. In most villages, the number of Maoist cadres who had been killed was far greater than that of people killed from other parties. The Maoists message to rural voters was:

> Previously we came to your house with a gun but now we have come here for your vote for peace. If you give us votes then we will take your issues to the parliament but if you don't then we will be forced to go back to the jungle.

However, there were reports that some Maoists engaged in underhand tactics, for example threatening voters committed to other parties. There were rumours that they had told illiterate voters that they could use modern technologies to see from a distance who they had voted for, and that they would take physical action against those who did not vote for the Maoists. As a result, the Commission had to conduct a voter education programme refuting such claims by the Maoists and assuring voters of the secrecy of the ballot.

The campaign of other *debutants* in the election field, for example the Madhesi regional parties, also grabbed the public's attention. The Madhesi Front started their election campaign late, due to their ongoing agitation. Their most effective campaign tool was the slogan *Jaya* Madhes! (Hail Madhes!), which attracted a large number of Madhesi people to their cause.

A somewhat *unusual* personality, who drew public attention during the campaign, was Devyani Rana—the youngest daughter of the pro-royalist party

President, Pashupati Sumsher Rana. It was Devyani who was said to be the reason why Crown Prince Dipendra killed his family and shot himself. She was seen on the campaign trail, campaigning for her father in Sindhupalchok district.

The Chief was kept busy during the election dealing with a succession of complaints about the Maoist youth wing's use of physical violence against the workers of other political parties, including attacks, beatings, maiming and even murder. There were also complaints about Maoist combatants leaving their cantonments and displaying their weapons, in order to threaten other political party workers and voters. Many political parties also said they were denied access to the rural hinterland, which the Maoists described as their electioneering *base area.*

The Nepali Congress sent a detailed, eight-page complaint about the Maoists *excesses* to the Commission. It claimed that the Maoists had used physical violence in constituencies of nineteen districts, to prevent Congress candidates and party workers from campaigning. In Solukhumbu, for instance, the complaint described how Congress candidate Bal Bahadur KC—a sitting Minister—was viciously attacked, sustaining critical head injuries and ended up in hospital. And in Gorkha constituency number 3, almost eighty YCL cadres surrounded Congress candidate Chinkaji Shrestha's house and threatened to burn his home and his family.

Unified Marxist Leninist candidates also filed a large number of complaints against the Maoists, saying they had attacked its candidates and party cadres in 15 districts. For example, Rajendra Pandey, a UML candidate from Dhading-3 constituency complained that the Maoists had injured a dozen of his cadres, breaking their legs, while threatening him with loaded pistols and demanding that he shall stop campaigning.

Other smaller parties also complained of attacks by the Maoist party. For example, the Nepal Workers' and Peasants' Party (NWPP)—a leftist party—complained that the Maoists had attacked their cadres and burnt their election office. And the Presidents of the *royalist* Rastriya Prajatantra party and its breakaway party Rastriya Janashakti—Pashupati Sumsher Rana, and Surya Bahadur Thapa respectively—complained to the Commission that they were prevented by the Maoists from going to their constituencies. They said the Maoists had blocked their way and looted campaign materials.

Not only did the Commission receive complaints from other parties against the Maoists but the Maoists also complained against other parties. They said election workers, mainly from the Unified Marxist Leninist party, had attacked Maoist cadres, albeit only on a few occasions. For example, the Maoists complained that the UML party's candidate and his henchmen in Chitwan had attacked five Maoist workers. They also said that when they complained about these attacks the UML-influenced local police officers let the attackers go scot-free. In another complaint, they said that in Kapilvastu, the Nepali Congress candidate used the local police and armed police (ostensibly NC supporters, or people bribed by the party) to shoot a Maoist Area Committee member.

When the campaigning intensified, the Maoists complained about more physical attacks and the murder of their cadres in several places including Solukhumbu, Dang and Surkhet. UN reports confirmed these complaints and stated that CPN-Maoists lost the greatest number of party workers during the campaign, even though all major parties suffered casualties.

After all is said, it remains a fact that the complaints from other parties against the Maoists far outnumbered the complaints made by the Maoists against other parties. The evidence still lies in a thick green folder in a corner of Bahadur Bhavan.

The campaign period, now seen as the *darkest part* of the Constituent Assembly election, must be seen—according to the Chief—within the wider context of Nepal's contemporary tension. Reflecting on the campaign period, the Chief later said:

> The fact that the Maoist party still maintained a standing army created a climate of fear among voters, party workers, election officials and government agencies. The legacy of war was strong.
>
> I must also mention that according to the reports we received, the Maoists used maximum violence against political opponents in the hills during the campaign, whereas the Madhesi Forum party resorted to a high level of violence in the Tarai region.
>
> In this context, the law enforcement authorities, primarily the Nepal Police, did not take any action against political party workers who repeatedly resorted to violence during the campaign. The passivity of the police in the face of the Maoists, and other abuses can partly be explained by their fear of retaliation. Partly, however, it was also a reflection of the Home Ministry's concern not to provide the Maoists with any excuse to pull out of the election process.
>
> Home Minister Sitaula, who was also the chief negotiator in the peace process, was deeply worried that if he took the slightest action then it could

provoke the Maoists to walk out of the peace process, as had happened in previous peace talks.

This meant that Returning and Polling Officers and the monitoring team—headed by the government's Permanent Secretaries, who were deployed by the Commission on the ground—hesitated to send us formal reports about incidents of violence. Even special investigation teams, deployed by the Commission and comprised of senior public officials, could not find the courage to send formal reports against perpetrators.

Honestly speaking, the Commission was also fairly reluctant to take action against the Maoists because they might have used it as a pretext for abandoning, or even wrecking, the election process. Due to our experience of the Maoists boycotting the November elections, we always felt insecure about what they might do, so we focused more on making them participate in the ongoing election process. We were ready to compromise for peace; and that was only possible to achieve if the Maoists took part in the election.

Having said all that, it is important to remember that violence during a campaign period was not new for Nepal. In past elections the Nepali Congress or UML had used violence in areas where they were strong, to secure results in their favour. I think it's not fair to criticise the Maoists alone for using violence in the campaign period. The culture of using violence during elections *preceded* the emergence of the Maoist party, but the intensity of violence used by the Maoists was certainly unprecedented.

The Chief also recalled the role of the UNMIN during this period:

The political parties had thought that once the Maoist combatants and their arms were under UN supervision, the former rebels would not obstruct the election process. The Commission also had high expectations about this. Without understanding the limitation of the UN's enforcement power, we just assumed that all security problems would be solved after the entry of the global body.

However, we received many complaints from the political parties about Maoist combatants leaving their cantonments and displaying their weapons publicly. When I brought that issue to the notice of Ian Martin, he was surprised, saying no formal complaint had been made. Martin explained that UNMIN's problem was that the NC and UML made allegations to the media, and to the Commission, which they did not make to UNMIN—so UNMIN staff had no knowledge of many alleged incidents.

Reports about the Maoist combatants leaving the cantonments floated everywhere throughout the campaign period, adding to public terror. It did not matter if these reports were true; rumours were enough to cause serious damage. Psychological terror spread like wildfire among voters.

The UNMIN criticised the Maoists' violent activities during the campaign, through press statements and UNMIN/OHCHR reports it published from time to time. Ian Martin also put pressure on the Maoist leaders, both at the central and local levels. Yet this did not stop the Maoists from engaging in violent activities against political opponents. Martin later told me that they had a mandate to investigate how the Maoist combatants were leaving cantonments, but that the parties to the peace process had not authorised enforcement action; so what could be done was limited. As a result of all these factors the election field contained unequal players.

Chapter 25

The inequality between the players created problems for the managers of the Constituent Assembly election. The Commission was ridiculed by the media and the civil society for failing to take effective action against the violations. The news reports carried disapproving headlines, like *Toothless Election Commission*, *Impotent EC* and *Feeble Commission*. The Commission began to lose what it valued most—its integrity.

Then, a complaint was filed by Dev Shankar Poudel, the UML candidate from the Rammechap-1 constituency, who stated that the Maoists had attacked his group while they were out campaigning. Poudyal said the Maoists had encircled them, and attacked him and his supporters with iron rods, heavy wooden sticks, large rough stones and *Khukuris* (Nepalese knifes), and stolen Nepalese Rupees 335,800 in cash.

That night, all the news channels showed Poudel lying in a hospital bed with injuries all over his body and a smashed and bloody head. When the Chief saw the images he was white with rage. He felt he had to take action, at any cost, to prevent a repetition of such an assault.

First, he planned to cancel the nomination of the Maoist candidate who was accused of being responsible for the attack on Poudel. The Chief was determined to use his executive prerogative to shorten the normally lengthy process of cancelling a nomination—in order to send a clear message to the perpetrators of violence.

The next morning, he invited the Commissioners to an emergency meeting, to discuss taking strong action against perpetrators of brutality. Three Commissioners supported this plan, believing it was time the Election Commission took a stance. They agreed the Commission could not simply stand by and watch such atrocities. But one Commissioner disagreed. He said:

> How can you single out the Maoists and take action against them when they are the ones who have lost more cadres in the election campaign than the others?

> All the national and international forces want to marginalise the Maoists and now the Commission is also trying to do the same... If you take this action, then the Maoists will probably not participate in the election.

This divided opinion represented a troubling split in the Commission. It revealed an internal weakness in the constitutional body mandated to hold elections. The practice of the Election Commission to make decision unanimously—a convention that had proved a handicap for the Chief on many occasions.

In the end, all the Commissioners were convinced, and no action was taken—despite the ongoing violations. None of the Commissioners wanted to be blamed for giving the Maoists the excuse to quit the election process.

Their inaction led to an increase in the intensity of violence—leading to a further deterioration of the security situation. This deterioration was reported by various international organisations, including the UNMIN which recorded 27 deaths, 30 abductions and 80 bomb explosions during the campaign. Another report, from the Washington-based organisation called International Foundation for Electoral Systems (IFES), stated that there were 99 incidents of violence during the campaign, over and above non-election related incidents which occurred at the same time.

In such a difficult political environment, election observation was an important task. Observers not only increased the credibility of the election process but also had a deterrent effect on election-related violence and irregularities. Most importantly, their presence increased the chance that the results would be accepted.

Therefore, although international observation in Nepal had been limited in previous elections, this time the country requested as many international observers as possible. In addition to around two dozen international agencies, three large international observation groups were accredited—the Carter Center (CC), the European Union (EU) and the Asian Network for Free Election (ANFREL).

The Carter Centre was invited because of the positive contribution it had made to Nepal's peace process. The European Union was seen as an effective alternative to the United Nations, so far as observation was concerned. And ANFREL was approached by UNMIN Chief Ian Martin in consultation with the ECN, because of his experience of working with the group in the East Timor elections. The Commission hoped that a South-East Asian observation group

Figure 14: International observers at ECN
Source: ECN, Photo by Suman Ghimire.

Figure 15: UN's Electoral Experts Monitoring team at ECN
Source: ECN, Photo by Suman Ghimire.

would understand Nepal's local conditions better than a Western group, and would thus be able to play a more effective role in the election process. And they would be cheaper to bring into the country than Westerners.

Apart from these three international missions, the UN also deployed a team of election monitoring experts, known as the Electoral Expert Monitoring Team (EEMT), which was independent of the UNMIN. This five-member team, headed by Dr. Rafael Lopez-Pintor, focused on four areas of election preparation—security of the election environment, development of a legal framework, electoral administration and public opinion and the media. The team conducted monitoring assessments in five phases and reported directly to the UN Secretary-General. In addition to the UN monitoring team and the three observation missions, two dozen other agencies were accredited to observe the election. Several donors and international organisations also supported the engagement of domestic monitors. On the advice of the UN, and the international observer groups, the Commission developed a liberal accreditation policy in order to attract a large number of domestic observers.

In anticipation of the April elections, over 60,000 local and around 800 international observers were fielded across Nepal, to observe the election process as well as to assist in ensuring fair election environment.

On election observation, the Chief later said:

> Everyone in the Commission agreed that we needed as many international observers as possible. In our culture, foreigners have a great deterrent effect; even if two people are fighting aggressively, they stop when they see a foreigner. So, we extended an invitation to all our international partners to provide as many observers as they could. Yet unlike other partners we did not make serious follow-ups in the case of observers from Nepal's immediate neighbours—India and China.
>
> In the case of India, particularly, there was always the worry that the neutrality of their observers could be questioned. All in all, Indian diplomats and their government had a poor track record of unwarranted interference in Nepalese politics. Moreover, some Indians were physically more or less similar to some Nepalese, a characteristic that would clearly decrease their deterrence effect. That is the main reason why the Commission didn't put an extra effort into importing observers from our closest neighbour.
>
> As far as China was concerned, its observers had the double disadvantage of being closely akin to many Nepalese of Mongolian stock, and of speaking a

language not understood in Nepal. Additionally, many Western countries were of opinion that there was no point in inviting observers from a rigidly authoritarian communist country like China, which had no experience of democratic elections.

It was the interested groups which had to apply with the Election Commission for accreditation to observe the election. Ultimately, we encouraged international observation groups only from distant countries, rather than from our neighbours.

We also asked all high level visitors during that period, including President Carter, to assist us by providing as many international observers as possible. We even approached the UN, to request that officials, including the Secretary General, use their office to mobilise observers for us. The Foreign Minister Ms. Sahana Pradhan, made an appeal during her address to the UN General Assembly.

These international observers played an important role in the election process in Nepal. Nepal's need for robust country-wide coverage, which was the demand from every candidate to field such observers in their constituencies, including in remote and conflict-affected areas, was of course difficult to meet. A large number of domestic observer groups were accredited by the Commission. These observers also played a crucial role in creating positive atmosphere for the elections.

Major domestic observer groups, some of which were also in collaboration with international observer groups, were mainly funded by international donors. Even though this was supportive to the overall election process, there were complaints that some of the internationally-funded domestic observer organisations did not maintain political neutrality and acted unprofessionally. In some cases we had to withdraw our permission for individuals who continued to act in such a manner. And there were also complaints that the process used for the selection of Nepalese observer organisations for funding by donors lacked transparency and a clear framework. The Commission had to expend a considerable amount of energy resolving conflict between organisations that received donor funds and those that did not.

Notwithstanding these shortcomings, deployment of long-term and short-term observers (LTOs and STOs respectively) provided legitimacy to the election process, as did the visits by President Carter and other distinguished members of international observation teams.

The UN election monitoring team was also comprised of experts with long experience of working in post-conflict election situations. That was why I referred to them whenever I faced difficult challenges, and they duly advised me.

Chapter 26

As the election day neared, security became the most pressing issue for the Commission. The fragile security—including the weak rule of law and human rights violations—was identified by different international organisations such as the UNMIN, the OHCHR-Nepal and Carter Center as the major challenge to a free and fair election. In December 2007, a report on human rights was also published, covering the period since the signing of the Comprehensive agreement by OHCHR-Nepal. The report said that the emergence of armed groups, the escalation of violence among them, and the growing social unrest about issues of exclusion posed a serious challenge for the government and state institutions responsible for maintaining law and order and protecting the rights of the population. The report also raised concerns about the impunity enjoyed by perpetrators of murder and other violence—be they the State, the Maoist cadres or the armed ethnic groups. According to the report, between January and October 2007 around 130 civilians were killed, including 60 people killed by armed groups. These findings indicated that an outbreak of large-scale violence was still the greatest threat to the election.

The already bad security situation worsened two weeks before the election when a bomb exploded in a Mosque in the eastern part of Nepal, killing two Muslims and injuring many others. The international community, and local political party leaders in Nepal started questioning the wisdom of trying to hold an election in such a tense environment.

The Chief responded, in early April, by inviting the leaders of the three main parties to a do-or-die meeting. He warned them, "If the three of you do not stop your violent activities against each other, the election will not be possible." The next day, the leaders signed a ten-point agreement, promising to abide by the election Code-of-Conduct and to support a free, fair, and impartial election. Unfortunately, this commitment was only limited to the paper.

Two days before the election, on 8 April, seven Maoist cadres were shot and killed by the police, who were deputed for the security patrol of the Nepali Congress leader Khum Bahadur Khadka, and over twelve people were injured during clashes between the Maoists and the Congress supporters in that same incident. The same day, the Unified Marxist Leninist candidate from Surkhet, Rishi Prasad Sharma, was killed during a violent street scuffle between the Congress and the UML workers. The Chief also received reports about Maoist and other political parties attacking party agents and stealing their election materials. These were serious incidents.

The Chief later recalled:

> Even though civil society activists like Daman Nath Dhungana and Padma Ratna Tuladhar, organisations like the UNMIN and the OHCHR and, most importantly, the Maoist leader Mahara played a crucial role in calming down the tense atmosphere in Dang district, the situation was explosive. Large-scale violence could erupt at any time.

In the past elections, the Nepalese Army had played a vital role in maintaining security. But the peace agreements explicitly forbade mobilisation of the army, and soldiers were not allowed to come out of their barracks during the election. The responsibility for election security was, instead, given to the Nepalese Police Force and the Armed Police Force. Around 75,000 temporary security personnel were also hired, to help enforce law and order on the day of election.

Although the government had overall responsibility for ensuring security, the Commission was also involved during the election, in a supporting role. As part of the election security plan, a security committee was formed—led by one of the Election Commissioners, also including Secretaries of the Home and Defence Ministries and Heads of agencies, such as the Nepalese Police Force, the Nepalese Armed Police Force and the Central Intelligence Department. The committee regularly reviewed and monitored the security situation throughout the country during this time.

Policies were devised to ensure a peaceful election and prevent an outbreak of large scale violence on the election day. Extra precautionary measures were also taken, including the following:

- Only vehicles permitted by security officials were allowed to move on that day.
- All international borders were closed.

- Helicopters patrolled, to give a sense of security in mountainous areas.
- A minimum of five security officials were deployed in every polling station.
- Back-up security officials were deployed in strategic locations.
- The Armed Police Force was used to assist the civilian Police Force, in case of an emergency.

The aim was to establish strong and sound communication channels, so that even people in remote areas would feel secure enough to vote. On the eve of the election the Commission held a press conference, during which voters were urged to participate without fear.

The Chief recalled:

> In the press conference, when I said that tomorrow's voting would be peaceful, around 300 reporters and journalists, both national and international, could not believe what I was saying and burst out laughing…That day I returned home late at night counting the number of things to be done if the election was cancelled yet another time.

Understandably, the Chief was preoccupied with improving security right up to, and throughout, the election. At one point, it had been hoped that the UN would assist with public security measures, and the Chief had discussed various options with Martin. UNMIN repeatedly offered to make available to the Nepali authorities the expertise of the UN Police Advisors. However, this offer was rejected by the Home Ministry and the Nepalese Police Force.

There were many reasons for this resistance to using the UN security personnel. Primarily, the Nepalese Police Force did not want to admit that they needed external support to maintain security. Also, the influential Indian authorities were not happy with the idea of the UN security advisors swarming their backyard. In retrospect, the Chief admitted:

> It was a mistake not to accept the UN offer to help improve the security environment for the election. The situation was really bad. On the one side were the former rebels who would not hesitate to use force to gain political control, and on the other were the newly emerged ethnic armed groups, who openly threatened to disrupt the election.
>
> As the election got closer, a few of my friends suggested it should be cancelled, because there was such a huge risk of unrest. They warned me that given the extremely poor security, anything could happen, and thousands of innocent people could be killed.

They had a point. Around 60,000 civil and armed police and about 75,000 poorly trained temporary police officers, were charged with election security. They were not capable of controlling or preventing violence if it erupted on E-day. But, despite the huge risk, there was no alternative because only the election could ensure peace.

To try to prevent large-scale violence we classified areas where polling booths were located into *normal, sensitive* and *highly sensitive* zones, and security arrangements were made accordingly. In highly sensitive zones, we stationed additional security forces which could be deployed instantly.

We also asked international bodies, including the UNMIN, to deploy their field staff in highly sensitive zones. We hoped that they would have a calming effect, as well as boost the confidence of our national staff.

Even the UN revised its security policy and agreed to deploy international staff in our sensitive areas. This helped, to some extent, to create a moderately conducive atmosphere for the election and marginally increased the confidence of national election staff.

Chapter 27

On the morning of 10 April 2008, over 10 million Nepalese women and men woke up to vote in the long awaited Constituent Assembly election. A significant number of these voters were from rural Nepal—peasants, labourers and craftsmen—who had lost family members in the Maoists' war or who had been subjected to physical violence from both the Maoists and the state army. Another important group of voters were those who were members of the state security forces and the rebel armed forces, who were held in barracks and makeshift cantonments throughout the country. For these men and women the election signalled an end to the continual fighting.

By 7 o'clock, the scheduled time for voting to begin, over 100,000 security officials were on duty in polling stations across the country. Helicopters whirred

Figure 16: Voters casting their ballots
Source: Photo by Dipesh Shrestha.

Figure 17: Voters from the Tharu community cast their ballots in an open space polling booth
Source: UN, Photo by Ky Chung.

Figure 18: Nepal Army personnels casting votes
Source: UN, Photo by Nayantara Kakshapati.

Figure 19: Maoist combatants casting votes
Source: UN, Photo by Sagar Shrestha.

overhead to ensure security, especially in the difficult mountainous regions. Security was the top priority; it was feared there would be clashes between armed political groups or between armed and non-armed groups, which could trigger large-scale violence and derail the election.

Most of the Returning Officers telephoned the Commission to say that enthusiastic voters had started queuing up from 5 o'clock, and that the situation was under control. Staff in remote locations had stayed overnight at the polling stations to make sure that the polling would open on time. In other areas they reached the polling stations as early as three or four in the morning, in order to make arrangements.

After collecting reports from across the country, the Chief went with his wife and daughter to vote at a polling station in a school near their home. When his car stopped outside the centre, the Chief saw a line of women dressed in brightly coloured saris or *salwar kameez*, waiting to go in. Some were holding babies, some even nursing babies, others were running after naughty children. Mostly it was women who voted that morning, as most of the young Nepalese men were out of the country, because of the legacy of the armed conflict.

The Chief entered the polling station to find voting taking place in a festive, carnival-type atmosphere. Diligent domestic observers with notebooks, and international observers with digital cameras and mineral water bottles, observed the process. The Chief voted in both the majoritarian FPTP and the proportional races.

The options for voting was wide-ranging. At one end there was the ultra-left Maoist party, which had launched a protracted armed struggle to restructure the Nepalese state. At the other end was the far-right Rastriya Prajatantra Party Nepal, which advocated for continuance of the monarchy. More moderate voices included the Nepali Congress party—which claimed to be democratic socialist but acted as a centre-liberal party—and the Unified Marxist Leninist party, which claimed to be Marxist-Leninist but acted as a moderate socialist party. Then there were the Madhesi regional parties, such as the Madhesi Forum party and the Lokatantrik party, which reflected the flavour of the New Nepal.

At the Election Commission's headquarters, a command post had been set up—through which all the polling stations could be monitored. There was also a round-the-clock special election hot line, receiving reports from different parts of the country. Reports from polling booths were largely positive, and voting *generally* took place in a more peaceful environment than was expected. Nevertheless, as the day progressed, the Election Commission received numerous reports of violence, malpractice, violations and irregularities, especially in the sensitive districts of Ramechhap, Dolakha, Gorkha, Rasuwa, Dhading, Rolpa, Rukum, Mahottari, Saptari, Sarlahi, Sunsrai, Dhanusa, Siraha, Rautahat, Bara and Parsa.

In Dhanusa district, the Nepali Congress candidate was shot and seriously injured. In Sunsari—Prime Minister Koirala's daughter's constituency—a Congress worker was killed. And in Sarlahi, an independent candidate was killed. Was death a low price to pay for electoral victory?

In Rautahat, a fight broke out between the Unified Marxist Leninist and the People's Front activists, and in Mahottari there was a scuffle between the aggressive youth-wing cadres of the Congress and the Unified Marxist Leninist party. This confrontation was so intense that the police had to fire blank rounds, in order to keep the situation under control. Again in Mahottari, a group of young boys threw ballot boxes into a pond. Voting in most of the districts badly affected by violence was either cancelled or postponed, on the recommendation of the polling staff.

Figure 20: Former US President Jimmy Carter and Roselyn Carter observing the election
Source: 2008 Deborah/The Carter Center.

By the late afternoon, the heads of various international observation missions—including Rafael Pintor of the UN, Jan Mulder of the EU, Chairman General Saiyud Kerdphol of ANFREL—had congratulated the Election Commission for staging a successful poll. Their comments were based on their own observations and reports from international and national observers.

At around three in the afternoon, President Carter and his wife Rosalynn visited the Commission, after observing polls in several stations around Kathmandu Valley. They congratulated the Chief and the Election Commission for holding a successful election. Although the Chief had met President Carter thrice before, he was meeting Mrs Carter, who was the co-founder of the Carter Center, for the first time. The Chief was eager to meet her because he had read that she was instrumental in introducing human rights into mainstream global affairs.

On the Carters, the Chief later reflected:

> For people in the East, like the Nepalese, who wrongly assume that Westerners do not care for family values or that their relationships, especially marital, do not last like those of Easterners, the Carter couple—married for over fifty

> years—stood as an imposing column of evidence to prove us utterly wrong. I was impressed by their long-lasting partnership, for their work on many noble causes, such as conflict resolution and peace building, especifically in Nepal.

The Chief also received a series of congratulatory calls from ambassadors, the head of UNMIN, civil society leaders and the Speaker of the parliament. When the polls closed at 5 o'clock the Indian Ambassador, Shiv Shankar Mukherjee, was the first one to call. In Hindi he said:

> *Aare Bhojraj sahib, aap logon ne bahut bada kaam kiya hai. Kisine bhi nahi socha tha ki elections itane peaceful honge. Hamare aur hamare sarkar ke taraf se aap logno ko badhaiyan.* [You have done a commendable job. No one had thought that the elections would be so peaceful. The Indian government sends its heartiest congratulations to all of you.]

On the same note, a statement issued by the UN Secretary-General Ban Ki-moon said:

> The Secretary-General congratulates the people of Nepal on today's Constituent Assembly election, which took place in a generally orderly and peaceful atmosphere. He commends the Nepalese for their enthusiastic participation in this historic event and appeals to all parties to remain calm while awaiting the results.

The heads of the domestic observer groups also congratulated the ECN team, but with some reservations. The head of one of the domestic observer group called National Election Observation Committee (NEOC), Surya Prasad Shrestha (a former Chief Election Commissioner), said, "Bhojraj *jee*, though there have been a few *gadbadi* [irregularities] the elections went well—especially given the challenges we had." The heads of the other domestic organisations also said that the elections went well, although they noticed some irregularities. Prominent political leaders also congratulated the Commission. The Democratic Alliance leader, Koirala, told the Chief, "*Socheko bhanda ta shanti purna nai chunab bhayo, tapai haru lai dhanyabaad.* [The elections were more peaceful than expected. Thanks to you all.]" Maoist Chairman Dahal also called. He said:

> You have fulfilled your responsibility with great success and efficiency. I would like to thank and congratulate you and the Commission on behalf of my party. Special thanks for fulfilling the people's desire for the Constituent Assembly election.

The Chief was relieved; it seemed the Maoists would accept the election results—something he had been concerned about since the beginning of the process. The international community, and the whole of Nepal, appeared to have accepted the legitimacy of the election, without reservation—at least that's how it appeared on the evening of 10 April 2008.

Information was still trickling in from various polling booths. But the Chief was tired and decided to have an early night. The following day he had to supervise the count. At midnight his phone rang; it was the Unified Marxist Leninist General Secretary, Madhav Kumar Nepal. He was the only one of the three big leaders who had not yet thanked the Election Commission. What followed was the most disheartening part of the Chief's day.

Nepal told him:

> The Election Commission is toothless. The Commission failed to take any action against the atrocities. Even after glaring violations of the Code-of-Conduct, the Commission could not do anything...There have been irregularities in two booths of my own constituency in Rautahat. So I want you to conduct re-polling there.

Recalling that incident later, the Chief said:

> My heart sank as I heard his words, although I was willing to consider what he said. On the one hand, it was not something big that Madhav *jee* had asked me to do—re-polling in some of his affected booths. I was ready to conduct re-polling in those areas if his claims turned out to be justified, because his presence was absolutely necessary in the new Assembly—he was an important element of the peace process.
>
> However, what disturbed me most was that he seemed more concerned about himself than the broader national issues, despite being a senior leader of his party. Many other UML candidates, or candidates of other parties, must have also gone through the same difficulties. How could he alone talk only about himself?

This incident was only one example of the numerous problems that the Chief faced on E-day. He recalled:

> Voting in Kathmandu, and a few other cities, was reportedly smooth—although there were problems like identification issues and the duplication of, or inaccuracies in, the names of voters, despite all the hard work of the Commission.

In the Tarai region particularly, there were reports that some parties had hired people from India to vote or brought in Indian gangsters to crush the opposition. The Commission also received reports about some parties stuffing ballot boxes with fake votes by threatening the election staff and security officials. In sensitive areas, security remained our greatest worry throughout the day. There were also complaints about Maoists combatants threatening voters.

Honestly speaking, the whole experience of conducting the election, which was postponed several times—was surreal for me. I felt numb all day; the kind of feeling someone gets when they experience too many emotions at the same time—excitement, relief, worry, anxiety.

When I lay in bed that night, I realised that the only reason the election was successful, and without large-scale violence, was the Nepalese people's desire for peace, and their commitment to the democratic process.

That's why the political leaders were committed to the Constituent Assembly election. There was no doubt that they were distracted at times but there was a strong desire amongst the top leaders, like Koirala, Dahal and Nepal, to hold the Constituent Assembly election in order to fulfil the people's desires.

I must also mention the role of the Nepalese monarchy and the Nepal Army. Throughout the process, I was worried about the Royal Palace and that the army might disrupt the election—as was widely expected. Truth be told, I received no reports of the involvement of the King, or his supporters, in any activity that disturbed the election. The royalist forces never put any pressure—direct or indirect—on me that could adversely affect the election.

The Nepal Army, in particular, showed great dignity and restraint throughout the process. The Chief of Army Staff, Rukmangad Katuwal, called me regularly to ask if I needed support for the election. The reason why they acted this way could be, again, due to the Nepalese people's overwhelming desire for peace that could be only ensured through democratic elections.

Chapter 28

Once the election was over, the priority of the Commission was to protect the will of the people, expressed through the ballot, and to complete the count and announce the results as soon as possible.

When the polling finished, the ballot boxes were taken—under tight security—to the headquarters of the 75 districts. In addition to the formal counting legislation, the Commission developed guidelines to assist the process. In rural areas, where literacy was low, it was necessary to be flexible, in order to reduce the number of votes which might otherwise be deemed invalid on technical grounds.

The first count began in Kathmandu-1, the only constituency using electronic voting machines. Two candidates in this constituency, Prakash Man Singh of the Nepali Congress and Pradip Nepal of the Unified Marxist Leninist party, were considered to be equally strong. Singh was from dominant Newar community and the son of the veteran democracy fighter Ganesh Man Singh. Nepal was a sitting minister and a senior UML leader. He appeared to be in a good position, as the UML had won five of the seven constituencies in Kathmandu in the last election in 1999.

The competition was tough. The counting of votes for Kathmandu-1 finally ended the next morning, when Singh was declared the first candidate to win in the historic Constituent Assembly election. The UML party came second and the Maoist party third, in both the FPTP and proportional race of Kathmandu-1.

Not surprisingly, given this victory, the Congress party was the first to organise a large celebratory rally after the election. Singh drove around the city in an open vehicle, adorned with red *abir* (powdered colour) and marigold garlands, the Nepali Congress flag fluttering from the car bonnet.

Immediately, political analysts, newspaper columnists and academics began predicting that the Congress would emerge as the largest party, followed by UML and then the Maoists. Some of them even started prescribing ways to engage the Maoists in the post-election process, to deal with what they foresaw would be their likely humiliating defeat. But within 24 hours these *best minds* of Kathmandu would be proved completely wrong.

As the counting of votes progressed, a remarkable trend began to reveal itself—the Maoists were *leading*. Most of the Maoist candidates were little known names with unknown faces, unlike many of the FPTP candidates of the Nepali Congress or UML party, who were well-known public figures.

In Jhapa-3 constituency, the Home Minister Krishna Sitaula lost to the never-before-heard-of Maoist candidate, Purna Prasad Rajbhansi. Rajbhansi had started his political career in 1990 after only completing grade seven. In Nuwakot-1 constituency, the influential leader and spokesperson of the Congress, Arjun Narsingh KC was beaten by a 28-year-old female, Bimala Subedi of the Maoist party. In patriarchal Nepalese society, this result was rather shocking.

The most unanticipated result came when UML General Secretary, Madhav Kumar Nepal was trounced, *twice*—losing to relatively unknown Maoist candidates in both Kathmandu-2 and Rautahat-6 constituencies. Nepalese law allowed a candidate to stand in two different constituencies. In the 1999 parliamentary election, Nepal, who had then stood for the first time, had won both the constituencies he contested in Rautahat. This was a complete turn-around. In Sunsari-5, Prime Minister Koirala's only child, Sujata Koirala lost to Madhesi Forum Chairman Upendra Yadav.

While the seats of the Nepali Congress and the Unified Marxist Leninist—both traditionally dominant parties—were being captured by formidable Maoists in the mountain region, in Tarai *their* seats were being snatched by the Madhesi parties. As dawn broke, entrenched Congress and UML politicians were being displaced one by one.

While the count continued, the election staff also conducted re-polling in stations where the ballot on the day of the election had been cancelled for some reason. Wherever candidates sensed that the voting was not in their favour, they pressed for a re-poll. Party leaders even tried to influence the Election Commission, and it was difficult to counter this kind of pressure. An example of this was when, shortly after voting closed, Home Minister Krishna Sitaula called on the Chief. Sitaula had not come to request a re-poll in his own constituency but rather, in that of the prime minister's daughter, Sujata Koirala's. Sitaula argued that there were irregularities in a few polling stations in Koirala's constituency. He said, "Please try to look into her case, if possible." But this complaint was not supported by the local authorities, so the Commission did not conduct a re-poll in junior Koirala's constituency.

The Chief later spoke of the count:

> One thing that I learnt in the days following the election was that counting is the most stressful part of the election process. It is the time when political parties demonstrate their worst behaviour, unbelievably bad.
>
> The security of the ballot boxes, and protecting the will of the people, was our prime concern throughout. In some rural areas the ballot boxes were stolen from the election staff; and in other areas they were intentionally damaged before they reached their counting, centres. In the Dhading-1 constituency, around 19 ballot boxes and election papers were stolen, while they were being transported to the district HQ for the count.
>
> In Dhanusa district, when the Madhesi Forum cadres saw they were losing, they snatched ballot papers and chewed them up. I just cannot describe how savagely political parties behaved, especially the newly emerged ones such as the Maoists and Madhesi Forum party.
>
> Apart from the security of the ballot boxes, the safety of the counting and re-polling center staff was also a challenge. In a counting centre in Birgunj an explosion occurred, which seriously injured two people and led to a storm of public indignation.
>
> Many of these things used to happen in elections before. But at such a politically sensitive time, we were worried that a small incident could trigger large scale violence unlike in the past.
>
> We received thousands of complaints from political parties. In most cases these complaints were filed by candidates who appeared to be losing. It was not possible for us to differentiate between genuine and fake complaints within such a short period of time. I had become a dutiful doctor who was immune to his patient's disease. Like a doctor, who at the end of his duty and just wants to go home, I wanted to finalise the results and finish the task in hand.
>
> However, I must admit that our complaints' mechanism was not adequate to meet the challenges of the post-conflict election. In an environment of extremely poor security enforcement, a strong party with adequate resources can influence

local officials with incentives or by threats, in order to get the outcome they want. Thus, in cases where the local level officials could stand up to bullies or avoid temptation, complaints were dealt with justice whereas the places where the local officials were partisan or felt threatened, complaints could not be dealt properly even if they were genuine.

Chapter 29

The final declaration of the three-tiered results was completed by the beginning of the monsoon season in 2008. The seats comprised 335 under the Proportional System, 240 under the FPTP and 26 Appointments by the Council of Ministers.

In the FPTP ballot, the Maoists got 120 seats, whereas the former ruling parties—the Nepali Congress and Unified Marxist Leninist got 37 and 33 seats respectively. The Maoists 120 seats, therefore, represented 50 per cent of the total FPTP seats—almost three times that of the Congress party or the UML party. This result implies that if the electoral system had not become a mixed system the Maoist party would have secured a clear majority in the Constituent Assembly election.

The newly emerged Madhesi Forum party secured 30 seats, making it the fourth largest party in the FPTP race, and the Lokatantrik party nine seats, making it the fifth largest party in the FPTP race. In the previous parliamentary elections in 1999, after the Congress and UML parties, the most successful party was the *royalist* Rastriya Prajatantra Party (RPP). Before this election, sensing public mood, the RPP removed from its constitution its policy of supporting constitutional monarchy. But still, the RPP—and other *royalist* splinter factions—made considerable losses.

Unfortunately, the representation of women, and other previously underrepresented groups, remained low in this FPTP race. In the case of women, for example, female candidates represented less than 10 per cent candidates nominated by all the parties. This surprisingly was true also for the Maoist party, which had boasted that nearly half its soldiers were women. It seemed women were *good* enough to be soldiers but not election candidates. The Madhesi parties presented an even more embarrassing picture. Despite being the strongest voice against marginalisation, the largest Madhesi party fielded merely three candidates for the FPTP race. Table 2 provides a summary of the results of the FPTP race.

In the proportional race, votes received were converted into seats, using a mathematical formula called the *Modified Sainte-Laguë Method.* Under this system, seats were allocated in direct relation to the number of votes received by a political party. The Maoist party won 100 seats, the Congress party won 73 seats, and the UML party won 70 seats. The difference in the number of seats, between the major parties, was much less in the proportional race than in the FPTP race.

Table 2: Results for the First-Past-The-Post race

Political party	*Total candidates*		*Winning candidates*		*Total**	*Percentage of seats*	*Percentage of votes*
	M	*F*	*M*	*F*			
Communist Party of Nepal (Maoists)	198	42	96	24	120	50.0	30.52
Nepali Congress	214	26	35	2	37	15.42	22.79
Nepal Communist Party (UML)	212	27	32	1	33	13.75	21.63
Madhesi People's Rights Forum, Nepal	100	3	28	2	30	12.50	6.15
Tarai Madhesh Lokatantrik Party	90	4	8	1	9	3.75	3.35
Sadbhavana Party	83	4	4	0	4	1.67	1.69
Janamorcha Nepal	175	28	2	0	2	0.83	1.33
Nepal Workers and Peasants' Party	71	27	2	0	2	0.83	0.64
Rastriya Janamorcha	107	15	1	0	1	0.42	0.91
Independents	774	42	2	0	2	0.83	1.20
Total					240	100.0	

Source: The Election Commission of Nepal (2008, 16–189).

Note: *Five candidates—two from the Maoist party, two from the MJF-Nepal and one from the Nepali Congress—each won in both the constituencies they stood in. According to the election law, candidates winning in two constituencies had to withdraw from one of them and by-elections had to be conducted. Accordingly, by-elections were held for five constituencies—plus, the constituency vacated by Ram Baran Yadav after he became the president. In the by-elections, the Maoist party won three seats, and the NC, UML and MJF won one seat each.

The proportional representation race (see Table 3) was intended to result in an increase in the number of female MPs, and MPs from the Madhesi community, indigenous groups, the dalits and people living in the backward regions. The Madhesi community was most advantaged with their representation in the PR race due to the provision of a short list in which parties fielding less than 100 candidates did not have to follow quota rules. Unfortunately, this increased representation did not accommodate excluded groups from the Madhesi community, who have always been excluded from the political makeup in Nepal.

Table 3: Results for the Proportional Representation race

Political party	*Quota-based proportional representation*			
	Votes	*Per cent*	*Seats*	*Per cent*
Communist Party of Nepal (Maoists)	3,144,204	29.28	100	29.85
Nepali Congress	2,269,883	21.14	73	21.79
Nepal Communist Party (UML)	2,183,370	20.33	70	20.90
Madhesi People's Rights Forum, Nepal (MJF)	678,327	6.32	22	6.57
Tarai Madhes Lokatantrik Party	338,930	3.16	11	3.28
Rastriya Prajatantra Party	263,431	2.45	8	2.39
Communist Party of Nepal (Marxist-Leninist)	243,545	2.27	8	2.39
Sadbhavana Party	167,517	1.56	5	1.49
Janamorcha Nepal	164,381	1.53	5	1.49
Communist Party of Nepal (United)	154,968	1.44	5	1.49
Rastriya Prajatantra Party Nepal	110,519	1.03	4	1.19
Rastriya Janamorcha	106,224	0.99	3	0.90
Rastriya Janashakti Party	102,147	0.95	3	0.90
Nepal Workers and Peasants' Party	74,089	0.69	2	0.60
Sanghiya Lokatantrik Rastriya Manch	71,958	0.67	2	0.60
Nepal Sadbhavana Party (Anandi Devi)	55,671	0.52	2	0.60
Rastriya Janamukti Party	53,910	0.50	2	0.60
Nepali Janata Dal	48,990	0.46	2	0.60
Nepal Communist Party (Unified)	48,600	0.45	2	0.60
Dalit Janjati Party	40,348	0.38	1	0.30
NepaRastriya Party	37,757	0.35	1	0.30
Samajbadi Janata Party Nepal	35,752	0.33	1	0.30
Churebhavar Rastriya Ekta Party Nepal	28,575	0.27	1	0.30
Nepal Lokatantrik Samajbadi Dal	25,022	0.23	1	0.30
Nepal Pariwar Dal	23,512	0.22	1	0.30
Total for parties winning seats	10,471,630	100.0	335	100.0

Source: The Election Commission of Nepal (2008, 190–292).

Before the election, the Maoists had demanded that the number of seats allocated under the proportional system should rise from 240 to 335. This increase ultimately benefited the Nepali Congress and the UML parties. Significantly, if the Nepali Congress had agreed to adopt a full proportional voting system the margin of their seat difference, compared to the Maoists, would have been less. For example, if the Congress had agreed use of a mixed member proportional system as outlined earlier, the Maoists would have secured only 169 seats overall while the Nepali Congress and UML parties would have secured a total of 123 seats and 118 seats respectively, making the margin of difference smaller in the number seats these parties had. These revelations demonstrate how important the nature of an electoral system is for shaping the outcome of an election.

By the end of the count of votes for all races, including the distribution of the appointed seats, the Maoists had secured the first position with 229 seats—nearly double the number of seats of its closest rival, the Nepali Congress, which secured 115 seats. In the third place was the Unified Marxist Leninist party, with 108 seats. With their outstanding victory, the Maoists established a clear leftist domination in Nepal's Parliament for the first time.

As far as the smaller parties were concerned, the Madhesi Forum party took the fourth position—with 54 seats—establishing itself as the largest Madhesi party in the parliament. The Forum party, along with the Loktantrik and Sadbhavana parties, took nearly 14 per cent of the seats. This was a huge increase for the Madhesi parties, which secured less than three per cent of the seats in the 1999 parliament. Twenty-five political parties were represented in the new parliament—the highest number ever in Nepal's parliamentary history. Table 4 provides a comprehensive picture of the final results.

Table 4: Final results

Political party	*PR*	*FPTP*	*Appointed by Council of Ministers*	*Total*
	Seats	*Seats*		*Seats*
Communist Party of Nepal (Maoists)	100	120	9	229
Nepali Congress	73	37	5	115
Nepal Communist Party (UML)	70	33	5	108
Madhesi People's Rights Forum, Nepal (MJF)	22	30	2	54
Tarai Madhes Lokatantrik Party	11	9	1	21
Sadbhavana Party	5	4	0	9
Communist Party of Nepal (Marxist-Leninist)	8	0	1	9

Political party	*PR*	*FPTP*	*Appointed by Council of Ministers*	*Total*
	Seats	*Seats*		*Seats*
Rastriya Prajatantra Party	8	0	0	8
Janamorcha Nepal	5	2	1	8
Nepal Workers and Peasants' Party	2	2	1	5
Communist Party of Nepal (United)	5	0	0	5
Rastriya Prajatantra Party Nepal	4	0	0	4
Rastriya Janamorcha	3	1	0	4
Rastriya Janashakti Party	3	0	0	3
Other parties/independents winning seats	16	2	1	19
Total for parties winning seats	335	240	26	601

Source: The Election Commission of Nepal (2008, 16–292).
Note: The number of appointed seats have been specified based on the interviews with the leaders.

The quotas in the proportional race also resulted in 33.9 per cent of elected 575 seats going to representatives of the Madhesi community; 33.9 per cent of the seats going to representatives of the indigenous community; and 8.9 per cent of seats going to representatives of the Dalit community as can be seen from the data in Table 5. Most impressively, women captured 33.2 per cent of the seats—making Nepal the first country in South Asia to have such a large number of women in its parliament (fourteenth in the global ranking of women representation in national parliaments). With these results, Nepal's parliament reflected, for the first time, the approximate *face* of the country.

Table 5: The approximate composition of different groups in the Constituent Assembly (only out of elected seats)

Group	*% of representation in the FPTP*	*% of representation in PR*	*In numbers out of a total of elected 575*	*% of a total of elected 575*
Women	12.5	48.1	191	33.2
Madhesi	30.8	36.1	195	33.9
Dalit	2.9	13.1	51	8.9
Janajatis	32.1	35.2	195	33.9
Backward regions (representing nine remote districts)	5.0	3.0	22	3.8
Others	41.7	28.1	194	33.4

Source: Vollan (2011, 140).

But the election results were also spectacular in other ways. The party that had fought an armed insurgency for ten years emerged as the largest party in the parliament. The ex-rebels became the first-ever Maoist party in the world to win a national election. One of the explanations of why the Maoists won the largest number of seats in the Assembly was that they were the most effective—through means fair or foul—on the ground, giving the assurances of peace and change that the Nepalese people wanted.

The Nepali Congress, the party that provided its distinct leadership in the peace process, lost the most. They had never before suffered such a humiliating electoral defeat. Their *fall from grace* was attributed to organisational weakness an inefficient, outmoded election model and strategy, and internal rifts that failed to take advantage of the divided leftist vote (of the Maoists and the UML parties) and the divided Madhesi votes (of the Forum, Lokatantrik and Sadbhavana parties).

The emergence of the Madhesi regional parties as the fourth political force in Nepal also marked an important shift in the locus of state power. It signified the end of the almost monopolistic dominance of the few hill community people. The strong representation of the Madhesis in the Constituent Assembly also established the influence of this previously marginalised ethnic group in future Nepalese politics.

Overall, the Nepalese cast their votes with considerable sophistication. Although they swept the Maoists into power, as the largest single party, they elected a pluralistic Constituent Assembly—giving none of the three major parties enough votes to pass far-reaching legislation without support from each other. The Nepalese people's message to the political parties seemed clear. Thoroughly *sick* of terror, deprivation and chaos, they wanted the politicians of all shades to work together to solve the country's problems.

Reflecting on the election results the Chief said:

> The results had come as a surprise to everyone. In fact, the results came as quite a surprise to the central level party bosses of the Maoists themselves. During our interaction with them, at the time of nominations, they confided in us that they hoped to do well in the proportional race but were not confident about the outcome of the FPTP race.
>
> The UML's internal assessment was that it would emerge as the largest party because of the continuing violence of the Maoists and the persistent non-performance of the Congress-led government.

For me too, the election results were big news. Throughout the election process I had been revising my strategy and devising tactical ploys, assuming that the Maoists would not be the largest party in the parliament and that they would be the most rebellious of the losers. The results proved that all our election strategies were based on incorrect assumptions.

The reason behind most analysts failing to predict the election outcome could have been because we banned pre-election polls. Since ours was a post-conflict election, I was worried that if pre-election surveys showed the weak position of any major party, like the Congress, the UML, or the Maoists, that party could abandon the election through some ruse or another. After two postponements, I did not want to take any risks. With the wisdom of hindsight, I think that we should have allowed these pre-poll surveys. This openness would have made the election result projections more confirmatory and more realistic.

Unlike the FPTP race, the declaration of the quota-based proportional results was not as simple. The first lists of candidates that the political parties submitted for the proportional race were a disaster. Not a single party was able to produce an accurate list, because of our complex quota system.

Due to the lack of a pre-ranking candidate list system, each candidate in the proportional list wanted to be selected. The party headquarters were besieged by party members. I also heard that some of these seats were even bought and sold.

We also faced other challenges during the process, related to the fluid political context. Some new parties did not even know if their nominated candidates were male or female. In the case of the Madhesi parties, although they only had to adhere to a quota for women, they failed to come up with names of female candidates. The Commission had to be really strict with them.

One important lesson we learnt was about the need to establish a threshold in the proportional race—that is the minimum percentage of votes that a party must receive to win a seat in the proportional race. In the post-conflict context we thought it was not necessary to establish such a threshold. We wanted our constitution-making body to include as many voices as possible. But due to the absence of a threshold, many smaller parties, even those with only 0.22 per cent of the votes—secured a seat in the proportional race.

That was clearly a mistake. There was no need for 25 parties to be in the parliament. Actually, we would have had five *more* parties in the parliament if we had adopted an *unmodified Sainte-Laguë method*, instead of the modified system we used. It was one of the members of the State Affairs Committee,

Minendra Rijal, who had the foresight to convince us to use the *modified Sainte-Laguë method*, fearing there would otherwise be too many small parties in the parliament. Undoubtedly, these small technical processes were more important than we thought.

Despite these shortcomings and complications, the quota-based proportional voting system resulted in the representation that the major political parties intended to have.

Of course, inclusion of excluded subgroups, within these broader groups, remains a challenge. But there is only so much that an election can do. If quotas were more specifically targeted, only at groups requiring affirmative action, they would be more effective for the marginalised. But instead of targeting the quotas the political parties had decided to divide them among the whole population of Nepal, in accordance with their share.

These election results put previously dominant parties in unexpected positions. Until the last day of the election, the prediction was that the Maoists would finish as a distant third. The international community was aghast, when the results were announced, and India was said to be in *panic mode*. They were not prepared for a Maoist victory and they didn't have any idea how they would deal with the triumph of the ex-rebels.

The same Congress and UML leaders, who had congratulated me on the successful completion of the election, now started protesting that it was not free and that it had been influenced by Maoist violence.

Their change of attitude made me wonder if these leaders would have accepted the overall results had the Maoists not won in the key constituencies of Kathmandu and Lalitpur—where, it should be said, several prominent international observers testified to a smooth and peaceful polling day.

The only person who did not change his tone, after the disastrous results of the Nepali Congress were announced, was Koirala. It is likely that on the eve of the election, he had already sensed his party's defeat. From my experience in the Home Ministry, I knew that as a prime minister, Koirala could access confidential reports from security and intelligence agencies. However, at that point in his life, a win by the Nepali Congress did not matter much to him. The only thing he wanted was the peaceful and meaningful completion of the Constituent Assembly election.

Koirala's attitude was an important reason why the election results were not violently opposed, as often happens in post-conflict countries. More importantly, the international community also encouraged acceptance of the results. When the UN legitimises an election, the rest of the international community cannot

Figure 21: Newly elected Constituent Assembly members from Tarai entering the Constituent Assembly hall premises to take the oath of office
Source: Photo by Bhashwor Ojha.

Figure 22: Newly elected Constituent Assembly members taking the oath of office
Source: Photo by Bhashwor Ojha.

Figure 23: The first meeting of the Constituent Assembly
Source: The Parliament Secretariat.

generally discredit the process. Positive reports from international observation missions also helped to create pressure for acceptance of the results.

When I called the Maoist chairman to congratulate him, I also reminded him that the international observers—whom he had accused of coming to help defeat the Maoists—were the ones who gave legitimacy to the election, making it possible for someone from an armed movement to become a democratically elected leader of the country.

To sum up, many critics pointed out *irregularities* in the election—such as allegations that the Maoist Deputy leader Bhattarai got more votes than there were actual voters in his constituency! I admit this election was not perfect. Yet, it achieved what was intended—making the former rebels accept the democratic process and put away their weapons forever.

Epilogue: Working Towards Peace

On the evening of 11 June 2008 the last King of Nepal—the last monarch of the centuries-old Shah dynasty—and his consort, the last Queen, drove out of the Narayanhiti Palace, en route to their new home in the suburbs of Kathmandu. Nagarjun Palace, a dilapidated old hunting lodge, was located amidst the pine trees of Rani Ban (Queen's Forest). The building had been provided, somewhat reluctantly, to the former Head of State by the Government of Nepal.

As they left Narayanhiti Palace a huge group of excited spectators and security officials surrounded the royal couple. The ex-King looked stern but largely

Figure 24: Gyanendra Shah during a press conference before vacating the Royal Palace
Source: Photo by Bhashwor Ojha.

Figure 25: Ram Baran Yadav taking the oath of office as the first President of the Federal Republic of Nepal from the Chief Justice. Vice President Parmananda Jha is next to him. *Source*: Photo by Chandra Shekhar Karki.

Figure 26: President of Nepal administering the oath of office to the newly elected prime minister from the Maoist party. Chairman of the CA Subhash Nembang in the Centre. *Source*: Department of Information, Nepal.

unaffected, while his wife wore an uncomfortable smile. As they passed by, the deposed King raised his hands in *namaste*, waving to the crowd—some of whom were celebrating the declaration of the republic and shouting anti-King slogans. Others were in tears, as they bid farewell to their beloved monarch.

Soon after ex-King Gyanendra Shah vacated the Narayanhiti Palace, the Nepali Congress General Secretary Ram Baran Yadav—a medical doctor by profession—was elected the new Head of State and the first President of Nepal. Yadav was the first person from the previously discriminated Madhesi community to hold such a high position.

Things began to change swiftly. Just a few months later, the Maoist Chairman Pushpa Kamal Dahal, an ex-rebel, became the Prime Minister of Nepal. The Nepalese saw a ray of hope in this strong and capable man, and in his committed party. Nonetheless, before he could make any notable impact, nine months later Dahal had to give up his prime ministership. He had controversially fired Army Chief Rukmangad Katuwal, a move which led nearly all other political parties to petition the President to reverse his decision. Clearly rattled, Dahal quit, and what can be characterised as *sharp political polarisation* followed. Street protests, political bickering and parliamentary deadlock virtually brought the processes of change to a grinding halt.

Both the peace process and the constitution-making exercise were adversely affected. How to achieve integration of the Maoist combatants remained undecided, and the constitution drafting deadline of May 2010 could not be met, and had be to extended several times. All in all, the post-Constituent Assembly election period was marked by nagging uncertainty, inter-party and intra-party squabbling, political and executive instability, a slowing down of developmental work, and a general lack of progress that further drained the energy of the Nepalese people and postponed the fulfilment of their hopes and dreams.

In January 2011, the United Nations Mission in Nepal departed the country, leaving the management of the Maoist combatants unresolved. India was blamed for being instrumental in pushing the Mission out of its backyard; the reason, it was supposed, was that the presence of the UN had thwarted India's desire to control the political process in Nepal.

After the UNMIN's departure, the onerous task of monitoring, integrating, and rehabilitating the restless Maoist combatants stationed in makeshift cantonments, was handed over to a special committee, comprised of leaders from major political parties. But this special committee failed to make any immediate progress on the management of the Maoist combatants, due to the ongoing political differences.

Time slipped by. After nearly three-and-a-half years of crippling political stalemate a seven-point agreement was signed by the major political parties in November 2011. The agreement was signed under the leadership of Deputy Maoist leader Baburam Bhattarai, who had become the prime minister in August 2011. The intention was to get things moving again. The agreement paved the way for the management of the Maoist combatants, who were still living in shabby cantonments—which had been hastily erected at the onset of the peace process. According to the agreement, 6,500 of the 19,602 (UN-verified) combatants would be integrated into the Nepal Army. The others could choose either voluntary retirement with cash incentives or a rehabilitation package. All the Maoist weapons would also come under government control. The new process to integrate and rehabilitate the Maoist combatants raised hopes that a new constitution could soon be agreed upon.

Unexpectedly, this progress in the management of the Maoist Army failed to reflect similar progress in the writing of the constitution. In November 2011, the term of the Constituent Assembly was again extended for a further six months—with the Supreme Court ruling that this fourth extension, which would end on 27 May 2012, would be the last. If the Constituent Assembly failed to finalise the constitution this time, the Supreme Court said there should be fresh elections to form a new Assembly, or a referendum, or another appropriate arrangement had to be put in place.

Unfortunately, the political parties again failed to agree on the content of the new constitution. The main difference remained disagreement about the nature of the formation of federal states. The Maoists demanded that federal states should be formed along ethnic identity lines, but other political parties, in particular the Nepali Congress and the Unified Marxist Leninist—rejected this idea. When the political parties failed to reach an agreement on the new constitution, they tried again to extend the deadline but their request was rejected by the Supreme Court, and around midnight on 27 May 2012 Prime Minister Baburam Bhattarai declared a new election for another Constituent Assembly. In effect, the Constituent Assembly elected on 10 April 2008 was considered to be dissolved.

Since then, the political landscape in Nepal has once again been marked by uncertainty and pessimism. This political crisis was further complicated by a split in the Maoist party in June 2012, between hardliners and moderates.

Particularly worrying has been the trend for some former Maoist soldiers to join the hard-line faction in the party. At the time of writing this book, the President is calling upon political parties to form a new consensus government, in preparation for a new election. But to date, the parties have failed to respond, creating a deep political vacuum in the country.

Despite these setbacks, the progress made on the management of the Maoist combatants, which was an important part of Nepal's peace building process, has offered some relief. Most Maoist combatants have opted for voluntary retirement with cash packages and have returned to their families. Over 1,400 have been integrated into the Nepal Army, and the few remaining combatants have chosen rehabilitation packages. All the Maoist weapons and cantonments are now under government control. This, perhaps, can be considered the main achievement of the Constituent Assembly election of April 2008. Equally importantly, the Maoist party had accepted the principle of multiparty democratic competition. After the fall of the Maoist-led government in August 2009, the Maoist party accepted the succession of two UML-led governments, reflecting their transformation into a democratic force. Hence, the Constituent Assembly election of 2008 can be said to have contributed not only to conflict resolution but also to consolidating democracy in Nepal.

Moving on to the three main protagonists of this narrative, Gyanendra Shah, Girija Prasad Koirala and Puspha Kamal Dahal, their lives changed greatly after the election. During the course of the research for this book the authors had the opportunity to speak to them. These interactions revealed many valuable memories, which can be stored for posterity.

Once King Gyanendra Bir Bikram Shah had become an *ordinary* Nepalese citizen, he moved out of the Nagarjun Palace into his own house in Maharajgunj. The government provided him with around 50 security personnel as a former Head of State, although they can be removed from his staff at any time. He was granted no other privileges.

When asked for an interview by the authors, to clarify a few issues, the former King was initially reluctant. According to his personal secretary, Sagar Timilsina, he had received countless requests for meetings and interviews—especially by foreign reporters and writers. It may have been Bhojraj Pokharel's public service reputation that finally persuaded the ex-ruler to agree to a meeting. Extraordinarily, Pokharel had never met the ex-King in person before, despite a long career in Nepal's civil service.

In 2009, a few months after the declaration of the republic, Pokharel went to meet the ex-King at Nirmal Niwas. He was confident about meeting the King but had a dilemma. As the person who had conducted the very election that had ended the monarchy, Pokharel felt he could not address Gyanendra Shah as a Maharajdhiraj—as if nothing had happened. At the same time, he did not want to offend his interviewee by calling him the *former King*, as the media had started to do. There was also the question of conducting the interview in either the honorific language used for royals (*hajur*) or the honorific language used for ordinary, but respected or elderly citizens or parents (*tapai*).

During the interview, Shah diplomatically curtailed the dilemma by speaking in English, which no longer has feudalistic connotations. And Pokharel managed to avoid addressing the former King directly. Shah openly shared his feelings but as he smoked his famous 555 brand cigarettes continuously, his restlessness and anxiety was evident.

The ex-King claimed that he was concerned about what was going on in the country. He said, "Political parties need to get together to solve the country's problems." Shah also revealed that senior leaders in the Maoist party had tried to meet him many times before. He explained, "I could not meet them because they were still branded as terrorists. As Head of State, I thought it would be inappropriate to meet them."

Shah also addressed the accusation that he had been against the transformation into a multiparty democratic system in 1990. He said, "...actually, during panchayat times, we were so tired of factionalism that His Majesty and I discussed whether liberal democracy could be better for Nepal." It was only later that he, and other royals, became dissatisfied with Nepal's democracy. This was mainly due to reports about rampant corruption at every tier of bureaucracy, within the police and the government, and the absence of basic law and order, which marked the post-1990 political scenario.

Apart from discussing politics, the dethroned ruler also shared his personal feelings. Shah said he was quite worried about his mother. He asked, "What did my old mother do to deserve such a punishment? Why was she subjected to so much humiliation?"

Shah also admitted that he was financially somewhat insecure, "I don't have as much money as people speculate." He also said that he might have to go to court to assert his civilian rights. He was referring to many royal properties which were being nationalised at the time. He explained, "As King, I tried to put all the royal properties into His Majesty's name, so they would be consolidated and institutionalised. But the people interpreted it differently."

Although it was not the intention to ask Shah about the Royal massacre, he did talk about it and seemed genuinely moved about the blood bath. He said, "People think that I masterminded the massacre but the reason for it was that the Crown Prince was unhappy about many things."

A palace official later confirmed Shah's comment, adding, "Crown Prince Diprendra looked quite disturbed that morning before the massacre happened because the Queen was talking about declaring the youngest Prince, Nirajan, the successor in his place if Crown Prince Diprendra married Devyani against her wishes."

Chairman Dahal became the first elected Maoist prime minister in Nepal. The authors met the former rebel leader several times. Dahal, unlike any other leader in Nepal, had the power to make people around him feel good. His greatest strength was that he knew how to please people, speaking the right words at the right time. In all our meetings, he seemed concerned about what had been going on in the country, and expressed a desire to solve the problems Nepal faced. But without mentioning names, he claimed he was constrained by many domestic and global factors that were contributing to the prevailing political problems.

He also explained:

> It was me who first mooted the idea of the Constituent Assembly election, as a unifying strategy for all political forces in the country. We were firm in our commitment to the Constituent Assembly election; that's why all this was finally possible. I have said this clearly to many international friends—we won't go back to the jungle. It seems some forces want us to abandon the path of peace.

Dahal also told the authors that the euphoria unleashed by the election was killed by the formation of a new government under the leadership of Madhav Kumar Nepal, who had been defeated from two constituencies in the election. On another occasion, Dahal spoke to the authors about the unsolved mystery of the Narayanhiti Palace massacre. He said:

> Personally, I have reasons to believe that the slaughter was politically machinated. We were to meet Birendra just a few days after the shoot-out took place. His brother Dhirendra was facilitating this parley, which was to be held in Pokhara . . .That whole week I had worked really hard preparing notes and scribbling

> talking points for my planned discussion with Birendra...Essentially, I wanted to tell him that we should get together, otherwise soon enough India was bound to finish the monarchy as well as the Maoists. Rather astonishingly, just before we were supposed to meet him, the bizarre massacre took place...How would anyone feel in such circumstances, which were too coincidental to ignore?

Dahal also shared his nervousness about the transition to a federal system. He said, "In the end, it is likely that there will be six or seven states. We have also made up our mind to move in that direction." In another conversation with the authors, Dahal reiterated his commitment to peace and multiparty democratic institutions.

He declared:

> Many people doubted us earlier as well, but the reason why we came to the peace process is because we have accepted the principles of peace and democracy, and we don't plan to renege on our commitment.

Girija Prasad Koirala was satisfied with the outcome of the Constituent Assembly election, even though the results were not favourable for his party. Above all he had campaigned for the peaceful and meaningful completion of the election. When we spoke to Koirala he was no longer the prime minister and there were reports that the Maoists would support him to become the first President of Nepal. But the Maoists backtracked, encouraged by New Delhi—which was not keen to see Koirala as President. Many political analysts have claimed that this led to the political polarisation that marked the post-Constituent Assembly election period.

The authors went to meet with Koirala several times. Although he was not in a position of power, he wielded considerable influence over the political circle that was. Attempts to weaken him in, and outside of his party had not dented his authority and he was frank during our conversations. However, he did sometimes ask that his comments not be reported.*

During another conversation, just after the Maoists had resigned from the Government, he told the authors:

> I tried to bring all the forces together but it was difficult. I don't know how to manage it further. Prachanda *jee* and Baburam *jee* come here...They agree about something, but then they do the complete opposite. What can I do, Prachanda's decisions change a lot?

* Sections of conversation which Koirala specifically requested should not be reported have not been shared in this book.

Koirala also talked about the Maoists withdrawal from the government. He said:

> I told Prachanda not to resign. I told him that even if you want to resign please come and talk to me for an hour. Then if you still want to resign, you can. But Prachanda resigned without even bothering to talk to me...I wanted to tell Prachanda that India would never agree to him interfering with the Nepalese Army, as that would threaten India's security. But Prachanda resigned without letting me discuss this grave issue with him. Later I lambasted Prachanda. Why did you resign without even talking to me, I asked? Then Prachandha *jee* replied, "*Thulo dhoka bhayo*." [That was a huge betrayal]. I said to Prachanda, I know how this betrayal happened. Didn't your party's problems start after you merged with the Nepal Unity Centre party? When I said this, Prachanda jee did not say a word. He just kept quiet.

Koirala was hinting that agents of some foreign forces had infiltrated the Maoist party, in order to weaken it. In one meeting, Koirala also shared his views about the abolished monarchy. He told us, "I was never for the abolition of the monarchy, but the circumstances pushed me." Then he related an incident about the former King that led to the deterioration of their personal rapport. He said:

> In December 2002, I was invited to the wedding of my grand-nephew, Niranjan's son, in Delhi. I informed the King about my personal visit to Delhi, as I always did when I went abroad. The King inquired if I planned to meet any Maoists there, which I denied because it was a purely social visit. Then, early next morning someone knocked on my door. It was the former Indian ambassador, Shyam Saran. He said he'd came to meet me because the King had told him that GP was planning to meet the Maoists during his visit to Delhi, and he wanted to know if that was true. I was shocked. I could not believe that the King could *double-speak*. I immediately called Prime Minister Lokendra and shouted at him. I told him that if the King behaved like this I would have nothing more to do with him. I said I had dealt with his father, and grandfather, but no one before had behaved like that.

In another conversation, Koirala talked about the political complexities associated with growing ethnic assertiveness. He said:

> What can I do? Identity politics have really made things complicated. Once some Koiralas came and said that we should make a Koirala Society, to ensure the representation of Koiralas. It made me so angry that I scolded them. I told them it is fine if you want to make a genealogy of Koiralas or a family tree but

> talking about this kind of representation is absurd. I also say this to Muslims and Christians—hasn't the state started giving you holidays on your major festival days? Doesn't that mean that the state has recognised your identity? The Maoist talk about ethnic federalism is foolish. They talk without understanding its full implications. Are you Prithivinarayan Shah? Are you trying to be one? I once asked Prachanda.

The next time, the authors met Koirala his health was not good. At the end of that meeting, he said:

> The only way Nepal's progress can be ensured is if the interests of India and China are complementary, vis-à-vis Nepal. I have tried to talk about this with Indian as well as Chinese diplomats. I once asked an Indian diplomat, isn't it beneficial for you if there is stability in Nepal? He replied, 'Yes.' I asked a Chinese diplomat the same question, isn't Nepal's stability in your own interest? The Chinese diplomat also said, 'Yes!' But when I ask them, why their interests cannot meet in Nepal, all that they say is that India and China have come quite close together because of their economic alliance and the sharing of military technologies. They say that but in practice they haven't been able to come together with a common set of interests relating to Nepal. I have tried my best; this is the one thing that I must try to do before I die, but it appears hard.

As the authors prepared to leave, Koirala told Pokharel, "You are leaving again to go to the US for study. Go . . . go! Stay there for four or five years; the situation in Nepal is bad."

That was the last time we saw Koirala. He died on 20 March 2010, in his daughter's home. Like his brother Bishweshwar Prasad Koirala, he had refused the doctors' advice to go to India for medical treatment because he knew that the end was near and he did not want to die in a foreign land.

Postscript: Bhojraj Pokharel

On the Constituent Assembly Election

The formation of an elected Constituent Assembly, which would draft a new constitution, has been an unfulfilled dream in Nepal for half a century. Finally, the 2006 Comprehensive Peace Agreement, which ended the decade-long Maoist insurgency, paved the way for its realisation. The political leaders desperately sought a person who could lead this process.

"This country has invested so much in you. And now when the country needs you, you are running away from your responsibilities. Aren't you betraying your motherland?" These were the powerful words of the octogenarian Prime Minister, Girija Prasad Koirala, the icon of Nepal's peace process—who pressurised me into accepting the position of Chief Election Commissioner. This was an offer I had turned down several times before. After serving almost 27 years in public service, I was not interested in going back into that sector. Furthermore, the King had used extra-constitutional powers to reject my name for the same position in 2003, so I had no interest in the post.

The day I was appointed, 30 October 2006, the Comprehensive Peace Agreement (CPA) was yet to be finalised and the Interim Constitution was far from being drafted. But I was strongly advised, by all the key political leaders, that I should not waste a single minute and start preparations as soon as possible for the Constituent Assembly election expected for mid-June 2007. I had to start in a *total vacuum* situation. There was no clarity on any issue, such as the nature of the electoral system; the number of seats there would be in the CA; the number of electoral constituencies there would be; the eligibility criteria for people permitted to vote; method of identifying an electorate; and legal and other tools required to make the election a success.

With time running out rapidly, if the election was to take place in June the following year, the major political parties—including the Maoists—agreed to grant voting rights to all people over eighteen years old on 15 November 2006. The Voter's Registration Act was passed in the first week of December 2006. Even today I shiver with anxiety when I remember the amount of work involved in putting together the voters' list within one month of the legislation being promulgated. We had to prepare the by-laws, design around seventy types of voter registration related forms, and print them off, so they could be used by around 28,000 registration staff around the country. Designing the training curriculum, identifying the voter registration staff, engaging the trainers and training these 28,000 staff, and deploying those officials to the registration process in a political context marked by deep insecurity was not easy to achieve. But we felt that if there was sincere commitment, and a great effort made, it could be done. In the end, the Commission was able to register about 17.6 millions voters on time.

The Interim Constitution, promulgated in January 2007, addressed macro level electoral issues. However, some key electoral issues were to be resolved later by legislation. Unfortunately, these issues were not addressed in time and the ECN was forced to postpone the election in June 2007. The parties later decided to hold the election in November that year. But even though the Commission was ready to hold an election in November, from a legal and technical point of view, political considerations forced the ECN to yet again, cancel the process on the day candidates were queuing up to submit their nomination papers. Finally, at the third attempt, we were able to successfully conduct the CA election in April 2008.

In the beginning, I misunderstood the political realities and aspired to create a new milestone in the electoral history of Nepal by conducting an exemplary election. This was the commitment I had made during the parliamentary hearing process before I was appointed. But soon I realised this post-conflict election would not be a *regular* election, but part of the ongoing peace process. As such it would be driven by political process, rather than by inbuilt electoral tools and technical boundaries. Any election, even with all technicalities and legalities resolved, will have no meaning if it is not politically acceptable. And political acceptance is more challenging in a post-conflict period. The ECN, which enjoyed the confidence of the political stakeholders, played a facilitating role in bringing the conflicting forces together. Thus, the election managers could not detach themselves from the management of the post-conflict political climate, even if that was beyond their formal role.

Every election is difficult to manage. Even elections in *older democracies* are not free from controversy. The Constituent Assembly election in Nepal was also an endeavour to bring the Maoist rebels into a democratic electoral process. Moreover, it was an electoral *game*, which the political actors had agreed to play even if they were unequal players. The background was a decade-long gun culture, with combatants housed in the UN-monitored cantonments. Some parties had electoral experience, some others had none. As the manager of this process, I became an *umpire* of these games. Striking a balance between the independent role of the Commission, the electoral norms, and the spirit of the peace process was difficult. This situation often required that the Election Commission be flexible and make compromises, in order to support the ongoing peace process. We tried to respond to the mood of political, as well as non-political actors—whether national or international. The aim was to bring the Maoists into the election process, whatever the cost. The ECN was often faced with the choice of accepting difficult demands, which were not generally acceptable in *normal* elections, or rejecting them and risk being blamed for allowing the rebels to boycott the elections. In these difficult circumstances our priority remained to support the peace process and bring all the political forces into the CA election.

In spite of serious political, security, technical, logistical and legal challenges finally the election was successfully completed. But in order to make it happen sometimes the EC, and even I, had to breach the traditional and constitutional limits of the Commission. I know that this proactive facilitating role was appreciated and encouraged by *almost* all the key players. There was hardly any progressive person who was not happy the day that the polling was conducted peacefully and successfully. But it did not take long for this happiness to turn into anger and hatred. Before the election, everyone's priority had been to conclude the process. The country's leaders often told me that the election should take place on a specified date, whatever the cost.

I clearly recall 10 April 2008—immediately after the poll—everyone, including key national and international actors, competed to extend their congratulations to the Commission, and especially to me. All of them said: "...you have done a great job. No one expected the election to be so peaceful or successful. You have performed magic. You deserve the highest reward for your work."

But gradually everything changed. And when the results started to come in, the same people who had commended our work started to condemn it. Instead they said: "This is the worst election I have seen in my life. Was it even an election? I am ashamed to call it an election. It was rather a show of force by a single party's gun."

I can understand why their stance changed so rapidly. It was not the decision of the ECN to hold an election without first resolving the management of the ex-combatants but of political actors who pushed the ECN into that position. This was because at that time the Maoist guns were useful to the politicians, who wanted to counter the King—their number one enemy.

But some of the leaders had *counted their chickens before they were hatched.* They were confident about their victory and expected lucrative presidential and prime ministerial positions immediately after the results. One of the biggest problems with political leaders, especially in the third world, is that if elections do not go in their favour, they turn their *barrel* towards the performance of the Election Commissions and their work, instead of evaluating their own performance. No one in Nepal, or in the outside world, had imagined that the Maoists would come out as the single largest party—everyone expected they would come a distant third. This was a *shocking* outcome for most people and very few were ready to accept the reality.

It is the job of the political pundits to analyse the election results, but I would like to share my views. Firstly, I believe people felt that the Maoists would be less threatening in parliament, and this influenced the voting pattern. Secondly, people may not have been voting in favour of the Maoists but rather against the continuous bad performance of other political parties who had been in power since the 1990s. Thirdly, the Maoists were able to convince voters that they would introduce good governance and focus on the people's agenda, which, unfortunately, they later failed to do. Fourthly, voting was also influenced by the Maoists psychological and physical threats—especially during the violent campaign period—or by the persuasive slogans the Maoists used. Finally, for years the Maoists had prevented other political parties being active in their strong-hold areas, and this limited campaigning. In remote areas, specifically for younger generations, the Maoists were the only political party they knew. All these factors combined to contribute to the Maoist victory.

It should be remembered that electoral violence is not new in Nepal and even previous elections—conducted in *normal* situations—had witnessed much violence. But this time we were managing an election in an extremely difficult and insecure period, during which the intensity of violence was far greater than ever before. It is sad that we failed to create an *enabling*, secure environment throughout the campaign period. Unless a culture of non-violence is developed, we will continue to see the will of the people and the outcome of the election stolen by fear and by influence of money, whether we like it or not.

The aim was to hold an election, and it was held. It has already become one of the major events in Nepal's history. But I feel that this history does not do injustice to anyone involved, and I believe that future generations should understand the reality of this election. So, I thought it was my duty to share what I knew as the manager of this process. I also wanted to share the reality of the context in which the election was held, and the challenges we faced and compromises we made in order to make this election possible. I also wanted to reflect on how an electoral process could help support a peace process. Thus, our account offers an important, if small part, of the modern political history of Nepal. It also provides a contribution to the global history of democracy.

The environment for the CA election was challenging and frustrating. However, the enthusiastic involvement of all actors, whether inside Nepal or external, made it a success. Some of the innovative approaches the Commission adopted made a positive impact on the overall election process. To cite a few of them: mobilisation of two teachers, proficient in local languages, in every community in order to educate voters about their choices; using seventeen different languages in media campaign for voter education; and extending a personal household invitation to voters. All these tactics helped to mobilise voters. In addition, sending government secretaries into the districts during the election period not only helped to build the confidence of the polling-station workers but also played a key role in creating an enabling election environment.

Although there are different opinions about the UNMIN's role in Nepal's peace process, I have no regrets about inviting them to provide technical assistance during the election. I must praise the work of the UN, and its dedicated staff, for helping to create the right environment for the election. My gratitude goes particularly to Ian Martin, the UN Secretary General's Special Representative to Nepal and Craig Jenness, Director of the Electoral Division at UNHQ, for their valuable contribution throughout. I am also grateful to the international community for its overall sincere support.

Disappointingly, soon after the election political parties seemed distracted from both the ongoing peace process and the constitution-making exercise, and began bickering for power. I wondered why I had put in so much effort into making the election a success, at a huge risk to myself, only for this to be the outcome. These feelings of frustration and revulsion about the performance of the leaders eventually made me resign from the post of CEC. But in retrospection, and within the larger *picture* of the peace process, I believe the election was successful in many ways, and helped to end the decade-long violent conflict in Nepal. The security situation has dramatically changed. The people who once relied on bullets came to the ballot, and are now engaged in a relatively peaceful democratic process. This change should not be overlooked.

On Why the Constituent Assembly Failed

Sadly, despite several extensions, the Constituent Assembly elected on 10 April 2008 failed to deliver the constitution on time—and was dissolved at midnight on the 27 May 2012. Unexpectedly, the 27 May 2012 became one of the saddest days of my life. Different people see different reasons for this failure, but I would like to share my observations of why the CA failed to deliver the constitution.

Due to their defeat in the election, many influential leaders of various political parties remained outside the CA platform, which was not a good sign for the drafting of a consensus document. Also the time-frame we planned, within which to deliver the constitution, was not realistic. We overlooked how the long legacy of armed conflict would impact on the process. And we did not realise that we were not *simply* writing a constitution but also that we had to reconcile two distinct political philosophies—radical communist thoughts and liberal democratic values.

The crisis of confidence among, and within, the various political forces, especially between the traditionally dominant parties and the Maoists, was a major barrier to the constitution-drafting process. The dilemma was in determining which should be first, the constitution-writing or the integration of the Maoist combatants. Political parties, who sensed the influence of the People's Liberation Army (PLA) during the CA election, feared that if the PLA issue was not managed first the Maoists would dominate the political process and dictate the writing of the constitution on its own terms. On the other hand, the Maoists were suspicious that if the PLA *card* was played first their bargaining power would be reduced, and the other political parties might not agree to write the progressive constitution they wanted. It was a *chicken and egg* discussion. Except for encouraging public consultation and the CA committees' work during the initial days, much time was spend *making and breaking* the government, rather than on writing the constitution.

Each of the major parties wanted to take the credit for finalising the constitution. Hence, none of the major political parties would agree the constitution promulgated under the leadership of another party. A culture of consensus, as stipulated by the Interim Constitution, was not adhered to and every political party's hidden agenda was to weaken the other parties, and benefit from that situation. Unfortunately, the country was the main victim of this strategy.

The other major mistake we made was to give two overarching responsibilities to the elected body, that of acting as a constitution-making body—writing the constitution—as well as being the parliament which enacted laws and formed the government. Related to this was the mistake of assigning two roles to the Chairman of the CA, who also had to act as the Speaker of Parliament. Parliamentary business, especially the making and breaking of government, became the main agenda of the House, instead of constitution-drafting—the primary purpose for which the House was elected. The thirst for power dominated the House. During this period we were forced to observe an election for a prime minister, which went to the seventeenth round without being conclusive. Grabbing power was the main priority of the political parties, and the constitution-making exercise was overshadowed from the beginning.

It should also be noted that the constitution-making process was hijacked by political leaders outside the CA, meaning the formal process within was handicapped by external mechanisms. The leaders of the key political parties never prioritised their attendance at CA Committee meetings that were intended to be the entry point for the raising of constitutional issues. They were over-confident, believing that in the end they, the party leaders, would finalise the constitution and everyone else would simply agree. But this back-fired when the leadership was inconsistent and limited their interests to partisan rather than national issues.

There was also a misunderstanding about the peace process. Some people thought that once the PLA was integrated the peace process would be concluded. But this was wrong. Key peace-related institutions, such as a Truth and Reconciliation Commission, and a Commission on Missing people were not formed. And transitional justice issues were not addressed. Social and economic issues (the root causes of the conflict) outlined in the Comprehensive

Peace Agreement (CPA) were never prioritised. Many provisions of the CPA were not met, for example, the return of seized property and land. Violation of these constitutional provisions began immediately after the promulgation of the Interim Constitution.

The state restructuring agenda was also not prioritised within the CA mechanisms. Extremists (those in favour and those against) have led the *fight* for federalism. Lapses in timely national leadership/ownership further complicated the issue, which gave enough space for both extremist sides to interpret it in their own biased way. As a result, our diverse society started fragmenting along the lines, for example, of identity, geography and caste, and by the end of the life of the CA, ethnic division had resurfaced on the streets. If, as provisioned in the Interim Constitution, the State Restructuring Commission had been formed in time—with a membership of independent scholars and experts—the damage would have been minimal. Likewise, if the formal due process of voting had been followed within the CA, the contentious issue of federalism would have been settled. However, finally the issue of federalism dominated the whole constitution-writing process, and later was perceived as the main reason for the failure of the CA to promulgate the new constitution.

It is important to note that internal factionalism *within* the various political parties also blocked the progress of the constitution-writing. All the major political parties were deeply divided internally. These factions inside the parties contradicted each other on almost every issue and hence, no agreement could be reached. This meant that the leaders of most of the major political parties failed to lead their members. In particular, different views within the Maoist party about the peace process and the issues of the constitution badly affected the drafting of the constitution.

There were absolutely no other *commanding* leaders like GP Koirala at this time. Notwithstanding his weaknesses, Koirala had the ability to see his decisions implemented both inside and outside the party. The absence of such a personality also affected the overall coordination of the political parties. The lack of a common enemy, like the King during the CA election process, allowed the political parties to drift further apart.

Differences among the CA members along ethnic lines also blocked the process. This problem arose due to the failure of the political parties to be *inclusive*—in terms of representation of diverse ethnic groups—and consultative and transparent. Internal democracy and functional communication systems hardly existed in the key political parties. This created a situation in which some CA members were prepared to exceed their party's mandates on some key issues of identity.

The size of the CA was also too big to work practically. Though the body appeared to be *inclusive*, owing to the presence of diverse groups, we failed to ensure the *quality* of members. Many lacked an understanding of, and commitment to, the new constitution-writing process. Some were mobilised by interest groups, which created further complications during key negotiations. Moreover, political leaders, with few exceptions, failed to understand the mood of the country.

Constitution-writing is a political process which, at times, necessarily goes beyond the boundary of legal frameworks. It is also dominated by many unexpected political issues which demand time-consuming, complicated negotiation. Only after progress in the integration of the PLA (post-November 2011) did the constitution-drafting process accelerate and negotiations began about the most critical issues on the table. Intervention (judicial activism) of the Supreme Court was not a welcome step at this stage. History itself will evaluate the action of the Supreme Court, but my opinion is that the court should not have intervened in an area to which it could not offer any tangible solution or remedy. The Supreme Court should have understood the sensitivities of the post-conflict complicated political context.

On the Current Situation in Nepal

Recently, I interacted with the Madhesi communities in the Tarai region, talking about the post-CA scenario in the country. I did not find any one who was hopeful about the future of Nepal. I was shocked when I heard comments like: "Yes, we removed one king through the elected CA, however, *several* kings have now started operating in the country. Managing one king was at least conceivable, managing several kings is quite challenging."

It is obvious that the leadership style of the country cannot cope with the changed political context. We abolished one form of monarchy but created several other *monarchs*: this is what people seemed to be saying. It is shameful that people feel this way within such a short time of the political changes that have taken place in the country.

If we look at our history, the Nepalese have always supported political change in the country—be it the People's Movements in 1990 and 2006, the Maoist Movement, or the Madhesi Movement. Nepalese people have come out fearlessly onto the streets to support those voices for change. However, instead of being rewarded with the *fruits of change* they feel they have been always subjected to more suffering. The CA was regarded as a unique opportunity to address the issues of exclusion and marginalisation, ignored by our forefathers. But instead, ethnicity became inceasingly divisive due to the short-sightedness of the political leadership.

The multiparty democratic system is said to be the best form of government, but to be effectively functional, a democracy also demands the pursuance of a certain set of standards, values and good practices. In the multiparty system, political parties are the engine and their leaders function as its driver. But the present driving style of political leaders in Nepal appears to be very dangerous and disruptive.

No wonder that Nepal today is at a major cross-road. Frustration is mounting, especially among young people—owing to increased corruption, injustice, bad governance and a psychological fear of violence based on ethnicity, or regionalism. During this transition period we have not been able to preserve the good values of our past nor have we been able to replace bad practices with good ones.

Nepal is a land of opportunities and Nepalese society is receptive to change. People possess strong qualities, including forgiveness and a desire to be at peace. We are rich in resources and are fortunate to have a large young population. Our strategic location, between two economic giants, is advantageous. What we lack is a visionary and credible leader, who can be trusted to guide the country towards progress.

When I think about the situation in Nepal, my thoughts are both positive and negative. On the positive side, I believe that the country has at least identified its past mistakes and has started to correct them. The strong walls of exclusion, and deep-rooted social discrimination—including the issue of *untouchables*—are being addressed. Even in remote corners of the country, people are talking about empowerment and rights. Community-based organisations have become active and are leading the social and economic change agenda. Even during the conflict, our social and economic indicators increased—and continue to do so, to the surprise of the international community.

However, on the negative side, after the *death* of the Constituent Assembly—without a constitution being finalised—there were reasons to be pessimistic. Due to the ongoing constitutional and political uncertainty, our political transition period will be longer than expected, leading to greater instability.

The behaviour of the political parties is also not encouraging, and the country could be led into anarchy.

Huge differences on various constitutional and political issues are prevalent among political groups. And the majority of the parties are further divided internally on these issues. It is difficult to get any agreement about anything. The nexus between crime and politics has also increased, and the dedicated political cadres are being sidelined and replaced by corrupt ones.

Still, I am hopeful that our political leadership will become more *sensible* about prioritising national interests. They must forget their partisan concerns and focus more on the national agenda. But the window of opportunity is very limited. Whatever the process, we should not delay the construction of a new constitution, that would meet the aspirations of the Nepalese people.

My Final Thoughts

Finally, I must explain a few things about this book. Immediately after the election, many of my friends encouraged me to write a book about my experience. Since Nepal's election was part of the ongoing peace process, I felt this could be useful for other countries going through a similar situation. Hence, I decided to write in English, in order to target a wider audience outside Nepal. In October 2008, I was introduced to Shrishti Rana through the Director of IFES Peter Erben, and a few months later we decided to collaborate on this work.

Initially, my plan was to limit this book to the managerial aspect of the electoral process. However, my role in the CA election was not only to manage technical processes but also to facilitate the political process, which supported the election. For any election to be successful, the political process is equally and at times—as I said earlier—even more important than the technical process. Hence, this book has focussed more on the *political* aspects of the election process, rather than the technical preparations.

I must, nevertheless, acknowledge the limitations of this work. Due to the limited information we could gather, this work has not been able to do full justice to all the forces or actors involved in the CA election process. I must mention members of the SPA—such as the NC-D, the UML, the NWPP, the Nepal Sadhvawana Party-Anandidevi (NSP-A), the Peoples Front, and the United Left Front (ULF)—and the civil society, the media, the electoral and security personnel, whose crucial roles have not been sufficiently covered in this book. Likewise, valuable contributions have been made by many important people, like civil society leaders Dr. Devendraraj Pandey, Daman Dhungana, Krishna Pahadi, Padama Ratna Tuladhar; government officials including Home Secretary Mr. Umesh Mainali and political leaders such as Amik Sherchan, Bharat Bimal Yadav, Bijaya Kumar Gachhedar, C. P. Mainali, Dinanath Sharma, Dev Gurung, Gopal Man Shrestha, Jhal Nath Khanal, Krishna Prashad Sitaula, Krishna Bahadur Mahara, Madhav Kumar Nepal, Mahant Thakur, Narayan Man Bijukchhe, Pradip Gyawali, Rajendra Mahato, Ramchandra Poudel, Ramesh Lekhak, Ramsaran Mahat, Sher Bahadur Deuba, Subhas Nembang and Upendra Yadav. I cannot ever tire of citing the example of Madhav Kumar Nepal and his party's sacrifice, during the formation of the interim legislative Parliament—when he agreed to give the Maoists (who had not even contested the election) equal seats with the UML. I hope that the gaps in our book will soon be addressed by other writers.

I also take this opportunity to express my gratitude to fellow commissioners, hundreds of thousands of electoral staff, security officials, the international community, international and domestic observers and civil society members as well as media. Their support was invaluable to ensure success of the Constituent Assembly election in a difficult political environment. I specially appreciate ECN secretary Sushil Rana and his efficient and dedicated team members who played a key role behind the scene to make this mega event a success!

While reading this book, it may appear as if we are focusing only on Girija Prasad Koirala. This is because most of my interaction during the election process was with him—as he was the prime minister at that time. Another reason for this is because Koirala, as leader of the SPA, represented all the major democratic forces in the country. In no way do we intend to glorify Koirala as the leader of the Nepali Congress. His role in this book is solely as SPA leader and prime minister.

It is also important to understand that the characterisation of different actors in this book is based on interviews, interaction with them, and available literature. Hence, what we present is our subjective interpretation as authors. I cannot claim that this is the most accurate characterisation of these personalities. I cannot claim to have shown the *whole* truth in our account. Moreover, since most conversations in this book are based on my recollections (not written records), they may not be perfectly accurate.

Lastly, as the manager of the election process, I cannot resist sharing some of my observations on the reforms required to ensure *better* elections in the future (if the similar system and processes are followed). These are:

- ***Restricting quotas to excluded and marginalised groups***

  We made a mistake by allocating quotas, or reserved seats, in the proportional part of the election to everyone. This meant reserved seats were not only used for marginalised groups but divided among the entire population. This system not only complicated implementation of quota seats but resulted in failure to do full justice to the excluded and marginalised groups, who deserved affirmative action. Communities that are capable of getting enough representation should not have been given reserved seats. Hence, quota seats (affirmative action) in future should only be allocated to recognised marginalsied and traditionally-excluded communities.

- ***Fixing the maximum period for reservation (Quota)***

  Reservation for different groups should not be for an unlimited time-frame. This policy should be reviewed after every two elections (or after each census) and those groups who graduated or who meet the agreed indicators should be dropped.

- ***Increasing the number of women representing the FPTP***

  The number of women representing the FPTP is historically very low—only 12.5 per cent in the CA election. A legal mandate should be introduced which ensures that at least 33 per cent of FPTP candidates are women.

- ***Banning the nomination of criminals***

  Legal provisions should be introduced to prevent the nomination of criminals as candidates in an election.

- ***Using a single ballot paper***

  During the CA election two different ballot papers (FPTP and PR) were used. As a result, election expenditure was doubled and the voting system became complicated. To reduce election costs, and to simplify the voting process, a single ballot paper should be used for both parts of the election. Even though this would deprive the right of candidates to stand as independents, the benefits of the single ballot paper outweighs its disadvantages.

- ***Introducing a No-Vote provision in the ballot***

  Provision should be made in the ballot paper for voters to indicate their preference for a no-vote—so they can register their dissatisfaction with all listed candidates.

- ***Fixing a threshold***

  For the CA elections, we wanted to ensure maximum representation of all voices, so a threshold in the Proportional Representation section of the election was not considered necessary. However, with hindsight, I realise that this was a mistake. If there had been a provision of only a 1.5 per cent threshold, the number of parties in parliament would have reduced to nine. We also failed to realise that if the large parties had most of the seats, the parliament would be more inclusive in terms of representation of excluded groups. So, a minimum threshold (2 per cent) is strongly recommended for future elections.

- ***Stopping by-elections and saving tax-payers' money***

  In the First-Past-The-Post race, candidates compete in two electoral constituencies. After each election, the ECN had to manage several by-elections, because candidates winning in both the constituencies would vacate one of the seats. This is a waste of tax-payers money. The solution is either to remove the provision which lets candidates stand in two constituencies, or make the winning candidates and their political parties bear the cost of a by-election.

- ***Exploring options to stop Code-of-Conduct violation***

  Enforcement of the election Code-of-Conduct has always been a major challenge for the ECN. One solution could be making the court responsible for adjudicating any violations of the Code.

- ***Removing the cap on election costs or making it a reasonable sum***

  The ceiling on election expenses for individual candidates as well as political parties, was fixed before the election—after consultation with the political parties. However, hardly any of them operated within this ceiling. Either the ECN should increase the cap to a more realistic level, or the cap should be abandoned. Policies to regulate the source of funding could be an alternative option. Additionally, if sources of funding for the election campaign and election expenses are transparent then this would also contribute to free and fair elections.

- ***Introducing heavy penalties and shifting the burden of proof***

  The maximum punishment for election-related offences is quite low in comparison to the seriousness of the crimes. Increasing the penalty would act as a greater deterrent. And, as with other serious crimes in Nepal, the burden of proof should be shifted to the perpetrators.

- ***Using election drones***

  The Election Commission should utilise new technologies like text messages, CCTV, YouTube and social network feeds as *election drones* to monitor the electoral violence and mal-practice. Legal actions, based on such electronic evidence, could then be taken against the guilty.

- ***Conducting an on-the-spot count***

  During the CA elections, counting, and especially the collection of ballot boxes from the polling booths to the counting centres (district headquarters)—was more challenging than conducting the election itself. Even if there was minor damage to the box re-polling had to take place. Security was another key challenge, especially while transporting the boxes. Counting at the polling stations themselves, immediately after the polls, would solve such problems.

- ***Prioritising quality over quantity***

  Domestic election observers have a huge responsibility to ensure that elections are free and fair. However, the ECN policy on domestic observation permitted some observers of questionable professionalism to be recruited. This policy needs to be refined, with the objective of attracting inscrutable professional observers.

- ***Removing the 10,000 signature requirement for party registration***

  The requirement that 10,000 voters' signatures should be submitted for party registration created an enormous problem for the Commission during the CA process. It was extremely difficult for the ECN to verify these signatures. A more practical solution should be adopted for party registration. It should either be dropped or request a smaller number but with a copy of citizenship of those signed, attached.

- ***Involving locally-elected bodies in election management***

  Gradually the responsibility for the technical management of an election should be shifted to local bodies, and the role of the ECN in this task should be minimal. Piloting the new scheme in a few selected areas of the country should begin as soon as possible.

- ***Recruiting university graduates as polling staff***

  Management of polling staff is a big issue. The system in Nepal means only the staff from the government or government owned or affiliated institutions are recruited for this task. The time has come to invite university students and graduates to volunteer for this process.

- ***Decentralising the voters list***

  Currently, the voters' list in Nepal is centrally prepared by the Election Commission. Under this mechanism, even if there are serious errors, holding staff accountable for mistakes is difficult. If collection of the voters' list is decentralised to the local bodies, this would make them more accountable and improve the quality of the list. The Election Commission would be responsible for capacity building of local level staff. This development would reduce the cost of the voter registration system and improve accountability.

- ***Target for a national ID***

  In the long-run, the government should provide multi-purpose ID cards and voting should be allowed based on these.

- ***Reducing the number of Election Commissioners***

  Nepal does not need a five-member commission. A maximum of three members is sufficient. Alternatively, one of the commissioners, the Chief Commissioner, could be permanent and the other two could be appointed and their services are taken only as required.

- ***Ensuring political neutrality***

  According to Nepal's Constitution, the Election Commission is an independent and neutral body. However, that was not quite my experience. Appointment of the Election Commissioners was based on the recommendations of the major political parties. Not surprisingly this created suspicion. In a society like ours, we need *neutral* personalities, who are not perceived as being close to a particular political party, to work in this respected democratic institution. Hence, the appointment process for Election Commissioners needs be reformed.

Annexures

Annex 1: Twelve-Point Understanding Reached between the Seven Political Parties and the Nepal Communist Party (Maoist) on 22 November 2005

The struggle between absolute monarchy and democracy continuing for a long time in Nepal has now taken a grave and unique turn. It has become the need of the day to establish peace by resolving the 10-year-old armed conflict through a forward-looking political outlet. Therefore, it has become an inevitable necessity that concepts of full democracy be effectively implemented through a forward-looking restructuring of the state, in order to resolve problems related to class, cast, gender and region in all sectors, including, the political, the economic, the social and the cultural sectors, by bringing the autocratic monarchy to an end and establishing full democracy. We hereby disclose that in the context of aforesaid conditions existing in the country, the following understanding has been reached between the Seven Political Parties within the parliament and the CPN (Maoists) through holding negotiations on various levels.

The points reached in understanding

1. Democracy, peace, prosperity, social advancement and an independent and sovereign Nepal is the primary wish of all Nepali people in the country today. We agree that the autocratic monarchy poses the main hurdle in achieving this wish. We believe that bringing about peace, progress and prosperity in the country is not possible until the absolute monarchy is brought to an end, and full democracy is established. Therefore, an understanding has been reached to establish full democracy by bringing the autocratic monarchy to an end by nation-wide agitation for democratic movements by forces that are against the autocratic monarchy, resisting it from their respective positions.

2. The agitating Seven Political Parties are fully committed to the fact that the existing conflict in the country can be resolved, and that sovereignty and state powers can be vested in the people by restoring the parliament through the force of agitation and by forming a powerful multiparty government, through its own decision, negotiation with the Maoists, and on the basis of agreement, holding the election of the Constituent Assembly. The CPN (Maoists) is of opinion that the aforesaid goal can be achieved by holding a national political conference of the agitating democratic forces, and subsequently, through its decision, forming an Interim Government and holding the election of a Constituent Assembly. On the issue of this procedural agenda, an understanding has been made to continue dialogue and seek for a common agreement between the agitating Seven Political Parties and the CPN (Maoists). It has been agreed that the force of People's Movement is the only effective option in achieving this goal.
3. The country, today, demands the establishment of permanent peace along with a positive resolution of the ongoing armed conflict. We are, therefore, firmly committed to establish permanent peace by bringing the existing armed conflict in the country to an end through a forward-looking political outlet. This can be done by establishing full democracy, by ending the autocratic monarchy and holding an election to form a Constituent Assembly that would take place on the basis of the procedure planned. The CPN (Maoists) has expressed its commitment to move forward in the new peaceful political stream through this process. In this very context, an understanding has also been made to keep the Maoist armed forces and the Royal Army under the supervision of the United Nations or similar reliable international supervisory bodies, during the process of the election of the Constituent Assembly. This would ensure that the elections are held in a free and fair manner and the results are accepted as reflecting free will of the voters. We also expect involvement of a reliable international community in the process of negotiation.
4. Making public its commitment to transparent institutionalism, its move towards democratic norms and values like competitive multiparty system of governance, civil liberties, fundamental rights, human rights, principle of rule of law etc., the CPN (Maoists) has expressed its commitment to direct its future activities accordingly.
5. The CPN (Maoists) has expressed its commitment to create an environment to allow the people, and the leaders and workers of the political parties, who have been displaced during the course of the armed conflict, to

return and live with dignity at their original places of residence. It has also pledged to return all homes, land, or properties that were seized in an unjust manner and to allow them to carry out political activities without any hindrance.

6. Through thorough self-assessment and rectification of past mistakes and weaknesses, the CPN (Maoists) has expressed its commitment for not repeating such lapses in its future course of action.
7. Through self-assessment of the errors and weaknesses committed while in power in the government, and in the parliament in the past, the Seven Political Parties have expressed their strong commitment for not repeating such mistakes and weaknesses henceforth.
8. A commitment has been made to fully honour terms of human rights and to value its norms in moving forward and also to respect freedom of press in the context of moving the peace process ahead.
9. As the announcement of municipal elections is pushed forward with the ill-motive of deluding common people and the international community, and of continuing the autocratic and illegitimate rule of the King, and as the rumour of the election of the parliament is being spread to be a crafty ploy, we announce boycotting it actively in our own respective ways, and appeal the general public to do the same and make such elections a failure.
10. The people and their representative political parties are the real guardians of the nation. Therefore, we are firmly committed towards the protection of the independence, sovereignty, geographical integrity and national unity of the country. It is our common obligation to maintain friendly relations based on the principle of peaceful coexistence with all countries of the world, especially with neighbouring countries, like India and China. But we request all patriotic people to remain cautious against false attempts of the King and the monarchists to create confusion by projecting an illusory, fake ('Mandale') nationalism in order to prolong the autocratic and illegitimate rule of the King and to raise a question mark over the patriotism of the political parties. We appeal to the international powers and the communities to support the democratic movement against the autocratic monarchy in Nepal in every possible way.
11. We wholeheartedly invite the civil society, the professional organisations, political parties, people of all communities and regions, the press, the intellectuals and in general, all common Nepali people to make the movement successful by actively participating in the peaceful People's Movement, which has been launched on the basis of these understandings

reached by placing democracy, peace, prosperity, forward-looking social transformation and the independence, sovereignty and dignity of the country at the centre.

12. Regarding inappropriate conducts that took place among the political parties in the past, a common commitment has been expressed to investigate all reported objectionable or offensive incidents and make the results of the investigations known publicly. An understanding has been made to resolve problems among parties through dialogues and discussions in the level concerned.

22 November 2005

Annex 2: Six-Point Agreement between the Seven-Party Alliance and the Communist Party of Nepal (Maoist) on 8 November 2006

Respecting people's mandate for democracy, peace and progress expressed by the Nepali population through the historic People's Movement and struggles launched from time to time since 1951,

Reaffirming commitments to the 12 points understanding, 8 points agreement, and 25 points Code-of-Conduct concluded between the Seven Political Parties and the Communist Party of Nepal (Maoist) along with all other agreements, understandings, codes of conduct and the letter sent to the United Nations stating similar opinion by the Government of Nepal and the CPN (Maoist),

Pledging for progressive restructuring of the state by resolving existing problems related to class, ethnicity, region and gender,

Reiterating commitments to competitive multiparty democratic governance, civil liberties, fundamental rights, human rights, complete press freedom, concept of rule of law and also all other norms and values of democratic system,

Guaranteeing the fundamental rights of the Nepali people to participate in the Constituent Assembly election in fear-free environment,

Today, on this 8th day of November 2006 (corresponding to Kartik 22, 2063 B.S.), the following decisions have been taken in the meeting of the high level leaders of the Seven Political Parties and the CPN (Maoist) in order to implement the commitments of both the parties to complete the election of the Constituent Assembly by 14 June 2007 in a free and fair manner having placed the democracy, peace, prosperity, progressive social and economic change, independence, integrity, sovereignty and prestige of the country in the centre point.

I. On implementation of the previous agreements

1. All the agreements, understandings, and codes of conduct made in the past shall be implemented or cause to be implemented.
2. A high-level commission will be constituted to investigate and publicise the whereabouts of citizens that were alleged to have disappeared by the State and the Maoists in the past.
3. The process of returning the houses, land and properties occupied in the past is to be accelerated. A condition enabling displaced persons to return to their homes shall be ensured. For this purpose, districtwise committees comprising representatives from both the sides shall be formed. All these tasks are to be completed within one month.
4. Withdrawal of all accusations and allegations charged by the State and the CPN (Maoist) against the political leaders and the cadres and release of all political prisoners of both the sides will be publicly declared.

II. On the management of Army and Arms

In order to hold the elections of the Constituent Assembly in a peaceful, free and fair environment and for democratisation and restructuring of the Nepali Army as per the spirit expressed in the 12 points agreement, the 8 points understanding, the 25 points Code-of-Conduct and the 5 points letter sent to the United Nations, the following actions shall be carried out:

On the Maoist army

1. As per the commitments expressed in the letter sent to the United Nations by the Government of Nepal and the Maoists on 9 August, the combatants of the Maoists shall be confined to temporary cantonments in certain specified places, and verification and monitoring of them shall be carried out by the United Nations. The main camps will be located in the following places: (1) Kailali, (2) Surkhet, (3) Rolpa, (4) Palpa, (5) Kavre, (6) Sindhuli and (7) Ilam. There will be three subsidiary camps located around of each of these main camps.

2. All arms and ammunitions would be securely stored and locked in the camps (with the key in the care of the parties concerned), except those needed for providing security at the camps holding the Maoist combatants. In order to facilitate monitoring by the United Nations Organization, a device with siren as well as with recording facility will be installed. When there is need to examine the stored arms, the United Nations shall do it in the presence of representatives of the party concerned. Other details of technical matters (including cameras for monitoring) will be decided through agreements between the Government of Nepal, the Maoists and the United Nations.
3. Until the completion of confinement of the Maoist combatants in the cantonments, the Nepali government will take up the responsibility of providing ration and other facilities to them.
4. The Interim Council of Ministers will form a special committee to carry out monitoring, adjustment and rehabilitation of the Maoist combatants.
5. Security arrangements of Maoist leaders will be provided in accordance with agreement reached with the government of Nepal.

On the Nepal Army

6. The Nepal Army shall be confined to the barracks as per the commitments of the letter sent to the United Nations. It is guaranteed that its arms shall not be used for or against any side. Arms of the Nepal Army equal to the number of stored arms of the Maoists shall be stored in the camp, sealed with a single lock and the key shall be retained by the party concerned. In the course of locking up the arms, in order to be monitored by the United Nations, a device with siren and recording facility will be installed. When there is need to examine the stored arms, it will be done by the United Nations in the presence of representatives of the party concerned. Other details of technical matters, including cameras for monitoring, will be decided by an agreement between the Government of Nepal, the Maoists, and the United Nations.
7. Control, mobilisation and management of the Nepal Army will be done by the Council of Ministers as per the newly enacted Military Act. The Interim Council of Ministers shall prepare and implement a detailed action plan for democratisation of the Nepal Army, having taken suggestions from the concerned committee of the Interim Legislature. This includes tasks like determination of the appropriate number of the Nepal Army, its democratic organisation and structure reflecting the national and inclusive

character, and to train them by democratic principles and human rights values.

8. The usual duties of the Nepal Army, such as border security, security of the conservation areas, national parks (protected areas), banks, airport, powerhouse, telephone tower, central secretariat and security of VIPs, shall be continued.

III. On the contents of the Interim Constitution

On the interim constitution

1. The Interim Constitution, presented by the Interim Constitution Drafting Committee, shall be finalised as per the agreements reached today.
2. The Interim Constitution shall be promulgated by the reinstated House of Representatives which shall consequently be endorsed by the newly constituted Interim Legislature.

On monarchy

1. No powers regarding ruling of the country shall be vested in the King.
2. The properties of the late King Birendra, late Queen Aishwarya and their family members shall be brought under the control of the Government of Nepal and shall be utilised for the benefit of the nation through a trust.
3. All properties acquired by King Gyanendra as a King (like palaces located in various places, forests, national parks (conservation areas), heritage sites having historical and archaeological importance etc.) shall be nationalised.
4. Matters like whether or not to continue the institution of monarchy, shall be decided by the first meeting of the Constituent Assembly by a simple majority vote.

On interim legislature-parliament

1. The Interim Legislature shall be an unicameral parliament with the following formation:
   a. The existing 209 members of the Seven Political Parties and others who are members of the House of Representatives and National Assembly (excluding those who were against the People's Movement) will form a considerable part. As the Left Front does not have its representation in the existing parliament, its representation shall be determined on the basis of understanding.
   b. Seventy-three members from and on behalf of the Maoists.

c. Forty-eight members from among the class organisations and professional bodies, oppressed ethnic communities and regions and political personalities (to be nominated on the basis of understanding). The total number of members would be 330.

Provided, that those who were against the People's Movement will not hold their office in the Interim Legislature.

2. The reinstated House of Representatives and National Assembly shall be dissolved immediately after the constitution of the Interim Legislature.
3. The people's government and the people's court, including all agencies related to power under the leadership of the CPN (Maoist) shall be dissolved since the day of activation of the constitution of the Interim Legislature.
4. The Interim Legislature shall be operated on the basis of political understanding.

On the interim government

The Interim Council of Ministers shall be formed on the basis of the understanding.

1. Structure and allocation of business of the Interim Council of Ministers shall be fixed on the basis of the understanding.
2. Operation of the Interim Government shall be consistent with the aspirations of the People's Movement, political understanding and the culture of joint efforts.

On the judiciary

1. The concept, norms and values of an independent judiciary shall be followed.
2. The judiciary shall be committed to the aspirations of the People's Movement, democraratic principles and the Interim Constitution.
3. A constitutional court to resolve disputes regarding the Constituent Assembly shall be constituted.

On the constitutional bodies

1. A new constitutional council shall be constituted comprising the prime minister, the chief justice and the speaker of the Interim Legislature and shall be caused through it to recommend appointments in the constitutional bodies. Such appointments will be based on specific criteria.
2. The appointments in the Election Commission will be completed on the basis of mutual understanding.

On the local bodies

1. Interim local bodies will be formed in district town and village levels on the basis of understanding between the Seven Political Parties and the CPN (Maoists).

On the citizenship problem

1. Citizenship certificates to all Nepal citizens who have hitherto been deprived of their citizenship shall be distributed before the election of the Constituent Assembly.
2. Distribution of citizenship certificates in simple manner, to all Nepalese citizens who were born before 13 April 1990 and who are continuously residing in Nepal since then considering that date as the base (cut off) year shall be arranged.
3. Other provisions regarding the acquisition of citizenship shall be in accordance with the provisions of the law.

On the election of the constituent assembly

1. The Interim Government shall be authorised to determine the date of holding the election of the Constituent Assembly by the last day of Jestha 2064 (14 June 2007).
2. The election of the constituent assembly shall be held on the basis of mixed electoral system. 205 members will be elected through the First-Past-The-Post system by casting votes to the candidates and 204 members will be elected under the proportional representation system on the basis of votes to be given to the political parties. A law in this regard will be enacted after consultation with the Election Commission.
3. While making a list of candidates, the political parties shall have to ensure proportional representation of women, oppressed tribes and regions, like the Madheshi, the Dalits and other groups.
4. Sixteen members will be nominated by the Interim Council of Ministers on the basis of understanding, from among distinguished persons in the national life.
5. The total number of members of the Constituent Assembly shall be 425.
6. Nepal citizens who have attained 18 years of age at the time when the Interim Constitution will be promulgated shall be eligible to be voters.
7. Monitoring of the election of the Constituent Assembly shall be caused to be done by the United Nations.

On the structure of the state

1. In order to end class-based, ethnic, lingual, gender-based, cultural, religious and regional discriminations and also to end the centralised and unitary structure of the state, it shall be restructured into an inclusive, democratic and progressive state.
2. A high level commission will be formed to make suggestions on the restructuring of the state.
3. Final decision regarding the restructuring of the state shall be made by the Constituent Assembly.

On the directive principles on socio-economic transformation

1. A common minimum program for socio-economic transformations to end all forms of feudalism shall be framed on the basis of mutual understanding and will gradually be implemented.
2. The feudal system of land ownership shall be eliminated and policies to implement scientific land reform program shall be formulated.
3. Policies that will protect and promote national industries and resources shall be adopted.
4. A policy to ascertain the rights of all citizens on education, health, housing, employment and food security shall be adopted.
5. Policies to provide land and socio-economic security to backward groups including the landless, bonded labourers, tillers, *haruwa-charuwa* and others who are socio-economically backward.
6. A policy to take strict action against those who have held the office of profit in the government and have collected huge amount of properties through corruption.
7. A common development concept that will ensure socio-economic transformation and justice and will also assist in ensuring the country's prosperity in a short period of time.
8. Policies to ensure the professional rights of workers and to increase investment for promotion of industries, trade and export, and to rapidly increase employment and income generating opportunities will be adopted.

IV. On management of the victims of conflict

1. Provisions will be made for ensuring proper relief, honour and rehabilitation of the family members of the people who were killed during the conflict and for those who have been disabled by injury in the course of conflict.

2. Relief will be provided for the family members of those who have disappeared during the conflict (on the basis of the reports presented by the investigation commission).
3. Special programs to rehabilitate people who have been displaced in course of the conflict, to provide relief in case of destruction of private and public properties, and to reconstruct the destroyed infrastructures shall be carried out.
4. A high level Truth and Reconciliation Commission shall be formed to conduct investigation about those who have committed serious violation of human rights at the time of the conflict and about those who were involved in crime against humanity during the conflict, and to create an environment for social reconciliation.

V. Miscellaneous

1. A high-level joint monitoring committee shall be formed under common agreement, to ascertain whether all understandings and agreements have been implemented or not.
2. The government will take action against activities that are contrary to the codes of conduct, understandings, agreements and laws, and shall punish violators.
3. At the time of the election of the Constituent Assembly, the political parties will be free to present their policies regarding republicanism, socio-economic transformations, referendum, election system and also other issues regarding which common agreement has not been reached at present.

VI. Time schedule

1. A comprehensive peace agreement between the Government of Nepal and the CPN (Maoists) shall be concluded by 16 November 2006.
2. The Maoist combatants as referred to in II.1 shall be confined to the camps along with their weapons by 21 November 2006 and all their arms are to be stored. The United Nations will verify and monitor them.
3. The Nepal Army as referred to in II.5 shall be confined in barracks by 21 November 2006, their specified arms shall be stored away and the United Nations shall conduct a monitoring of stored arms.
4. The Interim Constitution is to be completed by 21 November 2006.
5. Promulgation of the Interim Constitution, Constitution of the Interim Legislature and dissolution of the House of Representatives and the National Assembly shall be done by 26 November 2006.

6. The Interim Council of Ministers shall be constituted by 1 December 2006.

8 November 2006

Dissenting opinion

Having agreed to implement the matters referred above, which are also agreed upon by all other parties, our party has the following dissenting opinions:

1. The CPN (UML) is of opinion that the issue of whether to maintain the monarchy or not should be determined through a referendum along with the election of the Constituent Assembly.
2. The CPN (UML) has also expressed the view that adopting a proportional system for the election of the Constituent Assembly would be the most democratic of all available options.

Annex 3: The Comprehensive Peace Agreement between the Government of Nepal and the Communist Party of Nepal (Maoist) signed on 21 November 2006

Preamble

Respecting the people's mandate expressed in favour of democracy, peace and progress by the Nepali people through the historic struggles and People's Movement launched from time to time since prior to 1950 until now,

Reaffirming full commitment towards the 12 points Understanding, the 8 points Agreement reached between the Seven Political Parties and the Communist Party of Nepal (Maoist) (CPN Maoist), the 25 points Code-of-Conduct agreed between the Government of Nepal and the CPN (Maoist), the decisions of the meeting of high level leaders of the Seven Political Parties and the CPN (Maoist) held on 8 November 2006 including all agreements, understandings, codes of conduct concluded between the Government of Nepal and the CPN (Maoist), and correspondence of similar viewpoints sent to the United Nations Organization,

Expressing determination to carry out a progressive restructuring of the state to resolve the existing problems based on class, caste, region and sex,

Reiterating the commitment towards the competitive multiparty democratic system of governance, civil liberty, fundamental rights, human rights, full press freedom and concept of rule of law and also democratic values and norms,

Remaining committed towards the Universal Declaration of Human Rights, 1948, and the international humanitarian laws and basic principles and values relating to human rights,

Guaranteeing the fundamental rights of the Nepali people to participate in the elections of the Constituent Assembly in a free, impartial and fearless environment,

Keeping democracy, peace, prosperity, progressive socio-economic changes and the freedom, integrity, sovereignty and dignity of the country at the centre,

Expressing determination to implement the commitment of holding an election of the Constituent Assembly in free and impartial manner by 14 June 2007.

Declaring the beginning of a new chapter of peaceful collaboration by ending the armed conflict existing in the country since 1996 on the basis of the political understanding reached between both the parties in order to accomplish guarantee of sovereignty of Nepali people, progressive political outlet, democratic restructuring of the state and socio-economic and cultural transformation through the Constituent Assembly,

Now, therefore, this Comprehensive Peace Accord has been concluded between the Government of Nepal and the CPN (Maoist) with a commitment to transform the ceasefire reached between the Government of Nepal and the CPN (Maoist) into a long-term peace.

1. *Preliminary*

1.1. This Accord shall be referred as the *Comprehensive Peace Accord, 2006.* In short, the Accord shall be referred as Peace Accord.

1.2. The Accord shall come into force from today through a public declaration of the Government side and the Maoist side.

1.3. Both sides shall issue necessary directives to all the agencies under them to immediately implement and abide by this Accord, and shall implement or cause it to be implemented.

1.4. All the agreements, understandings, codes of conduct and decisions reached between the Seven Political Parties, the Government, and the Maoists, attached as an annex shall be deemed to be an integral part of this Accord.

1.5. The understandings and agreements to be reached in future necessary for the implementation of this Accord shall also be deemed to be a part of this Accord.

2. *Definitions*

Unless the subject or context otherwise requires, in this Accord

(a) **'Ceasefire'** means the act of prohibiting all terms of attack, kidnapping, act of disappearance, detention, mobilisation, strengthening, aggression and violent activities of armed forces and activities spreading destruction, incitement and instigation in the society through whatsoever means carried out between the Government of Nepal and the CPN (Maoist) aiming at each other.

(b) **'Interim Constitution'** means the Interim Constitution of Nepal, 2007 that is to be promulgated for the period until a new constitution is drafted and promulgated by the Constituent Assembly.

(c) **'Interim Council of Ministers'** means the Interim Council of Ministers to be constituted under the Interim Constitution.

(d) **'Both sides'** mean the Government of Nepal and the Communist Party of Nepal (Maoist).

(e) **'Law in Force'** means the Interim Constitution of Nepal 2007, and the Nepal laws in force that are not inconsistent to it. Provided that this definition shall not prejudice the legal provisions existing before the promulgation of the Interim Constitution, 2007.

(f) **'Verification'** means the matter of preparation of exact record after verification of army, combatants, and arms by the United Nations Organization.

3. *Political, economic and social transformation and conflict management*

Both sides agree to adopt the following policies and programmes for the political, economic and social transformation, and to manage the existing conflict in the country in a positive manner.

3.1. To ensure progressive political, economic and social transformation in the country on the basis of the decisions reached at the meeting of high level leaders of the Seven Political Parties and the CPN (Maoist) on 8 November 2006.

3.2. To constitute an Interim Legislature-Parliament on the basis of Interim Constitution, and to hold an election of the Constituent Assembly in a free and impartial manner by the Interim Government by 14 June 2007 and to ensure that in practice, the sovereignty of the nation is vested in the Nepali people.

3.3. To confer no ruling powers upon the King. The properties of late King Birendra, late Queen Aishwarya and their family will be under the control of the Government of Nepal and be utilised for the interest of the nation by forming a trust. All properties (like the palaces located in different places, forests and parks, heritages sites of historical and archeological importance etc.) acquired by King Gyanendra in that capacity shall be nationalised. The question of whether or not to maintain the institution of monarchy will be decided by a simple majority in the first meeting of the Constituent Assembly.

3.4. To adopt a political system that fully abides by the universally accepted concepts of fundamental human rights; multiparty competitive democratic system; sovereignty and supremacy of the people; constitutional balance and check; rule of law; social justice and equality; independent judiciary; periodic elections; monitoring of the civil society; complete press freedom; people's right to information; transparency and accountability in the activities of political parties; people's participation; impartial, competent and fair bureaucracy; and to maintain good governance by ending corruption and impunity.

3.5. To carry out an inclusive, democratic and progressive restructuring of the state by abolishing the current centralised and unitary form of the state in order to address problems related to women, the Dalits, the indigenous and ethnic (Janajatis) people, the Madheshi, the oppressed, neglected and minority communities, and people of backward regions by ending discrimination based on class, caste, language, gender, culture, religion and region.

3.6. To decide, through mutual agreement, a minimum common programme for the socio-economic transformation that ends all forms of feudalism and to implement it gradually.

3.7. To adopt a policy to introduce a scientific land reform programme by ending the feudal system of land ownership.

3.8. To follow a policy to protect and promote the national industries and resources.

3.9. To adopt a policy to establish the rights of all citizens to education, health, housing, employment and food.

3.10. To adopt a policy to provide land and other economic and social securities to the economically backward classes including the landless, the bonded labourers and the pastoral farmers.

3.11. To adopt a policy of severe punishment to persons who acquire wealth through corrupt ways while holding a government office of profit.

3.12. To build a common development concept for socio-economic transformation and justice as well as to accelerate development and economic prosperity.

3.13. To ensure the professional rights of labours and follow a policy for massive increase in employment and income generation opportunities by increasing investment in industries, trade, export promotion, etc.

4. *Management of armies and arms*

In order to hold the election of the Constituent Assembly in a peaceful, impartial and fearless environment, and for the democratisation and restructuring of the army to carry out tasks in accordance with the 12 points understanding, eight points agreement and the 25 points Code-of-Conduct concluded in the past, the five-points letter sent to the United Nations, and the decision taken in the meeting of high level leaders held on 8 November 2006, the following has been decided:

Concerning the Maoist army

4.1. As per the commitment expressed in the letter sent to the United Nations on behalf of the Government of Nepal and the CPN (Maoist) on 9 August 2006, combatants of the Maoists army shall be confined within temporary cantonments in the following places. They shall be verified and monitored by the United Nations. The main cantonments will be located in the following places: (1) Kailali, (2) Surkhet, (3) Rolpa, (4) Nawalparasi, (5) Chitwan, (6) Sindhuli and (7) Ilam. There will be three sub-cantonments around each of the main cantonments.

4.2. After confining the Maoist combatants within the cantonments, all arms and ammunition, except those required for the security of the cantonments, are to be stored in the cantonment, locked using a single lock, the keys of which are to be kept by the party concerned. In the process of installing such a lock, a device with a siren and video recording will also be assembled, for monitoring by the United Nations. To carry out any necessary examination of the stored arms, the United Nations will be required to act in the presence of members of the party concerned. Other technical details related to this process, including camera for monitoring, will be prepared through an agreement between the United Nations, the CPN (Maoist) and the Government of Nepal.

4.3. For the period of the Maoist combatants' stay in the temporary cantonments, the Government of Nepal will provide all supplies and cater to all other necessary arrangements.

4.4. The Interim Council of Ministers will work to supervise, integrate and rehabilitate the Maoist combatants.

4.5. Security provisions for the Maoist leaders will be made through mutual understanding with the government.

Concerning Nepal Army

4.6. The Nepal Army shall be confined within the barracks as per the commitment expressed in the letter sent to the United Nations. It will be ensured that their arms are not used for or against any one. The Nepal Army will also store their arms in equal numbers to that stored by the Maoists, which will then be locked with a single-lock and the key is to be kept in the care of the party concerned. In the process of installing the lock, a device shall be used along with a siren for the purpose of monitoring by the United Nations. While carrying out the necessary examination of the stored arms, the United Nations shall act in the presence of the party concerned. Other technical details related to this process, including a camera for monitoring, shall be decided upon through an agreement between the United Nations, the CPN (Maoist) and the Government of Nepal.

4.7. The control, mobilisation and management of the Nepal Army shall be done by the Council of Ministers in accordance with the newly enacted Military Act. The Interim Council of Ministers shall prepare and implement a detailed action plan for the democratisation of the Nepal Army having also taken suggestions from the respective committee of the Interim legislature. Under this scheme, activities like determination of an appropriate number of the Nepal Army, shaping its democratic structure and determining its national and inclusive character, will be developed. The army shall be trained on the basis of democratic and human rights values and other related tasks shall also be performed.

4.8. Continuity of the functions that are traditionally performed by the Nepal Army, like border security, security of the conservation areas, protected parks, banks, airports, power houses, telephone towers, central secretariat and security of very important persons shall continue.

5. *Ceasefire*

5.1. Termination of the military action and the armed mobilisation

5.1.1. Both sides express their commitments not to carry out the following activities:

a. Using any type of arms or weapons targeted against each other in either a direct or indirect attack;

b. Searching or confiscating weapons belonging to the other side, with or without weapons, at the place where the arms have been stored as per the understanding reached between the two sides;
c. Hurting or exerting mental pressure on any person;
d. Setting up ambush targeting each other;
e. Committing murder and similar violent activities;
f. Kidnapping/arresting/detaining/causing disappearance;
g. Damaging public, private, government or military property;
h. Making aerial attacks or bombardment;
i. Being involved in land mining and sabotage;
j. Spying on military activities of each other.

5.1.2. Both sides shall not recruit additional military forces or shall not transport arms, ammunitions and explosives or conduct military activities against each other; except in cases where the Interim Government may, in order to prevent illegal trafficking of materials like arms and weapons, explosives or part thereof or raw materials thereof, conduct patrolling, search, or confiscate them in international border or custom points by mobilising the security forces.

5.1.3. No individual or group shall travel with illegal arms, ammunitions and explosives.

5.1.4. Both sides shall assist each other to mark landmines and body-traps used during the time of armed conflict by providing necessary information within 30 days and defuse and excavate the same within 60 days.

5.1.5. Armies of both sides shall not be present with arms or in combat dress in any civil gathering, political meeting or any public programme.

5.1.6. Nepal Police and Armed Police Force shall continue to act for maintaining law, order and peace and conduct criminal investigation as per the spirit and letters of the People's Movement, the Peace Accord, as well as the prevailing law.

5.1.7. Both sides shall issue circulars to their respective armed agencies or personnel to stop addressing any armed person of the other side as 'enemy,' either directly or among members of the same side, and also to treat them in similar manner, without hostility.

5.1.8. Both sides express their consent to create an inventory of governmental, public and private buildings, land, and other properties occupied, locked up or not allowed to use in course of the armed conflict and to return them immediately.

5.2. **Measures for Normalisation of the Situation**

5.2.1. Both sides agree not to collect cash or kind forcibly and levy tax against one's will and contrary to the law in force.

5.2.2. Both sides agree to make public the status of the people taken in their custody and to release them within a period of fifteen days.

5.2.3. Both sides agree to make public the information about the real name, surname and address of the people who were made to disappear and those who were killed during the war, and to inform the family about it within 60 days from the date on which this Accord has been signed.

5.2.4. Both sides agree to maintain the peace in the society, normalising adverse situation caused by the armed conflict and to carry out relief work for, and to rehabilitate people victimised and displaced by the war, to constitute a National Peace and Rehabilitation Commission to perform the business related to it.

5.2.5. Both sides agree to constitute a high level Truth and Reconciliation Commission through mutual agreement, in order to investigate the truth about those who have seriously violated human rights and those who were involved in crimes against humanity in course of the war and to create an environment for reconciliation in the society.

5.2.6. Both sides pledge to renounce war, attack, counter-attack, violence and counter-violence of all forms in the country with a commitment to ensure democracy, peace and progressive change in the Nepali society. There is an understanding between the two sides in matters of assisting one another in peace building and maintaining law and order.

5.2.7. Both sides guarantee to withdraw accusations, claims, complaints and cases under consideration alleged against various individuals due to political reasons and to make public immediately the state of those who are in detention and to release them immediately.

5.2.8. Both sides express their commitment to allow people displaced due to the armed conflict to return voluntarily to their respective ancestral or previous places of residence without any political prejudice, to reconstruct the infrastructure destroyed as a result of the conflict and to rehabilitate and socialize the displaced persons with due respect.

5.2.9. Both sides agree to resolve problems that may occur in the above mentioned context on the basis of mutual agreement and to take responsibility, individually and collectively, for creating favourable environment for normalisation of mutual relations and reconciliation, and to implement it with the help of all political parties, the civil society and local organisations.

5.2.10. Both sides express their commitment not to discriminate against or pressurise any family by associating a member of the family with either of the sides.

5.2.11. Both sides agree not to create any kind of obstacle and allow any kind of obstruction to be created against the employees of the government of Nepal and public agencies in the course of their traveling to any part of the country to fulfill their duties and to perform their business, but to extend cooperation to them and facilitate their tasks.

5.2.12. Both sides agree to allow the United Nations, the International Donors Agencies, the Diplomatic Missions based in Nepal, national and international non-government organisations, press, human rights activists, election observers and foreign tourists unrestricted movement in the State of Nepal in accordance with law.

5.2.13. Both sides are committed to operate publicity programmes in a decent and respectable manner.

6. *End of war*

6.1. We hereby declare the end of the armed war continuing since 1995, giving permanency to the ongoing ceasefire reached between the Government and the Maoists on the basis of the Historical Agreement concluded between the Seven Political Parties and the CPN (Maoist) on 8 November 2006.

6.2. The decisions taken by the high level leaders of the Seven Political Parties and the CPN (Maoist) on 8 November 2006 shall be the main policy basis for long-term peace.

6.3. After the confinement of the Nepal Army in the barracks and the Maoist Army combatants in the cantonments, and the holding and displacing of their arms, creating fear, threat, and use of any type of violence and arms contrary to the understanding, agreements and law shall be legally punishable.

6.4. Armies of both the sides shall not be allowed to publicize for or against any party and to go for or against any side. However, they shall not be deprived of their voting rights.

7. *Observance of the human rights, fundamental rights and humanitarian law*

Remaining committed to the Universal Declaration of Human Rights, 1948, international humanitarian law, and fundamental principles and norms concerning human rights, both sides express their consent to the following issues:

7.1. **Human rights**

7.1.1. Both sides reconfirm their commitment to the respect and protection of human rights and commitment to the international humanitarian laws and accept that nobody shall be discriminated on the basis of colour, gender, language, religion, age, race, national or social origin, wealth, disability, birth or other status, opinion, or faith.

7.1.2. Both sides agree to create an atmosphere for the Nepali people to enjoy their civil, political, economic, social and cultural rights and are committed to create an atmosphere where such rights are not violated in the future under any condition.

7.1.3. Both sides express the commitment that impartial investigation and action shall be carried out in accordance with law, against the persons responsible for creating obstructions in exercising the rights envisaged in the Accord and ensure that impunity shall not be encouraged. Apart from this, they are also committed to ensure the rights of the victims of conflict and torture, and the family of disappeared persons to obtain relief.

7.1.4. Both sides agree to not carry out acts of torture, kidnapping and forced labour against the public in general and to take necessary action to discourage such acts.

7.1.5. Both sides shall, on the basis of norms and values of secularism, respect social, cultural and religious sensitivity, religious sites and beliefs of individuals.

7.2. **Right to life**

7.2.1. Both sides agree to respect and protect an individual's fundamental right to life. No one shall be deprived of this fundamental right and no law shall be made that sanctions capital punishment.

7.3. **Right to individual dignity, freedom and movement**

7.3.1. Both sides are to respect and protect the right to individual dignity. In this connection, no person including those deprived of their freedom in accordance with the law, shall be subjected to torture or any other cruel, inhuman or degrading treatment or punishment. Right to privacy of the citizen shall be respected and legally protected.

7.3.2. Both sides shall, respecting fully the individual's right to freedom and security, not keep anyone under arbitrary or illegal detention, or kidnap or take anyone as hostage. Both sides agree to make public the status of every disappeared person and those held as captive and inform the matter to the victims' family members, legal advisors and other authorised persons.

7.3.3. Both sides will respect and protect the right to freedom of movement, freedom to choose a place of residence (subject to legal norms) and express commitment to respect the rights of the persons displaced by the conflict and their families to return to their original residence or to settle in any place of their choice.

7.4 **Civil and political rights**

7.4.1. Both sides are committed to respect and protect every person's freedom of opinion and expression, to form unions and associations, to peaceably assemble and to respect the right against exploitation.

7.4.2. Both sides agree to respect the right of every citizen to take part directly or through one's nominated representative in matters of public concern, to cast vote, to be elected and to enjoy the right of competing for entering into public service.

7.4.3. Both sides are committed to respect a person's right to be informed.

7.5. **Socio-economic rights**

7.5.1. Both sides are committed to respect and protect right to livelihood of a person through freely chosen or accepted employment.

7.5.2. Both sides are committed to respect and guarantee the right to food security of all people. They ensure that no interference shall be made in use, transportation and distribution of food grains and food products.

7.5.3. Both sides acknowledge that the right to health of citizens is to be respected and protected. Both sides agree not to hinder supply and to assist medicine and health-related campaigns, and express their commitment for treatment and rehabilitation of those who were injured because of the conflict.

7.5.4. Realising that the right to education for all should be ensured and respected, both sides are committed to maintain appropriate academic environment in educational institutions. Both sides agree to guarantee that the right to education shall not be violated. They agree to immediately put to an end activities like taking the educational institutions under control and using them, causing teachers and students to disappear or taking them under control or abduction and not to establish military barracks in the schools and hospitals in a way so that it would impede their normal functioning.

7.5.5. Both sides agree that private property of any person shall not be seized or controlled except in accordance with law.

7.5.6. Both sides believe in ensuring continuity for production activities without disturbing the industrial environment in the country, respecting the right to collective bargaining and social security in the industrial enterprises, encouraging industrial enterprises and labour to solve the problem arising between them, if any, in a peaceful manner and respect the right to work determined by the International Labour Organization.

7.6. **Rights of woman and child**

7.6.1. Both sides fully agree to provide special protection to the rights of women and children, to immediately prohibit all types of violence against women and children, including child labour, as well as sexual exploitation and harassment, and not to include or use children who are of eighteen years or under, in the armed force. Children so affected shall, immediately, be rescued and necessary and appropriate assistance shall be provided for their rehabilitation.

7.7. **Right to personal liberty**

7.7.1. Both sides agree to maintaining freedom of belief and opinion, freedom of speech and publication, freedom to assemble peaceably and without arms, freedom of movement, freedom to practice any profession or occupation of one's choice, freedom to acquire and use property, freedom to participate in peaceful political activities, freedom to be equal before the law; and to operate or cause to operate a tolerant system of justice.

8. *Mechanism for dispute settlement and implementation*

8.1. Both sides express their consent to be individually and collectively responsible for not repeating in future mistakes that were committed in the past, and for correcting them gradually.

8.2. The National Peace and Rehabilitation Commission may create mechanisms as necessary, to make the peace campaign successful. The constitution and procedures of the Commission shall be as determined by the Interim Council of Ministers.

8.3. Both sides are committed to resolve all types of mutual differences or problems that may arise at present or in the future through mutual dialogue, understanding, agreement and negotiations.

8.4. Both sides express their commitment to the fact that the Interim Council of Ministers shall, in order to implement this Accord, the Interim Constitution, and all the decisions, agreements and understandings concluded between the Seven Political Parties, the Government of Nepal and the CPN (Maoist), constitute the National Peace and Rehabilitation Commission, the Truth and Reconciliation Commission, a high-level Recommendation Commission for the Restructuring of the State and other mechanisms as per necessity, and may determine their working procedures.

9. *Implementation and monitoring*

Both sides agree to the following arrangements for the implementation and the monitoring of the agreement referred to in this Accord.

9.1. Both sides agree to give continuity to the task of monitoring provisions concerning human rights referred to in this Accord by the Nepal based United Nations Office of the High Commissioner for Human Rights.

9.2. Both sides agree to cause to monitor the management of armies and arms by the Nepal based United Nations Mission as referred to in the five-points letter sent to the United Nations earlier and in this Accord and express their commitment to assist.

9.3. Both sides agree to cause supervision of the election of the Constituent Assembly by the United Nations.

9.4. The National Human Rights Commission shall, in addition to its responsibilities as determined by law, also carry out such works as are related to the monitoring of human rights as referred to in this Accord. The Commission, in the course of performance of its business, will coordinate with national and international institutions on human rights, and obtain necessary help.

9.5. Both sides agree to receive the reports submitted by all above-mentioned bodies, to provide information requested by them, and to implement the suggestions and recommendations to be provided by them on the basis of agreements and discussions.

10. *Miscellaneous*

10.1. Both sides agree not to operate parallel or other forms of mechanism in any areas of the state or government machinery, as per the spirit of the decisions taken on 8 November 2006 and the essence of the Peace Accord.

10.2. Both sides agree to sign any complementary agreements, as necessary, for the implementation of the present Accord.

10.3. This Accord may be amended at any time with the agreement of both sides. Both sides agree to provide the other party a written notice of amendment if an amendment is desired. Amendment to the Accord may be made with the agreement of both sides after receiving such a notice. The provisions to be made by such an amendment shall not be below than that of the minimum standards of recognised international human rights and humanitarian laws and main spirit for establishment of peace.

10.4. If any dispute arises in interpretation of this Accord, a joint mechanism consisting of both sides shall make the interpretation on the basis of the preamble and the documents included in the annex to this Accord, and such an interpretation shall be final.

10.5. The concept of 'two sides' and 'situation' as referred to in this Accord shall, ipso facto, cease after the making of constitution of the Interim Legislature-Parliament. Thereafter, all responsibility for implementing the obligations referred to in this Accord shall be as per the arrangements made by the Interim Council of Ministers. It shall be a duty and responsibility of all the political parties to extend cooperation in the compliance and implementation of the Accord.

10.6. At a time when the entire country is centred in the main campaign of the election for the Constituent Assembly, we hereby heartily request all to resolve their problems and demands through dialogues and negotiations and to extend cooperation to the election of the Constituent Assembly and to maintain peace and security in all situations.

10.7. We hereby heartily appeal to the political parties, civil society, professional groups, public-class organisations, journalists, intellectuals and all Nepali people in general to actively participate in this historic campaign to build a new Nepal and to establish sustainable peace through the election of the Constituent Assembly, and by ending the armed conflict.

10.8. We heartily urge all friendly nations as well as the international community, including the United Nations Organization, to extend their support to Nepal in this campaign for establishing full democracy and sustainable peace in the country.

Taking cognizance of the responsibility of the future of the country and its people, and being fully committed to the text of this Comprehensive Peace Accord, we hereby execute this Peace Accord on behalf of the Government of Nepal and the Communist Party of Nepal (Maoist), and make this Comprehensive Peace Accord public.

Annex 4: Agreement on Monitoring of the Management of Arms and Armies

8 December 2006

Preamble

In keeping with the letters to the United Nations (UN) Secretary General of 9 August and the Comprehensive Peace Accord of 21 November 2006,

Guaranteeing the fundamental right of the Nepali people to take part in the Constituent Assembly elections in a free and fair environment without fear,

Declaring the beginning of a new chapter of peaceful democratic interaction by ending the armed conflict taking place in the country since 1996, based on the Comprehensive Peace Accord between the two parties in order to accomplish, through the Constituent Assembly, certainty of sovereignty of the Nepali people, progressive political outlet, democratic restructuring of the state and social-economic-cultural transformation, and,

Affirming the will to fully observe the terms of this bilateral agreement witnessed by the United Nations:

The parties agree to seek the UN assistance in monitoring the management of the arms and armies of both sides by the deployment of qualified UN civilian personnel to monitor, according to international norms, the confinement of Maoist army combatants and their weapons within designated cantonment areas and monitor the Nepal Army (NA) to ensure that it remains in its barracks and its weapons are not used against any side.

1. *Modalities of the agreement*

1.1. Principles

1. Neither of the parties shall engage in movement or redeployment of forces resulting in tactical or strategic advantage.
2. Any claims or reports of violations of this agreement will be reported to the UN monitors, substantiated or not substantiated, and subsequently reported to the parties through the appropriate representative of the UN Mission in Nepal.
3. The security forces deployed by the Interim Government shall have authority to conduct routine patrol, to explore in order to prevent illegal trafficking of the weapons, explosives or raw materials used in assembling weapons, at the international borders or custom points and seize them.
4. Both parties agree to allow the United Nations, international donor agencies and diplomatic missions based in Nepal, national and international non-governmental organisations, press, human rights activists, election observers and foreign tourists to travel unrestricted according to law in the state of Nepal. The parties will ensure the safety, security, freedom of movement and well-being of the UN Mission and associated personnel, goods and services in all parts of Nepal.

5. The parties shall immediately take all necessary measures to cooperate with efforts aimed at controlling illicit trafficking of arms and the infiltration of armed groups.
6. Both parties fully agree to not include or use children who are 18 years old and under, in the armed forces. Children thus affected would be immediately rescued and necessary, appropriate assistance will be provided for their rehabilitation.

1.2. Definitions

The following definitions are accepted:

1. *Cantonment* (Maoist *army*) is a temporarily designated and clearly defined geographical area for encampment and provision of services for the Maoist combatant units including weapons, ammunition and equipment. The cantonments are provided for all echelons of the Maoist army.
2. *Barracking* (NA) is the deployment of Nepal Army units to barracks, with weapons, ammunitions and equipment. No units below a company level will be independently deployed unless for activities specified elsewhere in this agreement or otherwise mutually agreed upon by the parties.
3. *Secure arms storage areas* are either military barracks with regular armoury stores used for storage of weapons, munitions and explosives, or storage containers established in special perimeters at cantonment sites controlled and guarded by the responsible unit.
4. *"The parties"* refers to the party of Government of Nepal (including the Nepal Army) and the party of the Communist Party of Nepal (Maoist) (including the Maoist Army).
5. *UN Monitoring* refers to all efforts by the United Nations Mission in Nepal to determine relative compliance with the terms spelled out in this agreement and to report to all the parties and others concerned, its findings.
6. *The Joint Monitoring Coordination Committee (JMCC)* is the monitoring, reporting and coordinating body chaired by the UN with membership of the parties. The JMCC is responsible for supervising compliance by the parties to this agreement, in accordance with provision 6.1 of this agreement.
7. *Joint Monitoring Teams* (JMTs) are the bodies that will assist in monitoring the cessation of hostilities. The Joint Monitoring Teams will be active at the regional and local levels and in mobile

teams. Each team will comprise of one UN monitor serving as team leader, one monitor from Nepal Army and one monitor from the Maoist Army. Joint Monitoring Teams will not be used for weapon storage inspections. Inspections at Maoist army cantonments will take place in presence of a UN monitoring team and a representative of the Maoist army. Inspections at Nepal Army barracks will take place with a UN monitoring team and a Nepal Army representative.

8. *Maoist army combatants:* For purposes of this agreement this will include regular active-duty members of the Maoist army who joined service before 25 May 2006, who are not minors, and who are able to demonstrate their service, including members of CPN(M), by identity cards and other means agreed upon by the parties.

1.3. Promotion

1. The parties shall promote awareness of this agreement, and adherence to its provisions, among their commanders, members and affiliated groups.
2. The parties, Government of Nepal, Nepal Army (NA), CPN(M) and the Maoist army, shall design, in cooperation with the UN Mission, an awareness programme to ensure that local communities and the parties' commanders, members and affiliated groups understand the mandate of the UN Mission and all of the obligations of the parties spelled out in this agreement. The information programme shall include the use of meetings, and the use of print and electronic media in local languages.

1.4. Phases

This agreement shall come into force upon signing. Thereafter, it shall be implemented in phases, segmented as follows:

1. reporting and verification;
2. redeployment and concentration of forces;
3. Maoist army cantonment, NA barracking and arms control; and
4. full compliance with the agreement.

A complete and practical timeline will be established by the parties for all of these activities to take place in consultation with the UN.

2. *Reporting and verification*

The parties will report detailed information about their troops and this information will be treated with appropriate confidentiality by the United

Nations. The parties will provide maps and sketches showing current dispositions, including

2.1. order of battle/military structure, organisation, deployment and number of troops;
2.2. minefields, landmines, unexploded ordinance, standard explosives, improvised explosive devices and exact location of such items;
2.3. all necessary information about roads, tracks, trails and passages related to encampments;
2.4. information regarding armed or unarmed groups working along with the parties, the Nepal Army (NA) and the Maoist army, including their responsibilities; and,
2.5. other information required by the UN Mission for proper monitoring of the disposition of arms and armies.

The UN Mission shall check this information immediately after monitors are deployed.

3. Redeployment and concentration of forces

3.1. Comprehensive plans, timelines and routes for the redeployment and concentration of forces will be provided by both the NA and the Maoist army to the UN Mission.
3.2. The redeployment and concentration of all combatants in Nepal, with the NA in barracks and the Maoist army moving in to cantonment sites, shall be carried out in consultation with the UN. The redeployment and cantonment of forces will be monitored by the UN agents after they are deployed.
3.3. Both sides express an understanding to create a record of government, public and private buildings, land and other properties and return them immediately.
3.4. The parties will withdraw all military and paramilitary checkpoints (unless explicitly permitted in this agreement) to promote and guarantee free movement and create an environment free of fear and intimidation.
3.5. The Nepal Police and Armed Police Force shall continue the task of maintaining law and order and conduct criminal investigations as per the spirit and sentiment of the *Jana Andolan* and the Peace Accord as well as the prevailing law. Both parties agree not to operate parallel or other forms of mechanism in any areas of the state or state machinery as per the spirit of the decisions of 8 November 2006 and the essence of the

Peace Accord. All sides agree to let employees of the Nepal government, and public agencies travel freely to any part of the country to fulfil their duties and not to create any obstacles or obstructions for them, or not to let obstructions arise, and to facilitate their work.

4. *Maoist army cantonment, barracking of the NA and arms control*

4.1. Maoist army cantonment

In accordance with the commitment expressed in the letter sent to the United Nations, the Maoist army combatants and their weapons shall be confined within designated cantonment areas. The cantonment shall be based on comprehensive planning and preparation before implementation. After the Maoist army combatants begin staying in the temporary cantonments, the Government of Nepal will provide food supplies and other necessary arrangements. When implemented, the comprehensive concept shall ensure good communications and proper logistics. UN monitors will have access to any and all cantonment sites for purposes of monitoring.

4.1.1. *Commanders' responsibilities*

a. The normal Maoist army chain of command, control, communication and information will be utilised to control the Maoist army cantonment, using the normal Maoist army structure in administration of the sites.

b. There will be seven main cantonment sites and 21 satellite cantonment sites, three for per main cantonment site. The satellite sites will be clustered within no more than two hours driving distance from the main sites, unless otherwise agreed by the parties.

c. The designated seven main sites will be under command, control, communication and information of the Maoist army site commander and the satellite sites by the designated satellite commanders. The site commanders shall provide the following information in detail for each site, to the UN Mission:

1. Command structure for the unit and sub-units plotted on a map;
2. Names of commanders down to company level;
3. Communication system;
4. Complete list of personnel;
5. Complete list of weapons, i.e. types, numbers, serial number and calibre under storage at the main cantonment sites;
6. Ammunition inventory type, lot number and amount;

7. List of names for the site security guards detachment, and complete list of weapons and ammunition for the detachment (main and satellite cantonment levels).

Site commanders' responsibilities include:

1. providing camp security, including access control to the site;
2. ensuring the security, freedom of movement, and well-being of the UN Mission and associated personnel, goods, and services;
3. providing information in cooperation with the UN Mission in accordance with section 2;
4. maintaining of discipline, morale and normal training in the spirit of the Comprehensive Peace Accord, excluding live fire exercises;
5. supervising daily routines and control of troops; and,
6. attending to logistics and camp services (in cooperation with the Government of Nepal and other assisting agencies).

4.1.2. *Weapons storage and control*

The parties agree upon the safe storage of all Maoist army weapons and ammunition, in the seven main cantonment areas under UN monitoring, except as mentioned below for perimeter security purposes. Both sides shall assist each other to mark landmines and booby-traps used during the time of armed conflict by providing necessary information within 30 days and to defuse, remove/lift and destroy them within 60 days. All improvised explosive devices will be collected at designated sites a safe distance from the main cantonment areas. These sites shall be agreed upon by the parties, in consultation with the UN Mission. Unsuitable devices will be destroyed immediately. Stable devices will be stored safely and under 24-hour armed guard provided for by the guard arrangements cited below. The parties, in consultation with the UN, will determine a timeline and process for the subsequent destruction of all improvised explosive devices. To ensure the safety of both the monitors and the Maoist army personnel, no improvised explosive devices or crude bombs will be brought inside the cantonment sites.

In the main cantonment sites the weapons and ammunition storage area will be secured by the following system:

a. A solid fence will surround the specified area, including a gate with a lock. There will be signs on the fence clearly identifying the restricted area.

b. The weapons storage depot will be composed of storage containers painted white and furnished with shelves for safe weapons storage and easy control, and with a complete inventory (weapon type, calibre and serial number).
c. A single lock provided by the UN will secure each storage container. The key will be held by the designated main cantonment site commander. A 24-hour surveillance camera provided by the UN Mission will cover the storage site and will be monitored from the UN office in the cantonment site. Floodlights will be switched on automatically during hours of darkness.
d. The UN Mission will provide an inspection registration device mounted on each container door indicating when the storage container has been opened.
e. An alarm system provided by the UN Mission will be connected to sirens in both the UN office and the camp commander's office. The system will be activated if the container door is opened without a "safe button" having been switched off in connection with regular inspections.
f. UN monitors will carry out the inspections of the arms storage area and containers in the presence of a Maoist army representative.
g. Each main cantonment site will be allowed 30 weapons of the same make and model to be used only for clearly defined perimeter security by designated guards, with each satellite allowed 15 such weapons under the same conditions. These weapons will all be properly registered with their make and serial number noted, and locked in a guardhouse when not in use. The parties, in consultation with the UN, will periodically review the number of weapons needed for perimeter security purposes on the basis of a shared threat assessment.
h. Security provisions will be made for the CPN(M) leaders through understanding with the government.
i. The UN Mission shall monitor these commitments with a full-time presence at the Maoist army main cantonment sites and through field visits and regular inspections. These inspections will be carried out randomly and without warning.

4.1.3. *Registration of Maoist army combatants at cantonment sites*

a. All Maoist army combatants will be registered at the main cantonment sites. This registration will include the provision of age, name, rank, responsibilities within unit/formation, date of entry into service and will provide the basis for a complete list of personnel. Maoist combatants will be registered regardless if they are in possession of weapons or not. If with weapon, the type and condition of weapon will be specified. The total number of weapons will be categorised by unit/formation. Only those individuals who were members of the Maoist army before 25 May 2006 will be eligible for cantonment. The parties will agree as to how this pre-existing service is to be confirmed in consultation with the UN.

b. As part of this registration, all Maoist army combatants will present their Maoist army identity card to be marked by the UN. The process for marking the cards will need to be determined. This registration card will be the basis for any assistance received by Maoist army members. Unregistered persons will not be eligible for assistance or permitted to remain in cantonments.

c. Only those Maoist army combatants who have been properly registered at cantonment sites will be eligible for possible integration into the security forces fulfilling the standard norms. Any discharged personnel will be ineligible for possible integration. Those who are eligible for integration into the security forces will be determined by a special committee as agreed in the Comprehensive Peace Accord. This integration process will be determined in subsequent agreement with the parties.

d. Upon registration, Maoist army combatants, if found to be born after 25 May 1988, will be honourably and automatically discharged.

e. Discharged Maoist army combatants must release all weapons, uniforms and other military gear; and, agree not to return to cantonment sites unless mutually agreed upon by UN monitors in consultation with the parties. The assistance packages to be provided to voluntarily discharged personnel will be agreed by the parties in advance of cantonment.

f. The Interim Council of Ministers will form a special committee to supervise, integrate and rehabilitate the Maoist army combatants.

4.2. Barracking of the Nepal Army

4.2.1. *General regulations*

In accordance with the commitment expressed in the letter sent to the United Nations, the Nepal Army shall remain in its barracks and its arms are not to be used in favour of or against any side. UN monitors will have access to any and all NA barracks for purposes of monitoring whether Nepal Army forces or weapons are being used for or against any party. Upon visiting any Nepal Army barracks for inspection, the site commander will be duly notified, and the UN inspections will relate only to matters regarding the disposition of forces and weapons.

The Council of Ministers will control, mobilize and manage the Nepal Army as per the Army Act of 2006 (*Sainik Ain* 2063) or its successor legislation. The Interim Council of Ministers are to prepare and implement the detailed action plan of the Nepal Army's democratisation by taking suggestions from the concerned committee of the Interim Parliament/Legislature. The purpose is to carry out activities like assessing the appropriate number of the Nepal Army, to train the army in democratic and human rights values while developing democratic structure, national and inclusive character.

4.2.2. *Commander responsibilities*

The normal NA chain of command, control, communication and information will be utilised to monitor the NA deployment to barracks. The commanders shall provide the following information in detail to the UN Mission:

1. Command structure for the unit and sub-units plotted on a map;
2. Names of commanders down to company level;
3. Communication system;
4. Order of battle/military structure, organisation, deployment and number of troops;
5. Minefields, landmines, unexploded ordnance, standard explosives, improvised explosive devices and exact location of such items; and,
6. Other information required by the UN Mission for proper monitoring of the disposition of arms and armies.
7. The NA will ensure the safety, security, freedom of movement and well-being of the UN Mission and associated personnel, goods and services, and provide information in cooperation with the UN Mission according to Section 2.

8. The UN Mission shall monitor these commitments through daily presence in selected NA barracks, field visits and regular inspections.

4.2.3. ***Weapons storage and control***

The Nepal Army will remain within the barracks as per the commitment expressed in the letter sent to the UN to ensure that their arms are not used for or against any party. The Nepal Army is to store arms in equal numbers to that of the Maoist army, to seal it with a single-lock and give the key to the concerned party. In the process of installing the lock, they are to assemble a mechanism including a siren and register for monitoring by the UN. While carrying out the necessary examination of the stored arms, the UN will do so under the presence of a Nepal Army representative. The barrack/barracks where NA arms will be monitored under the conditions spelled out in section 4.1.2 will be identified and agreed by the parties. The arms will be stored in storage containers.

4.2.4. Deployment and concentration of forces—NA permitted activities

In accordance with the spirit of the Comprehensive Peace Accord, continuity will be given to functions of the Nepal Army including border security, security of the conservation areas, protected areas, banks, airports, power houses, telephone towers, central secretariat and security of VIPs. A detailed list of these institutions and installations will be kept by the Secretary Ministry of Defence, along with the number and types of forces assigned to such duties. The list of such institutions and installations will be kept by the NA under seal, and this list will be made available to UN monitors when they deem necessary on a case-by-case basis.

Permitted NA activities are as follows:

1. Routine military activities within the barracks and regular training in barracks and camps. The JMCC will be notified 48 hours in advance before undertaking limited live fire exercises at designated live firing ranges.
2. Participation in official ceremonies, parades, etc., as directed by the government.
3. Provision of Border Security as directed by the government.

4. Relief of troops on a one-to-one basis, including transport as mentioned.
5. Regular maintenance and replacement of non-lethal equipment, including transport as mentioned. Maintenance and replacement of lethal weapons will take place only as determined by the Interim Government or agreement by both parties.
6. Execution of development and construction tasks as directed by the civilian authorities, on central regional and local levels.
7. Provision of support in relief work in times of natural and other disasters as directed by the government.
8. Participation in peacekeeping operations called for by the United Nations, and all preparations, transport, training, transfer of equipment, etc., connected to this.
9. Provision of security for VVIPs and VIPs.
10. Provision of security of vital installations as directed by the government.
11. Provision of security of transportation of Nepal Rastra Bank funds.

For all of the activities mentioned above, the rules regarding notification of troop, air movements and exercises spelled out in section 5.2 apply.

5. *Compliance with the Agreement*

5.1. Prohibited activities

In the spirit of the Comprehensive Peace Accord, and in light of this agreement, after the placement of the Nepal Army in the barracks and the Maoist combatants in cantonment, the parties shall scrupulously refrain from the following activities:

1. Holding and carrying arms is in violation of the law. Displaying arms, intimidation and any type of use of violence is prohibited, and use of arms is legally punishable.
2. Targeting or threatening to attack any type of arms and weapons against each other in a direct or indirect way is prohibited.
3. Harming or intimidating any person, including internally displaced persons, humanitarian and development workers and other non-combatants, and any seizure of their equipment and property.

4. Ambushes, murder or violent operations.
5. Kidnapping, unlawful detention or imprisonment, disappearances.
6. All offensive military flights within and over Nepal.
7. Damaging or seizing public/private/government, military or the UN property and all attacks on the UN and associated personnel.
8. Planting mines or improvised explosive devices, conducting sabotage or military espionage.
9. Recruiting additional armed forces or conducting military activities against each other, including transporting weapons, ammunitions and explosives. (Unless mutually agreed by the parties and notified in advance according to the terms of this agreement.)
10. Collecting cash or goods and services or levying tax against one's wishes and against the existing law.
11. Any actions that impede or delay the provision of humanitarian assistance or protection to civilians.
12. Any restrictions on the safe, free and unimpeded movement of humanitarian or development agencies undertaking activities approved by the Interim Government or its successor.
13. All acts and forms of gender-based violence.
14. Any restrictions on the free movement of people and goods.
15. All activities that obstruct the efforts of the UN Mission and amount to a failure to cooperate with the UN Mission, including the prohibition of the UN Mission patrols and flights over any location.
16. Any attempt by a party to disguise its equipment, personnel or activities as those of the UN Mission, other United Nations agencies, the International Committee of the Red Cross/Crescent or any other similar organisation.
17. Any attempt to redeploy military forces and equipment or occupation of any positions out of their respective deployment positions without the consent of the Joint Monitoring Coordination Committee.
18. The use of children who are below 18 years of age, in the armed forces.
19. All hostile propaganda and incitement to military action.

The parties shall also refrain from all activities that are prohibited elsewhere in this agreement.

5.2. *Permitted activities*

The key principle that will underpin permitted activities for both sides shall be to alleviate the effects of the armed conflict on civilians and the war-affected areas and to galvanise popular support for peace. Permitted activities for both sides will be conducted as per the decisions of the Interim Government. Troop, air movements and exercises have to be properly notified and approved by the Joint Monitoring Coordination Committee at least 48 hours in advance.

Permitted activities include:

a. De-mining and decommissioning of military hazards;
b. Development activities to include improvement and opening of roads, rehabilitation of bridges and passages and airstrips according to the decisions of the Interim Government;
c. Humanitarian relief;
d. Socio-economic activities such as assisting free movement of people, goods and services;
e. Free movement of unarmed soldiers in plain civilian clothes who are on granted leave, medical referrals, or visiting families—no more than 12 per cent of the total retained force at a given cantonment or barracks will be on authorised leave at any given time unless mutually agreed by the parties;
f. Supply of non-lethal items to military units, food, water, medicine, petrol, oil and lubricants, stationary, uniforms etc.; and,
g. Medical evacuation.

5.3. *Violations*

The following acts shall constitute violations of the agreement:

1. Any act that contravenes this agreement;
2. Unauthorised troop movements;
3. Unauthorised recruitment, conscription or mobilisation;
4. Unauthorised replenishment of military equipment;
5. Violation of human rights, humanitarian law or obstruction of freedom of movement of people, goods and services;
6. Espionage, sabotage, air surveillance and acts of subversion; and,
7. Military flights, or military flights utilising civilian aircrafts over cantonment sites without 48-hour notification to the parties and the UN mission, except in emergency situations or medical evacuations.

6. The United Nations mission

Monitoring of compliance with this agreement will be carried out:

a. by UN Monitors; or,
b. by Joint Monitoring Teams, if so decided by the JMCC and in keeping with other provisions of this agreement.

The UN Mission will submit reports to the parties on compliance with this agreement. It will do so either directly, or through the JMCC.

6.1. The Joint Monitoring Coordination Committee

The nine-member Joint Monitoring Coordination Committee (JMCC) will have a chairman appointed by the UN Mission. There will be two vice-chairmen, one each from the Maoist army and the NA. The remaining six members will be two UN, two NA and two from the Maoist army, all as selected by the parties respectively.

The JMCC shall reach its decisions by consensus. In the event of a deadlock, the representative of the UN Secretary-General shall have final authority for reporting on the compliance of the parties with this agreement to the Secretary-General and to the Interim Government for resolution. The chairman shall report regularly to the representative of the Secretary-General and to the designated representatives of the parties regarding the activities of the JMCC.

The JMCC shall serve three main functions:

1. To assist the parties in implementing this agreement. The JMCC shall be the central coordinating body for monitoring arms and armies in accordance with the terms of this agreement and to approve, where appropriate, those activities specified in Section 5.2.
2. To serve as a dispute resolution mechanism. The JMCC shall resolve all disputes and military or operational difficulties, complaints, questions, or problems regarding implementation of this agreement.
3. To assist in confidence building. The JMCC shall work to gain the trust and confidence of the parties and promote the overall goals of this agreement among the people of Nepal.

In order to achieve these goals, the JMCC shall operate according to the following basic principles:

1. Resolve all problems and disputes at the lowest level possible, i.e., delegation of authority to the JMTs;

2. Promote joint problem-solving and build trust and confidence through active efforts to appropriately investigate and report on all incidents of concern to the parties; and,
3. Build on lessons learned in the process.

The Joint Monitoring Teams (JMTs) will assist the Joint Monitoring Coordination Committee at the local level and through site visits. The JMTs will comprise one international monitor as the team leader and one monitor from the Nepal Army and one monitor from the Maoist Army. The number of JMTs and their deployment will be determined by the chairman of the JMCC in consultations with that body.

The tasks of the JMTs will include:

1. Village and community visits and liaison with the civilian community;
2. Cooperation with other UN-agencies, and liaison with international organisations and non-governmental organisations;
3. Assistance to the parties in creating a favourable operational environment for the conduct of the ceasefire by information sharing and defusing local tension;
4. A pro-active concept for initiation of conflict management at the local level; and,
5. Investigation of complaints linked to possible alleged violations of the agreement, reference paragraph 5.1, and to recommend measures to ensure compliance.
6. Joint Monitoring Teams will not be used for designated weapons storage inspections.

7. *Miscellaneous*

1. This agreement can be revised at any time with the consent of both parties. Both parties agree to provide to each other prior written information if they wish to make any change. Amendments can be made to the agreement with the consent of both parties after receiving the information. The provisions to be made by such an amendment will not fall below the minimum standards of accepted international human rights and humanitarian laws.
2. Both parties consent to sign any complementary understandings, as necessary, for the implementation of the present agreement.
3. This agreement will be signed by both parties in Nepali and English. The United Nations will witness the English language version of this agreement

and, accordingly, the English-language version of this agreement will be considered as authoritative in matters of dispute.

4. The spirit of the Comprehensive Peace Accord shall guide the interpretation and implementation of this agreement by all the parties.
5. This agreement shall come into force upon signature, and it supersedes the agreement of the same name done on the 28th day of November 2006 (12 Mangsir 2063 BS).

Done in Kathmandu, Nepal on the 8th day of December 2006 (22 Mangsir 2063)

Source: Agreements and Understandings on Peace Negotiations of Nepal, Government of Nepal, Peace Secretariat, Singha Durbar, Kathmandu, Nepal http://www.peace.gov.np/uploads/Publication/cover%20and%20con.pdf

Notes on References

This book is mainly based on the recollections and reflections of Bhojraj Pokharel on his experience of conducting Nepal's Constituent Assembly election, in his role as the Chief Election Commissioner (from October 2006–June 2008)—including his personal notes from those days. Additionally, some chapters in this book draw on interviews with the following people: Amresh Kumar Singh (Nepali Congress Member of Parliament, 2007–08), Baburam Bhattarai (UCPN-Maoist Deputy leader), Baburam Khanal (Section Officer, Election Commission of Nepal), Bhogendra Yadav (UCPN-Maoist District Committee member, Biratnagar), Bharat Pathak (Rastriya Prajatantra Party member), Bibek Shaha (Secretary, Military Secretariat, Royal Palace), Chandra Kishore Lal (writer and columnist), Chakra Bastola (Nepali Congress Central Committee member), Chum Narayan Tabedar (Madhesi Janadhikar Forum member), Devi Khadka (UCPN-Maoist Constituent Assembly member), Dhala Kumari Shah (Wife of *Mukhya Chautariya* Khagendra Jung Parakram Shah), Dilli Raj Belbase (District Election Officer, Nawalparasi), Ek Raj Bhandari (UCPN-Maoist Constituent Assembly member), Ganesh Acharaya (UCPN-Maoist District General Secretary, Biratnagar), Geeta Gurung (District Election Officer, Dolakha), Ghanshyam Khatiwada (CPN-UML District General Secretary, Biratnagar), Girija Prasad Koirala (Nepali Congress President), Gokarna Poudyal (Girija Prasad Koirala's personal secretary), Gyanendra Bir Bikram Shah (former Head of State), Harish Chandra Ghimire (District Election Officer, Kavre), Hiradevi Poudel (District Election Officer, Mustang), Hisila Yami (UCPN Central Committee Member), Ian Martin (UNMIN head, 2007–09), Indira Acharya (Girija Prasad Koirala's sister), Jhalak Sharma (communist activist), Jyoti Koirala (Girija Prasad Koirala's nephew), Khadka Bahadur Basnet (CPN-UML, District Secretary, Biratnagar), Kåre Vollan (Election Expert), Khim Lal Devkota (UCPN-Maoist Chairman of Nepal National Intellectual Organization), Laxman Ghimire (Nepali Congress Central Committee member), Laxmi Pandey Gautam (District Election Officer, Gulmi), Krishna Sitaula (Nepali Congress Central Committee member), Mahendra Dhoj Singh (political observer), Indrakumari Thapaliya (District Election Officer, Jhapa), Ishwor Pokharel (CPN-UML General Secretary), Mahendra Marasini (Girija Prasad Koirala's Security Officer, National Intelligence Department), Mahesh Timilsina (District Election Officer, Morang), Manushi Bhattarai (UCPN-M student leader), Minendra Rijal (Nepali Congress Central Committee member), Nabin Uprety (UCPN-Maoist Municipality-in-charge, Biratnagar), Om Bahadur Khadka (District Election Officer, Bardiya), Padma Ratna Tuladhar (human rights activist), Pradip Nepal (CPN-UML Central Committee member), Pradip Gyawali (CPN-UML Central Committee member), Prahlad Lamichhane (UCPN-M District Committee member, Makawanpur), Prem Luitel (District Election Officer, Sunsari), Puspha Kamal Dahal (UCPN-Maoist Chairman), Raghu Chandra Bahadur Singh (Retd. Major General, Nepal Army), Sagar Timilsina (Private Secretary of the Narayanhiti Royal Palace), Radheshyam Adhikari (Member of the Interim Constitution Drafting Committee from the Nepal Congress), Sanjaya Bhattarai (Nepali Congress, District General Secretary, Biratnagar), Sarun Batha (UCPN-M District Member Rukum), Shambu Pokharel (Nepali Congress National Convention member), Shanta Kumar Malla (Rtd. General and former aide-de-camp to King Birendra), Shanta Nepal Marasini (District Election Officer, Rasuwa), Shashank Koirala (Nepali Congress Central Committee member and Girija Prasad Koirala's nephew), Shekhar Koirala (Nepali Congress Central Committee member and Nona Koirala's son. Sekhar Koirala was also engaged with the peace process closely.), Surya Prasad Shrestha (former Chief Election Commissioner), Tamrat Samuel (former Deputy Head, UNMIN, Head of Asia Pacific Division, Political Department, UN), Uma *didi* (close associate of Koirala family, Biratnagar), Yubraj Karki (CPN-UML Central Committee member). Interviews were also conducted with former aide-de-camps to King Gyanendra, former Royal Palace staff, and the Maoist leaders' security officials—whose names have not been revealed at their request. Most importantly, this book has relied heavily on the archives of newspapers such as the *Annapurna Post*, *Himal Khabarpatrika*, *Kantipur*, *Nepal Weekly* and the *Nepal News* and others, including the *Nepali Times*, *Rajdhani*, *Republica* and *Samay*.

Bibliography

Alex, Perry. 2005. 'Extended Interview with King Gyanendra.' *Time Magazine*, 16 April. Accessed 24 December 2009. See http://www.time.com/time/magazine/article/0,9171,1050194,00.html

Asian Network for Free Elections (ANFREL). July 2008. *Nepal Constituent Assembly Elections 10th April 2008*. Bangkok: ANFREL. Accessed 15 October 2009. See http://newmediaauthority.com/anfrel/wp-content/uploads/2012/02/2008_nepal.pdf

Baral, Lok Raj (eds). 2005. *Election and Governance in Nepal*. New Delhi: Manohar Publisher.

Bhattarai, Baburam. 2005. 'Princely Tendency and Democracy.' In *Monarchy vs. Democracy: The Epic Fight in Nepal*. New Delhi: Samkaleen Teesari Duniya.

Dahal, Ram Kumar. 2001. *Constitutional and Political Developments in Nepal*. Kathmandu: Ratna Pustak Bhandar.

Devkota, Khimlal. 2012. *A Perspective on the Maoist Movement in Nepal*. Kathmandu: Apollo Offset Press.

Democracy and Elections Alliance, Nepal. 2008. *The Constituent Assembly Election Observation Final Report*. Kathmandu: Democracy and Elections Alliance, Nepal.

Einsiedel von, Sebastian, Malone M. David and Suman Pradhan (eds). 2012. *Nepal in Transition: From People's War to Fragile Peace*. New Delhi: Cambridge University Press.

Electoral Expert Monitoring Team (EEMT). June 2007. *Nepal Electoral Expert Monitoring Team First Assessment Report*. Kathmandu: EEMT. Accessed 19 October 2010. See http://un.org.np/unmin-archive/downloads/eemt/2007

———. 27 July–6 August 2007. *Nepal Electoral Expert Monitoring Team Second Assessment Report*. Kathmandu: EEMT. Accessed 19 October 2010. See http://un.org.np/unmin-archive/downloads/eemt/2007-08-

———. 27 September–9 October 2007. *Nepal Electoral Expert Monitoring Team Third Assessment Report*. Kathmandu: EEMT. Accessed 19 October 2010. See http://un.org.np/unmin-archive/downloads/eemt/2007-

———. 3–17 March 2008. *Nepal Electoral Expert Monitoring Team Fourth Assessment Report*. Kathmandu: EEMT. Accessed 19 October 2010. See http://un.org.np/unmin-archive/downloads/eemt/2008-03-

———. 5 April–8 May 2008. *Nepal Electoral Expert Monitoring Team Fifth Assessment Report*. Kathmandu: EEMT. Accessed 19 October 2010. See http://un.org.np/unmin-archive/downloads/eemt/2008-

European Union, Election Observation Mission (EU EOM). September 2008. *Nepal-Constituent Assembly Election 10 April 20008*. Kathmandu: EU EOM. Accessed 15 October 2009. See http://www.eeas.europa.eu/eueom/pdf/missions/eu_eom_final_report.pdf

Government of Nepal, Ministry of Law, Justice and Parliamentary Affairs. 2007. *Nepal ko Antarim Sambidhan, 2063* (In translation: Interim Constitution of Nepal, 2007). Kathmandu: Ministry of Law, Justice and Parliamentary Affairs, Nepal Government.

———. 2011. *National Action Plan on Implementation of the United Nations Security Council Resolutions 1325 & 1820 [2011/12-2015/16]*. Kathmandu: Government of Nepal, Ministry of Peace and Reconstruction.

———. 2012. *Shanti Prakriya ma hal samma bhayeka samjhauta, sahamati, samajdhari, ghosana ra nirnaya haru ko sankalan* (In translation, Compilation of all peace agreements, understandings, declarations, decisions, 2012) Kathmandu: Government of Nepal, Ministry of Peace and Reconstruction.

Hachhethu, Krishna. 2006. *Political Parties of Nepal*. Lalitpur: Social Science Baha.

Koirala, Girija Prasad. 2007. 'My Political Gamble.' In *Simple Convictions—My struggle for Peace and Democracy*. Kathmandu: Mandala Book Point.

Kumar, Dhurba. 2010. *Electoral Violence and Volatility in Nepal*. Kathmandu: Vajra Publications.

Lamb, Christina. 2006. *House of Stone: The True Story of a Family Divided in War-Torn Zimbabwe*. US: Lawrence Hill Books.

Martin, Ian (ed.) 2010. *Nepal's Peace Process At the United Nations—Volume I*. Lalitpur: Himal Books.

National Election Monitoring Alliance. 2008. *The Constituent Assembly Election 2008 Observation Report*. Kathmandu: National Election Monitoring Alliance.

Nepal, Jagat. 2010. *Girija Prasad Koiralaka Afnai Kura* (In translation: Girija Prasad Koirala's Own Personal Account). Lalitpur: Jagadamba Prakasan.

Ogura, Kiyoko. 2001. *Kathmandu Spring: The People's Movement of 1990*. Lalitpur: Himal Books.

Pandit, Lok Darshan, compiled. 2010. *Nepalko Sansadiya Nirbachan Ko Darpan* (In translation, Nepal's Parliamentary Elections) Kathmandu: Sopan Press Pvt. Ltd.

Press Council Nepal. 2008. *A Public Report on Media Monitoring for Nepal's Constituent Assembly Polls*. Kathmandu: Press Council Nepal.

Roy, Anirban. 2008. *Prachanda: The Unknown Revolutionary*. Kathmandu: Mandala Book Point.

Seddon, David. 2005. *Armed Violence and Poverty In Nepal: A Case Study for the Armed Violence and Poverty Initiative*. Bradford: Centre for International Cooperation and Security, University of Bradford. Accessed 28 April 2009. See http://www.brad.ac.uk/acad/cics/publications/AVPI/poverty/AVPI_Synthesis_Report.pdf

Shaha, Rishikesh. 1990. *Modern Nepal: A Political History (1769–1855)—Volume I*. New Delhi: Manohar Publications.

———. 1990. *Modern Nepal: A Political History (1885–1955)—Volume II*. New Delhi: Manohar Publications.

Sharma, Ganeshraj, compiled. 1998. *Bishweshor Prasad Koirala ko Atmabirtanta* Kathmandu: Jagadamba Publications.

Shrestha, Ananda and Hari Uprety. 2003. *Conflict Resolution and Governance in Nepal*. Kathmandu: Nepal Foundation for Advanced Studies.

Stiller, Ludwig F. 1973. *The Rise of House of Gorkha: A Study of Unification of Nepal, 1768–1816*. New Delhi: Manjushree Publishing House.

———. 1993. *Nepal: Growth of a Nation*. Kathmandu: Human Resource Development Centre.

Surendra, K.C. 2006. *Nepalko Rajya Punarsamrachana Ra Sambidhan Sabha* (In translation, Re-structuring of the State and the Constituent Assembly in Nepal). Kathmandu: Pairavi Publications.

Thapa, Deepak (ed.). 2003. *Understanding the Maoist Movement of Nepal*. Kathmandu: Modern Printing Press.

Thapa, Deepak and Bandita Sijapati. 2004. *A Kingdom Under Siege: Nepal's Maoist Insurgency, 1996 to 2003*. London: Zed Books.

Thapa, Manjushree. 2005. *Forget Kathmandu: An Elegy for Democracy*. India: Penguin Books.

———. 2011. *The Lives We Have Lost*. India: Penguin Group.

The Cater Center. May 2009. *Observing the 2008 Nepal Constituent Assembly Election April 2008*. Atlanta: The Cater Center. Accessed 20 November 2009. See www.cartercenter.org//election_reports/FinalReportNepal2008.pdf

The Central Bureau of Statistics. 2003. *Population Monograph of Nepal*. Kathmandu: Nepal Planning Commission/The Central Bureau of Statistics.

———. 2007. *Statistical Year Book of Nepal*. Kathmandu: The Central Bureau of Statistics, National Planning Commission Secretariat.

———. 2011. *Poverty Trends in Nepal (1995–96 and 2003–04)*. Kathmandu: The Central Bureau of Statistics, National Planning Commission Secretariat.

The Election Commission of Nepal. 2008. *The Constituent Assembly Members Elections, 2064, Election Results Handbook*. Kathmandu: The Election Commission of Nepal.

———. 2008. *The First Annual Report*. Kathmandu: The Election Commission of Nepal.

———. 2009. *The Second Annual Report*. Kathmandu: The Election Commission of Nepal.

———. 2009. *The Election Commission's Report of the Constituent Assembly Election, 2006–2009*. Kathmandu: The Election Commission of Nepal.

United Nations Security Council. October 2007. *Report of the Secretary-General on the request of Nepal for United Nations assistance in support of Its peace process*. New York: United Nations Security Council.

United Nations Office of the High Commissioner for Human Rights in Nepal (OHCHR). December 2007. *Human Rights in Nepal: One Year after the Comprehensive Peace Agreement*. Kathmandu: OHCHR–Nepal.

———. April 2008. *Constituent Assembly Elections of 10 April 2008: Summary of Human Rights Monitoring*. Kathmandu: OHCHR–Nepal.

United Nations Mission in Nepal (UNMIN). March 2008. *UNMIN Election Report No 2*. Kathmandu: UNMIN.

———. April 2008. *UNMIN Election Report No 3*. Kathmandu: UNMIN.

———. October 2008. *The United Nations and Nepal's Peace Process*. Kathmandu: United Nations Mission in Nepal (UNMIN).

UNDP, Electoral Support Project, Election Commission of Nepal. 2010. *Report on Gender Mapping in the Field of Elections*. Kathmandu: UNDP, Electoral Support Project, Election Commission of Nepal.

Vollan, Kåre. 2011. 'Case Study Nepal.' In *Electoral Quotas and the Challenges of Democratic Transition in Conflict-Ridden Societies—A Nordem Special Report 2011* by Nils A. Butenschøn and Kåre Vollan. Oslo: University of Oslo.

Whelpton, John. 2005. *A History of Nepal*. UK: Cambridge University Press

World Bank Country Study. 1991. *Nepal Poverty and Incomes*. Washington, D.C: The World Bank.

Websites

Baburam Bhattarai. 2010. *Biography*. http://www.baburambhattarai.com/

Election Commission of Nepal. http://www.election.gov.np/EN/

International Convention Center. 2010. *About Us. http://www.bicc.com.np/*

United Nations Mission in Nepal (UNMIN). 2013. *Electoral Assistance*. http://un.org.np/unmin-archive/?d=activities&p=electoral

United Nations Mission in Nepal (UNMIN) Archive. 2010. *Secretary-General Reports to Security Council, Secretary-General Statements on Nepal, and Peace Process*. http://un.org.np/unmin-archive/?d=official&p=peace\

Index